ADVENTURES
IN SMALL TOURISM

SMALL CITIES SUSTAINABILITY STUDIES IN COMMUNITY AND CULTURAL ENGAGEMENT

SERIES EDITORS:

W. F. Garrett-Petts, Professor of English, Thompson Rivers University
Nancy Duxbury Carreiro, Senior Researcher, Centre for Social Studies, University of Coimbra, Portugal, and Co-coordinator of its Cities, Cultures, and Architecture Research Group

Published with the support of Thompson Rivers University.
ISSN 2561-5351 (Print) ISSN 2561-536X (Online)

This series is interested in discovering and documenting how smaller communities in Canada and elsewhere differ from their larger metropolitan counterparts in terms of their strategies (formal and informal) for developing, maintaining, and enhancing community and cultural vitality, particularly in terms of civic engagement, artistic animation, and creative place-making.

No. 1 · *No Straight Lines: Local Leadership and the Path from Government to Governance in Small Cities*
Edited by Terry Kading

No. 2 · *Creative Tourism in Smaller Communities: Place, Culture, and Local Representation*
Edited and with an introduction by Kathleen Scherf

No. 3 · *Adventures in Small Tourism: Studies and Stories*
Edited and with an introduction by Kathleen Scherf

UNIVERSITY OF CALGARY
Press

Adventures in Small Tourism

STUDIES AND STORIES

EDITED AND WITH AN INTRODUCTION BY
Kathleen Scherf

THOMPSON
RIVERS
UNIVERSITY

Small Cities Sustainability Studies
in Community and Cultural Engagement
ISSN 2561-5351 (Print) ISSN 2561-536X (Online)

University of Calgary Press
2500 University Drive NW
Calgary, Alberta
Canada T2N 1N4
press.ucalgary.ca

Library and Archives Canada Cataloguing in Publication

Title: Adventures in small tourism : studies and stories / edited and with an introduction by
    Kathleen Scherf.
Names: Scherf, Kathleen Dorothy, 1960- editor.
Series: Small cities sustainability studies in community and cultural engagement ; no. 3.
Description: Series statement: Small cities sustainability studies in community and cultural
    engagement, 2561-5351 ; no. 3 | Includes bibliographical references and index.
Identifiers: Canadiana (print) 20230472486 | Canadiana (ebook) 20230472516 | ISBN
    9781773854755 (hardcover) | ISBN 9781773854762 (softcover) | ISBN 9781773854786
    (PDF) | ISBN 9781773854779 (Open Access PDF) | ISBN 9781773854793 (EPUB)
Subjects: LCSH: Tourism—Case studies. | LCSH: Culture and tourism—Case studies. |
    LCSH: Small cities—Case studies. | LCGFT: Case studies.
Classification: LCC G155.A1 A38 2023 | DDC 910—dc23

The University of Calgary Press acknowledges the support of the Government of Alberta
through the Alberta Media Fund for our publications. We acknowledge the financial support
of the Government of Canada. We acknowledge the financial support of the Canada Council
for the Arts for our publishing program.

This book is published with financial support from Thompson Rivers University.

Alberta Government   Canada   Canada Council for the Arts   Conseil des Arts du Canada

Copyediting by Ryan Perks
Cover Art: Colourbox 56765828
Cover design, page design, and typesetting by Melina Cusano

For Dana Scherf-Silk

Contents

Acknowledgements

Thanks to Thompson Rivers University, especially the Research and Graduate Studies Office, for granting me a sabbatical in 2022, during which I completed a good deal of the work for this volume. I am also grateful for its support of my research assistant, Brendan Coulter. Thompson Rivers University is located on the unceded land of the Secwepemc, within Secwepemc'ulucw, the traditional territory of the Secwepemc people.

Much of the labour on both this book and its predecessor, *Creative Tourism in Smaller Communities: Place, Culture, and Local Representation* (University of Calgary Press, 2021), occurred at my sunny loft flat in Mainz, Germany, in the house owned by my good friend Dr. Stephanie Doetsch. It is such a pleasure to acknowledge the affection and encouragement she regularly extends around my scholarly work and its attendant thrilling details. I am also happy to thank my colleague and friend Dr. Nancy Duxbury for her continuing participation in my scholarly projects. She is usually busy editing her own books, but always makes time to share her expertise in mine.

Twenty-eight authors contributed to this international volume, and all have endured scores of my emails and deadlines in order to co-create this book; not a single one of them has let me down. I am very grateful to them for all their work.

Once again, I want to acknowledge with gratitude my long and strong relationship with the University of Calgary. This is my second book with University of Calgary Press, headed by its director, the inimitable Brian Scrivener. He and his stellar staff, including Helen Hajnoczky, Melina Cusano, and Alison Cobra, work every day to bring peer-reviewed writing to all readers through open access—they are stardust, they are golden. Unsung heroes Ryan Perks and JoAnne Burek once again bring their copy-editing and indexing expertise to this volume. The comments made by both scholarly reviewers were also helpful.

Finally. My son Dana Scherf-Silk has accompanied me on this long academic career; I was still an assistant professor when he was born. Clearly one can never really reflect the full scope of experience a child brings, but I can and do, with love, celebrate Dana by dedicating this book to him.

Small Tourism: Local, Localism, Neolocal, and a View Toward Regeneration

Kathleen Scherf

The Context for Small

This book is the companion volume to 2021's *Creative Tourism in Smaller Communities: Place, Culture, and Local Representation*, also published by the University of Calgary Press. That book offered a variety of authorial perspectives on a central question: In what ways are creativity and place-based tourism co-engaged to aid sustainable cultural development in smaller communities? (Scherf 2021, 3). We defined "creative tourism" as

> an experiential subset of cultural tourism that demonstrates four characteristics: 1) it involves the transfer of culture-based, place-specific endogenous knowledge to the visitor; 2) it includes the experiential participation of the visitor in activities that embody such knowledge; 3) it operates in a collaborative paradigm in some manner; and 4) it demonstrates a longer view beyond the actual tourist experience toward the host community's cultural sustainability. (4–5)

Although the current volume does not focus intentionally on only creative tourism, its studies and stories of small tourism enterprises, located in small communities, and offered to small groups of visitors, almost universally echo the characteristics of creative tourism. The appeal and advantages of small tourism speak to the nature of creative tourism: experiencing the

unique attributes of a circumscribed destination, taking part in local traditions and activities, engaging visitors with residents, and revitalizing or sustaining a community's tangible and intangible cultural assets. The ten studies
in *Creative Tourism in Smaller Communities* offered two basic approaches to
the question the volume posed. First, authors emphasized the importance
of community- and culture-led planning in developing successful and sustainable creative tourism enterprises. Second, they argued that the creative
representation of place through tourism could develop cultural capital for the
host community.

In his conclusion to that volume, Greg Richards spoke of the ability of
smaller places to engage in the collaborative identification and expression of
cultural assets to provide a sense of place for visitors, as well as for residents.
The analyses in the volume revealed five interrelated circumstances that,
when present in a smaller community, could provide a favourable climate in
which the combined interests of tourism and local sustainability could thrive.
First, the community must recognize that its attraction to tourists depends
on its cultural assets, those tangible and intangible characteristics that make
the place uniquely itself. Second, those assets should be identified through a
collaborative, community-led process of cultural mapping, engaging all willing residents and incorporating their various perspectives on how their place
is best and most authentically represented. Third, the host community should
support or develop cultural networks or clusters, leveraging extant cultural
capacity and mitigating the lack of density in smaller communities. Fourth,
the positive relationship between visitors and residents must be prioritized.
Residents are community stakeholders, but visitors, when they want to engage with the everyday life of a place, are also community stakeholders—in a
way, they are temporary residents. As Greg Richards has commented in many
of his articles and presentations, locals and visitors co-create place. Visitors
wishing to experience the authenticity of a particular place, or communities
wishing to help sustain their culture through tourism, will both be sorely
disappointed if a negative relationship exists between locals and visitors. The
cultural failure of mass tourism bears ample witness to this fact. Fifth and
finally, and again with reference to mass tourism, tourism can best assist a
community's sustainable cultural development and social inclusion if visitors
willingly recognize their agency as contributors to a destination's cultural sustainability. Where co-creation of place exists, where tourism is beneficial to
a community, the authors of *Creative Tourism in Smaller Communities* argue

that a collaborative paradigm for tourism is not only about local clusters and networks, but also about the community and the visitor. As the introduction to that volume concludes,

> This may require a new mindset for being a *visitor*. Tucking into a local culture in this way as a visitor can only happen when the participative arena is manageable—or, put another way, when it is small. As the tourism industry struggles to recover from calamitous reality of *Coronazeit*, we might find that small is the new big. (23)

And that is the point at which we begin the present consideration of small tourism in small places. More specifically, we aim to explore the opportunities and issues faced by providers of creative tourism experiences, and especially by micro-enterprises (defined below) to a small number of participants (in this volume, we define that as under twenty-five), in a tightly defined geographical place.

Small Places, Small Enterprises, Small Numbers

This volume presents both academic studies and personal stories about small tourism. Rather than separating the two approaches by type, I have categorized them thematically, presenting first a study, and then a story that exemplifies and provides an example of some of the concepts discussed in its matching study. As such, I hope the volume is interesting to students and practitioners interested in contemporary tourism issues. I will introduce the chapters shortly, but first some discussion of small tourism in the context of this book.

Small tourism is hardly a new phenomenon. Retreats of various sorts, safaris, voluntourism, and genealogical tourism are all examples that, while perhaps not always creative, generally involve small numbers of tourists. And alternative approaches to tourism have certainly been informed by reactions against the over-tourism much analyzed since the 1970s. Over-tourism is poignantly demonstrated in international cities like Amsterdam and Barcelona, where local tourism councils have developed plans to decentralize the physical impact of visitors in their respective central cores, and where the overwhelming number of visitors have had a hand in *barriocide*, or the death of neighbourhoods, to which residents often react negatively.

Over-tourism wreaks havoc on both physical and cultural sustainability, as *Creative Tourism in Smaller Communities* discussed. The sustainability of physical infrastructures can be threatened by mass tourism. A huge issue is the ability of locals to live in their neighbourhoods, as the experience of Barcelona's Gràcia neighbourhood shows. Local tenants can sometimes no longer afford to live in their community, as landlords may prefer to use their buildings to provide relatively expensive short-term accommodation for tourists, thus both increasing costs and decreasing housing stock for residents. Aside from housing issues, mass tourism can also stress municipal infrastructures in central districts, which are often tourist zones. This situation is well-documented in municipal tourism plans and in tourism studies, but it is also perfectly visible to the untrained eye. For example, one Sunday morning in the winter of 2017, when I was coming down the hill in an empty bus from Barcelona's El Carmelo neighbourhood, the bus, halting at Tirso/ Pl Laguna Lanau, a stop for Gaudi's Parc Güell, became suddenly engorged with tourists descending toward central Barcelona. Filled to capacity, the bus could not even admit all those lined up, nor could it stop for residents as it proceeded on its route. At the next few stops, ebony- and lace-clad elderly local ladies, clearly heading to church, watched the bus drive past, unable to stop for them. Their dismay and their attitude toward tourists was roundly evident in their facial expressions. The driver could only shake his head and shrug. The point is not that tourists should not visit Parc Güell, of course, but rather that the inability of Barcelona's physical infrastructure to support both permanent and temporary residents (as the city now terms its visitors) is increasingly clear. Tourism on a smaller scale is less damaging to local infrastructure, both built and natural, so while it is perhaps not exactly aiding its physical sustainability, it is at least less ruinous to it.

Preserving endogenous culture is also a sustainable development goal, and tourism has been affected by the desire to support and sustain local cultures. Large tourism practices encourage the "tourist gaze" described by John Urry in the 1990s and vividly expressed in popular culture by the American television show *Rick Steves' Europe*,[1] in which tourists are guided to basically consume—or gaze upon—a popular destination's tangible cultural assets. But small tourism, specifically creative tourism, not only reduces negative guest impact on local culture, but actually seeks to strengthen and revive cultural practices by weaving together the perspectives of guest and host. As the experience economy seeped into the tourism industry at the turn of this century, visitors began to seek memorable and transformative experiences when travelling, experiences in which they did not merely gaze and graze the tangible, but actually engaged with the intangible cultural assets of place. Instead of purchasing a product, tourists started to purchase experiences. Relational or creative tourism pushed this idea further, such that residents and visitors were seen to co-create a sense of place, in terms of consciously engaging in local activities offered by locals, yes, but with visitors also contributing their own perspective and history to the moment, thus enriching the experience for both sides, and for the community more broadly. A great attraction of such an approach to tourism is that it is seen to contribute to cultural sustainability; as we learned in *Creative Tourism in Smaller Communities*, and as we will see in this volume with regard to small tourism, successful creative tourism enterprises are largely community-based and collaboratively determined, with locals actively engaged in identifying and participating in their own endogenous cultural assets to share with visitors, thus creating cultural capital and establishing or supporting cultural networks. This participative approach to tourism by informed residents develops political agency, and also allows them to shield their cultural assets from the exploitation that mass tourism often inflicts.

Barcelona can provide another instructive example here. Las Ramblas, the central urban avenue in the Ciutat Vella (old town), stretching just over a kilometre from Port Vell to Plaça de Catalunya, used to be a local destination for Barcelonians to enjoy Sunday walks and leisure time with their families and friends. Since the city's rise as an international tourist destination with the 1992 Summer Olympics, Las Ramblas has been reduced to a street of cheap souvenir kiosks, fast food outlets, hordes of cruise passengers on their outings, and pickpockets—in short, a location avoided at all costs by permanent residents. Its decline, and that of the neighbourhood on its eastern side, El Gótico, are vividly documented in Eduardo Chibàs Fernández's 2014 documentary *Bye Bye Barcelona*.[2] On the east side of Las Ramblas—so on the El Raval side of the Ciutat Vella—is the historic Mercado de la Boqueria, a large, covered food market that has been operating on the same site since the 1200s. Once the visitor penetrates through the vendors selling candy, Iberico ham, and fruit snacks situated just inside the Las Ramblas entrance (conveniently located, for tourists, across from the Erotic Museum of Barcelona), one finds that the stall keepers farther off the main thoroughfare are verbally adamant that visitors do not take photographs of their offerings, unlike those at the front of the market, who encourage the snapping of pictures. I am well aware of that situation, because the first time I was there, in 2013, I was absolutely gobsmacked by the abundance and variety of fresh seafood so attractively displayed on beds of crushed ice. As I raised my phone to take a picture, the fishmonger put up her hand to block the photo, and sternly admonished me: "No tourist! No tourist! No picture!" I have been there many times since to purchase fresh fish for my dinners, and have seen that scenario play out time and again. Such is the stultifying effect of mass tourism on a local culture, as Fernández's short film so poignantly demonstrates. But with small tourism, this does not have to happen. Consider another market in Barcelona, this time in a small neighbourhood in the Ciutat Vella, El Born, which lies just to the east of El Gótico, a locally trendy but less-Disneyfied place where actual Barcelonians still live. In 2018, I was looking for some small tourism experiences, and as has been amply documented in the literature on creative tourism, local cooking classes fit the bill: small groups, offered by small enterprises, led by locals, and sharing both tangible and intangible endogenous cultural assets via foodways. I participated in the "Born to Cook"[3] experience, in which our group of six participants purchased the produce and seafood required to make our paella during a tour of the Mercado de Santa Caterina, at which we were introduced to various vendors, before we gathered in a cozy basement kitchen to cook our food together. It was an informative market tour and a wonderful opportunity to see the chef's local food cluster working together in this small tourism enterprise (we will see a similar enterprise in Bogotá, Colombia, in chapter 6, but in a more compromised neighbourhood). In this sustainable small tourism experience, we kept tourism dollars in the local economy, did not overly stress the physical environment or infrastructure, and respectfully shared the local culture in a way that supported, rather than hampered, its continued existence. Such are the possibilities of small tourism with regard to sustainable development.

In addition to its roles in supporting sustainable development as an alternative to mass tourism, the importance of small tourism has become heightened in the wake of COVID-19 and the havoc the pandemic has wreaked on the tourism industry. Lockdowns in various places have prevented any travel whatsoever, excluding perhaps to the grocery store or to the pharmacy. After those lockdowns, travel was for a year restricted to "local" movement, which of course has different meanings depending on where you live. In British Columbia, Canada, during the summer of 2021, people could only travel within their region, but those are pretty big regions. The idea of the road trip as a form of tourism once again gained currency. Likewise, camping regained its former popularity. The pandemic encouraged travellers to discover, or perhaps rediscover, the delights of their own places. Writing for the *New York Times* in July 2021, Alexander Lobrano described the effect of COVID-19 on travel:

> This kind of small-brush-stroke travel is intimately valuable, too, because it teaches us where we live and who we are. During the last few decades, the glamour of the exotic and far-flung has often prevailed as the grail of travel, when the truth is that it can be just as interesting to hop on a train to New Haven from New York City for a day trip as it is to go to Thailand. . . . What the Covid years have taught me again is that any journey, no matter how brief or local, is a success if it provokes and feeds my curiosity, and that yes, for me it will always be wonderful to just go, anywhere.

Ivan Baidin, writing for *Forbes* in 2021, noted the surge in attendance to state and national parks in the United States, and predicted that domestic tourism and the "staycation" would be the dominant trend in tourism for 2022. Sixty-four per cent of the experts interviewed by the United Nations World Tourism Organization (UNWTO) believe that it will take until 2024 for international arrivals to regain 2019 levels. In January 2022, the UNWTO stated that

> domestic tourism continues to drive recovery of the sector in an increasing number of destinations, particularly those with large domestic markets. According to experts, domestic tourism and travel close to home, as well as open-air activities, nature-based products and rural tourism, are among the major travel trends that will continue shaping tourism in 2022. (UNWTO 2022)

This context is a fertile ground for the kind of small tourism products we examine in this volume. For now, small tourism appears to be well positioned to challenge big tourism.

But small tourism providers and the tourists they serve are sadly no panacea for travel during COVID-19. Small tourism has also suffered, although it has perhaps, as a function of the characteristics of small tourism that we will be exploring, had a less trying time. For example, McCormick and Qu (2021), in researching the impact of COVID-19 on creative tourism micro-enterprises in Japan's rural island of Naoshimo, found that the local cluster of providers, collaborating at the grassroots level, were able to leverage their networks in order to find innovative ways around the disarray and inaction with which the local government failed to support their small businesses during the worst of the pandemic in Japan. While we are still not fully out of the grip of COVID-19, the creative tourism micro-enterprises on Naoshimo are presently intact, bowed but not quite broken.

While it is highly unlikely that mass tourism will ever disappear, it does seem that, taken together, the pandemic, the consumer drift toward relational tourism, and the unsustainability of mass tourism have created a perfect storm in the face of which small tourism enterprises could advance. While small tourism experiences have of course been extant in various forms, we suggest that the profile of small has been heightened, and as such provides opportunities that are good for communities and visitors alike. That is really what this book is about.

How Small Is Small?

In this volume, we focus on the provision of small-scale creative tourism experiences that are thematically rooted in the specific location in which they are hosted. We understand these providers to be micro-enterprises that offer locally based experiences highlighting tangible and intangible cultural assets to either small groups of people or to individuals, in specific limited destinations, such as urban neighbourhoods, rural contexts, or peripheral locations. They concentrate on local cultural assets, both tangible and intangible. As defined by the European Commission (2015), a micro-enterprise is an independent business (to be clear, we also consider non-for-profit organizations) that employs fewer than ten people, and whose annual balance sheet does not exceed EUR 2 million, or somewhere around CAD$2,800,000. Every tourism provider represented in this book can be defined as a micro-enterprise. Further, micro-tourism enterprises generally share a philosophy:

> Tourism micro-firms typically design and deliver experiences that are based on local nature and culture and which involve other local actors (Komppula, 2014; Yachin & Ioannides, 2020). Through their operations, tourism micro-firms help to protect,

maintain and communicate the essence of the place (Middleton, 2001). Thus, tourism micro-firms have a meaningful contribution to the economic, social and environmental wellbeing of their localities (Hallak et al., 2013; Morrison, 2006). Their role is particularly significant in rural areas, where tourism is often seen as a development strategy, and micro-firms hold the potential to generate activity (Bosworth & Farrell, 2011; Cunha et al., 2018; Morrison et al., 2010). (Yachin 2020)

Compared with our rather succinct understanding of small enterprises, our consideration of the *number* of tourists served is a little more difficult to categorize. In terms of numbers, the present volume examines cases that serve from one to about twenty-five participants. Two chapters discuss small arts festivals that nonetheless attract larger numbers, but these visitors are dispersed over several days across many events. COVID-19 has affected one of these festivals, which takes place in Hungary, and while continuing, the number of attendees has been reduced, and safety measures are in place. A couple of chapters do not actually discuss numbers of tourists, but rather address what we might term "niche" markets, groups that are sometimes difficult to identify, or that are not a marketing target, such as gay travellers in rural British Columbia. In this volume, we consider a niche group of the travelling public as "small." Or at least smaller, especially with regard to destination marketing. Intentionally serving small numbers of visitors at one time is an important element of small tourism, as it allows for a deeper connection between the people thus engaged; small visitor groups is a stated feature of many of the creative tourism cases described in this volume.

Finally, we come to the most contested element of small tourism: the question of what counts as a small destination. The concept of a "micro-destination" is attractive, but Hernández-Martín et al. (2016) clearly define a micro-destination as a place that services tourists, quite apart from residents. The authors in this volume very much see small destinations as facilitating connections between resident, visitor, and place. They view small tourism as community-based, or as local tourism. In their book *Reinventing the Local in Tourism: Producing, Consuming and Negotiating Place*, Russo and Richards (2016) set out the characteristics of local tourism, which they correlate with the "creative turn"—as discussed in *Creative Tourism in Smaller Communities*—in tourism. Local tourism can mean that any place in a given locality, and not only its flagship cultural attractions, might be a destination. A community itself may determine what is noteworthy to share with visitors, based on its everyday culture and, most importantly, grounded in local points of connection between visitors and residents that occur in spaces, activities, and in social constructions. The local becomes more of an idea than a geographically bounded area. As Freya Higgins-Desbiolles and Bobbi Chew Bigby suggest (2022), a "local turn" in tourism studies allows us to "reconceptualize the local," and to empower the community to define, express, and offer itself to guests. The local, after all, is more than a host community or a destination:

> In our articulation of the local community as the linchpin of the local turn, we mean more than just a certain group of people associated with a place. Instead, we are more broadly inclusive of the local community, the local ecology (living air, land and waterscapes and more-than-human beings) and all generations pertaining to that place (including future ones). Using this broader articulation of the local opens up potential for enlivening forms of tourism. (2)

No longer are rural towns, urban neighbourhoods, and small cities the main points of connection in small tourism; these can now be found in much more unassuming sites, such as a certain corner, monument, cemetery, shop, or even the knowledge of how to create a traditional craft, prepare a dish, or carry out work that is endemic to the life of those who live locally. It can be a small arts festival, or a community centre. It can be a farmers' market. It can be any small thing—and that is what we are focusing on in this book—that expresses the sense of place for locals and that, when that cultural asset intersects with the community's desire to engage in tourism, results in creative tourism experiences that are sustainable, that are rooted in local nature and culture, and that strengthen, not deplete, the community's sense of place and its local culture—very unlike the situation at Mercado de la Boqueria. I like the German concept of *der Ort*—the place, the point. In this case, a point of connection. So for us, a small tourism destination is a point at which locals, through micro-enterprises, have decided to share their place with a small number of visitors at one time. The following chapters share various perspectives on small creative tourism.

The Chapters

Small Tourism: Supporting Diversity Outside the Mainstream

Our first study, "The Development of Inclusive Small Rural Destinations for Gay Tourists in Canada," authored by Spencer J. Toth, Josie V. Vayro, and Courtney W. Mason, is joined by its companion story, Katja Beck Kos, Mateja Meh, and Vid Kmetič's, "Rajzefiber: A Community Hub for Small Tourism in the Small City of Maribor, Slovenia." Toth, Vayro, and Mason explore perceptions of tourism in small rural communities in the interior of British Columbia, Canada, from the perspectives of both visitors and destination marketing organizations. More than eight thousand kilometres to the east, Kos, Meh, and Kmetič take readers through the concept, establishment, and activities of their micro-tourism enterprise in Slovenia. Both chapters are set in areas known for winter and summer outdoor tourism activities, as well as for adventure tourism. As both sets of authors point out, the tourism marketing agencies for both districts slant heavily toward such activities.

British Columbia is known to be culturally liberal, but Toth, Vayro, and Mason are examining small communities in the interior of the province, which are generally reliant on resource-extraction industries that are now in decline. Like many rural communities in that situation, tourism has provided another source of income. But the chapter's research shows that the social conservatism that often exists in these cultures has raised concerns for gay travellers. While there certainly exist international small communities that purposefully cater to gay tourists—Sitges, Key West, Provincetown—interior BC communities are generally not considered in this light. Gay travellers to these rural BC communities comprise a niche market, a small and non-self-disclosing minority of visitors. Gay travellers, the authors show, want to travel to gay-friendly places where they can encounter familiar communities, feel safe, know they are accepted, and sense that the small community will welcome them for who they are and how they want to live. They feel somewhat apprehensive about engaging in tourism activities in rural British Columbia, often relying on gay-oriented social media like Grindr to find out about safe and welcoming places in the destination community. The authors suggest that small rural communities could see the interest of gay travellers, who want to expand their tourism world beyond "gay utopias," as a potential growth market. However, marketing adjustments would be required in order to better reach this small niche market. In their interviews with represent-atives of the destination marketing organizations (DMOs) responsible for these rural communities, Toth and his co-authors find that, although sym-pathetic, the DMOs suffer from a number of limitations. Marketing tools are based on analytics, and privacy legislation prevents questions about sexual orientation on consumer surveys. As well, gay tourists may well feel wary about self-disclosure. As such, this niche group is not only relatively small, but also quite hidden, so it does not turn up on surveys as an interest group, in contrast to, say, snowmobilers, skiers, fishers, or family groups. Funds fol-low numbers when determining destination marketing. Gay tourists in rural British Columbia are revealed in this chapter to be outside the mainstream of tourism, and as a small niche group are not marketed to, and thus often do not travel to where they might be interested in visiting, resulting in a loss for consumers, providers, and communities.

Readers may not think that, at 110,000 people, Maribor, a small city lo-cated in eastern Slovenia and the stepsister of the more popular Ljubljana, the country's cultural, political, economic, and administrative centre, would have much in common with rural BC communities in terms of tourism. But it does. The Slovenian Tourism Organization, the national DMO, offers an annual "Slovenian Incoming Workshop" for foreign tour operators, but it concentrates mostly on the western side of the country. The workshop focus-es on known, tangible cultural assets, and the outdoor tourism assets abun-dant in Slovenia. The authors assert that as a result, "untypical, small-scale tourism places and enterprises must try to help themselves . . . with only scarce marketing funds, making it difficult to attract an international audi-ence" (page 62). The concerns of the Rajzefiber authors in this chapter echo those enumerated by Toth, Vayro, and Mason; in order to expand markets and to meet the expectations of tourists who seek a safe and authentic local connection with a place, micro-tourism enterprises need the help of DMOs. DMOs, in turn, require funding to expand their campaigns and appropri-ately train staff. Both sets of authors, in these two widely distanced locations, offer the same suggestions to improve the problems they have identified. Toth and co-authors mention the use of Grindr by their survey respondents; the Rajzefiber crew also stress the need to use social media to connect with niche groups, but point out that as a micro-enterprise, they lack the funds, time, and expertise to leverage social media to their benefit. In both cases, there is a need for DMOs and other tourist promotion organizations to assist with marketing and promotion to niche tourists outside the mainstream of what is generally promoted. For the DMOs, funding is the problem. Where tourism marketing dollars go is generally associated with the number of visits reported. So big tourism begets big tourism. Data that expresses the niche status of certain tourist groups is not available, and so they remain invisible. Small tourism requires the assistance that big tourism commands, both chapters affirm.

Both chapters also emphasize that social inclusion is a desirable effect of small tourism, the first chapter in terms of feeling at home in a destination community, and the second in terms of local authenticity of the tourism product. The need for the social inclusion of both residents and visitors is also highlighted. Including residents and visitors in shared enterprises is a challenge, although it always sounds very good in the scholarship of creative tourism in smaller places. In Maribor, Kos, Meh, and Kmetič share how much effort they put into encouraging community-led tourism planning, establishing credibility with residents, and forming partnerships with other community organizations. In rural British Columbia, Toth, Vayro, and Mason point out that while gay residents of small rural communities may feel uncomfortable publicly sharing their own clusters and networks with outside tourists, festivals are seen as a more general way to invite niche groups into the community and to engage visitors with it, all while establishing community partnerships. In Maribor, Razjefibre has developed the Festival of Walks to do exactly that. While micro-tourism enterprises and tourists who engage with them clearly make a choice alternative to mainstream tourism, in order to be sustainable and to contribute to their small communities, such enterprises need support to consistently attract the niche groups to which they cater. As Kos and co-others point out, it is hard to believe that the pandemic may have had any positive effects on the tourism industry, but perhaps the opportunity to reimagine strategies for more sustainable and inclusive tourism, including supporting small tourism, was one such benefit.

Small Tourism: Altruism, Education, and Restoring the Culture of Place

The broader understanding of "local" articulated by Higgins-Desbiolles and Bigby, discussed above, allows us to think of a place as including its history and its landscape. This definition of the local is particularly relevant to the two chapters that comprise our second study-story set. In their chapter "Sustaining

Castello Sonnino: Small Tourism in a Tuscan Village," John S. Hull, Donna Senese, and Darcen Esau introduce us to Castello Sonnino, an ancient wine estate in a small Tuscan village, a place where the restoration of old traditions shared among the village, the land, and the residents is linked to educational tourism through the Sonnino family's micro-tourism enterprise, the Sonnino International Education Centre (SIEC). The theme of expressing a local sense of place through cultural and ecological restoration and education reverberates in Moira A. L. Maley, Sylvia M. Leighton, Alison Lullfitz, Johannes E. Wajon, M. Jane Thompson, Carol Pettersen, Mohammadreza Gohari, and Keith Bradby's "Revealing the Restorers: Small Tourism in Restored Lands of the Noongar Traditional Area of the Fitz-Stirling in Southwestern Australia," a story about the people who have been restoring land and its relationship to Indigenous cultures disturbed over three decades of government-sponsored agricultural development. These restorers are also micro-enterprise providers of educational tourism. In maintaining and restoring both *mezzadria* (the linkage between land, resident, community—a living landscape) in Italy and the *Boodja* (the combined entity of land and Noongar culture) in Australia, both sets of providers, who have taken on their endeavours as family units, work on the local scale, integrating practices of sustainable economy, ecology, culture, and society. They bring in guests to educate them about the integration of the local landscape and culture, in hopes that highlighting their preservation efforts will benefit the local community and contribute to the sustainability of its traditional way of life, while at the same time providing a transformative travel experience. Small creative tourism optimizes experiential potential for tourists, so the size of visitor groups is kept small, and the pace slow, which in turn reduces the negative impacts often caused by larger tourism.

Hull, Senese, and Esau's fulsome literature review on altruism and tourism identifies a reciprocal relationship between providers, guests, and communities, which can provide both direct (between two actors, including within community networks) and indirect (for the community as a whole) benefits. They point out that there is scant literature on intentional altruistic tourism—outside volunteer tourism—and they hope their chapter makes a contribution to this topic. Through their case study of a summer school at SIEC, the authors show how the Sonnino family is motivated to preserve their ancestors' relationship with the land and the village of Montespertoli and sustain the community's collaborative sharecropping system. As Hull and his co-authors write,

> These participatory tourism experiences developed at Castello Sonnino have helped diversify small-scale tourism offerings in the region, and have transformed the estate into an economically viable and internationally recognized rural centre for sustainable development. Importantly, this case study has demonstrated that altruism—in this case, between hosts and students at the SEIC—plays an important motivating role in small tourism and shows how it can help preserve the environment and cultural heritage for future generations. (104)

The guests, in this case the participants and instructors at the 2018 SIEC summer school, fully participate in the operations of the estate and engage with the local community through experiential education. This three-way collaboration between provider, visitor, and community produces direct and indirect benefits for all, while at the same time co-creating what we can understand to be the "local," a defining feature of creative tourism.

This altruistic intentional motivation to provide small tourism experiences is reflected in the personal stories of the land restorers recorded by Maley and her co-authors. The three families of restorers deliberately undertake the reparation of land and Noongar culture—together forming the *Boodja*—to its natural state. By hosting small visitor groups (typically ten to fifty visitors dispersed over a month) in the family-run restored areas, the authors report that,

> in the context of small, relational tourism, we follow a journey of landscape and cultural reconnection that focuses on tourists' brief immersion with land restorers at the site of recreation. This creative approach is strategic, aligning with the principles of sustainable tourism (Bradby 2016, 316) and with those of altruistic tourism, yielding mutual benefits for the restorers and their visitors. (112)

Later in their chapter, they make a strong argument for indirect community benefit, another characteristic of altruistic tourism, as exposure to, experience with, and reflection on local *Boodja* reparation creates a ripple effect encouraging strategies of sustainability in the wider Australian community.

In both the Italian and Australian cases, more than fifteen thousand kilometres apart, slow tourism allows time for the reflection and the relational aspects that small tourism engenders. There is no need to cover a lot of ground or to check items from a list. These small tourism adventures are more about feeling and experience, and quality above quantity. When altruistic providers offer slow tourism, they are more apt to master their art and provide quality—they think and feel deeply about the passion projects and lifestyles they are sharing. The authors in this set of chapters contend that the same is true for the consumers of these experiences. Guests have the feeling that they are making a genuine contribution within a continuum of sustainable development. Strong, long-lasting, and transformative change in these examples occurs both within and outside of the visitor, the resident, and the community. These chapters highlight the role of altruism in informing and supporting small-scale creative tourism, especially in rural areas. But small tourism also happens in cities.

Small Tourism: Sustaining Local Culture and Social Inclusion in Urban Neighbourhoods

Neighbourhoods in cities are often understood to be destinations for tourists: the red-light district in Amsterdam, Gastown in Vancouver, or El Gótico in Barcelona. However, the neighbourhoods in which residents actually live not only comprise geographical units of cities, they also contain elements of the local as described by Higgins-Desbiolles and Bigby. Indeed, tourists seeking immersion in local culture will look for the smaller nooks and crannies of cities, in hopes of engaging in authentic experiences on a human—or small—scale. The DMO for Copenhagen, in fact, bases its entire campaign on this idea through the concept of "localhood."[4] Both chapters in this study-story set explore small tourism in neighbourhoods of larger urban centres. Andre Principe examines how a neighbourhood cultural association is actually an actor in local tourism in "The Role of Cultural Associations in the Promotion of Small Tourism and Social Inclusion in the Neighbourhood of Bonfim, Oporto: the Case of Casa Bô." In their story of creating local tourism experiences in "Small Tourism in a Big City: The Story of 5Bogota," Diana Guerra Amaya and Diana Marcela Zuluaga Guerra show how their experience operating a tourism micro-enterprise reflects many of the themes

Principe identifies in his chapter, most notably how locals have taken control of the tourism experiences offered by their own neighbourhood. In exploring the creation of tourism in these small locales in Oporto and Bogotá, we see strands of the neolocalism investigated by Linda Ingram, Susan L. Slocum, and Christina Cavaliere in 2020. Susan L. Slocum explains:

> Neolocalism involves the crafting of the tourism product that reflects the culture, history, and value system inherent in a destination. Neolocalism is defined as "the reaction of individuals and groups to consciously establish, rebuild, and cultivate local ties, local identities, and local economies." (2020, 208)

In this deliberate decision to circumvent the traditional tropes of tourism, and in the political decision to take the sharing and consumption of their own locale into their own hands, residents of neighbourhoods create authenticity by offering their own experiences of their localhoods, their ways of life, as a tourism product. The local is the most authentic offering tourists can encounter—a cultural association in a parish of Oporto, or a farmers' market in a compromised neighbourhood of Bogotá, provide glimpses into a genuine way of life, as does a relationship between visitors and residents that benefits both, as well as the community. Such subtle expressions of a particular place are not available through larger tourism experiences, nor can they be furnished by traditional tourism providers. Small creative tourism knits a shared community experience.

Principe presents the parish of Bonfim, challenged by COVID-19, an aging population, and swaths of deserted buildings. Guerra and Zuluaga describe how Bogotá has suffered not only from COVID-19, but also, famously, from the insecurity and danger caused by drug trafficking and guerilla activity, as well as decades of international isolation as a result. As they explain, "Most of its population lives in financially vulnerable conditions, where they are viewed as a mass, closer to being numbers than persons" (page 156). Though separated by seventy-five hundred kilometres, both locations host communities whose members endure social exclusion and economic insecurity. The authors of both chapters are of the opinion that tourism micro-enterprises developed via community-led planning contribute to social inclusion and sustainability in urban neighbourhoods, and that such enterprises provide at least one strategy to reclaim the social agency that is often muted, if not buried, by the homogeneity of big tourism.

Principe's study describes the Casa Bô cultural association, a non-profit or third-sector organization responsible for providing Bonfim with programs that support culture, environmental sustainability, and social solidarity. Run by volunteers and locally led, it offers what for-profit or municipal bodies do not. Principe's research reveals that its activities also serve small numbers of tourists, as Oporto's burgeoning tourism industry expands outside its extant infrastructure, in the city's centre, and as tourism consumer trends embrace local authenticity. While challenging traditional tourism patterns and offering new touristic options, the activities in which visitors engage at Casa Bô also support neighbourhood residents through community engagement to create social inclusion and connect locals and residents for a more sustainable tourism that brings some tourism wealth into the community. Visitors tread the paths of the everyday life of the place and experience events as local residents do. With economic profit not being the main motivator at Casa Bô, it is free to create social capital by engaging residents in its activities, which serve the interest of the residents, the visitors, and the community.

Guerra and Zuluaga's story provides a how-to guide that mirrors Principe's findings, and it is firmly grounded in neolocalism in both content and intent. After detailing the challenges of under-served populations in Bogotá, and asserting that the big tourism offerings of beaches and nightlife do not serve these residents, the authors explain

> That is why we at 5Bogota decided to create a project that opens the possibility for real and everyday people to break into the tourism industry through the concept of small, creative tourism.
> . . .
> 5Bogota is a small tourism start-up that connects travellers with local hosts who showcase the country realistically and uniquely. At 5Bogota, we design tours and experiences that are completely authentic, through which travellers learn about our culture and our people while supporting local development. This has the potential to transform the Colombian travel industry, making it more inclusive and participative. (157)

Guerra and Zuluaga proceed to provide a step-by-step guide for practitioners interested in developing a tourism micro-enterprise that furnishes small-scale experiences based on local tangible and intangible cultural assets to modest numbers in local neighbourhoods. Their methodology is based on utilizing or creating clusters of partners who wish to share their everyday experience with visitors, and who engage in a collaborative cultural mapping process to determine the final shape of the tourism products. This strategy not only results in authentic local experiences, but more importantly, it also creates agency, social inclusion, and cultural capital. The authors then provide three examples of their products. Like the Razjefibre tours in Maribor, one of the goals of 5Bogota is to bring and keep tourism dollars in the neighbourhood.

5Bogota and Casa Bô rely on collaborative, community-led planning to present their micro-tourism products; both cite workshops[5] and gastronomic experiences as ways to engage small groups of visitors and residents at the same point in space and time, sharing local endogenous knowledge. As Principe explains about the social dinners hosted at Casa Bô:

> Greater social interaction takes place most prominently at the vegetarian dinners that occur before evening cultural events. Event artists, members of Casa Bô, and the audience share a long table with seating for about sixteen people, or other tables around the kitchen and library room. During dinner, everyone sits at a table with no marked places, and usually the members of Casa Bô sit and interact with visitors so that there is more interaction and contact between all. This initiative allows for the beginning of new friendships between residents, tourists, artists, and volunteers of the cultural association. (138)

Guerra and Zuluaga on the same topic:

> Gastronomy is one of the crucial elements to research if you want to share with your visitors the customs of local culture; meals can foster moments of profound connection with locals and their customs. These moments happen organically as visitors and residents enjoy the flavours and scents of a meal, snack, or beverage. During these activities, language barriers are also reduced for both foreigners and locals, increasing social inclusion for all. (163)

Small tourism in these examples not only offers visitors an authentic local experience, but also provides one strategy for creating a more informed, active, and socially inclusive community. In urban centres, such neighbourhood engagement can also help disperse tourists from over-touristed central areas, as these two chapters demonstrate.

Small Tourism: Networking and Arts Festivals in the Periphery

Our next set of chapters takes us out of urban neighbourhoods and into peripheral areas. Large and well-known arts festivals create their own cultures, to which participants flock annually, such as the Burning Man music festival in the Black Rock Desert of Nevada. The cultures of such huge festivals are formed from self-generated practices, guided by the philosophies of their leaders, and can be mobile. So the cultural assets they produce and reproduce are not endogenous; they may be "local" to the festival, but they are not particularly tied to place. Burning Man's "10 Principles," on which its activities are based, does not mention any real geographical location; instead, they construct "Black Rock City" every August.[6] But when they are tied to location, especially to geographically peripheral ones, are intentionally connected to community cultural assets, and are developed as a result of community-led planning, small arts festivals in small places can be powerful engines to express a sense of place, to create cultural capacity, to facilitate social inclusion, and to encourage visitor-resident co-creation.

In their contributions to the book *Neolocalism and Tourism: Understanding a Global Movement* (2020), both Ros Derrett's and Guanhua Peng, Solène Prince, and Marianna Strzelecka's chapters explore this theme in New South Wales, Australia, and Öland, Sweden, respectively. Their work contributes to the literature on arts festivals in the periphery, which is also the topic of the first study in our fourth set of chapters, Emese Panyik and Attila Komlós's "Cultural Festivals in Small Villages: Creativity and the Case of the Devil's Nest Festival in Hungary." Panyik and Komlós point out that "little is known about the potential of festivals to draw attention to underdeveloped, small, and isolated regions," and that, like the authors in *Neolocalism and Tourism*, they "aim to address that research gap" in their chapter. They believe, like most authors in the present volume, that "authentic experiences are often segregated, hidden in isolated places far from urban areas or popular tourist attractions or destinations. Larger tourism enterprises are typically ill-suited for small, creative tourism experiences" (pages 173–74).

Panyik and Komlós's chapter details the importance of creative clusters and community networking in producing this annual festival. Networking in small communities is a feature of small creative tourism experiences, and it is that networking that binds not only residents to visitors, but, arguably more importantly, residents to each other and to their place. Peng, Prince, and Strzelecka's case study of the Skördefest harvest festival, which celebrates local foodways, mirrors Panyik and Komlós' work on the Devil's Nest Festival, which "was born in a remote limestone quarry located about twenty kilometres from the closest city, Pécs, as a small-scale arts festival, through the collaboration of four neighbouring villages and two wineries" (page 174). Even though Pécs is two thousand kilometres southeast of Öland, our study echoes Peng, Prince, and Strzelecka's, showing, as Panyik and Komlós assert, that

> in order to create an authentic experience, tourist events should reflect the origins of the place. As interactivity and community-led planning and participation are among the chief festival objectives, various new creative forms of artistic expression have been developed in which local entrepreneurs, visitors, and residents actively co-create, mostly by means of open-air performances, with minimal design and accessories, drawing on local resources. (185)

Both of these studies in two different books offer calls to action for small festivals in small places, which these authors argue support local creative clusters through visitor-resident engagement, resulting not only in financial benefits to the community but also in cultural sustainability.

These ideas reverberate in the story that accompanies Panyik and Komlós's chapter, Donald Lawrence's "Artistic Micro-Adventures in Small Places," a memoir about his experiences as a visual artist participating in three Canadian small arts festivals in the relatively remote communities of North Bay, Ontario, St. John's, Newfoundland, and Dawson City, Yukon. Lawrence has three objectives in sharing his story, and they pair resoundingly with the accompanying study by Panyik and Komlós:

> First, the context of this volume may simply be a good opportunity to call attention to such arts events as these for practitioners and scholars of tourism, in the hopes of interesting tourism

promoters in small arts festivals. Second, in some respects, these sorts of events work best because they are organized by a small collaborative network in a local community, including artists, and perhaps some artists from other places. The tourists, maybe small in number, who purposefully or otherwise find themselves in the middle of such events, will experience something special, something genuinely experimental and/or local in conception—often a one-time-only experience. Third, though the artists and curators who come from away to participate in such events may not be tourists in the typical sense, they are often highly engaged visitors to such communities, contributing to local economies and intent on building important linkages between small places, networks comprising members of an extended cultural community, which may be an important ingredient for the sustainability of small tourism in small places. (192)

Lawrence's "micro-adventures," placed in the context described by Panyik and Komlós, and considered in relation to studies such as those by Ros Derrett, which demonstrates that "community-led festivals celebrate the community's social identity, its historical continuity, and its cultural resilience" (2020, 103), make real and give experiential substance to the concept that small arts festivals in small places "are socially constructed and negotiated phenomena that can be staged in everyday places that also become tourist places" (103). Lawrence's piece "One Eye Folly," located a half-mile offshore from North Bay on the ice of frozen Lake Nipissing, demonstrates the potential of community-based small tourism in the close-knit places that not only celebrate but also rely on their local traditions, such as life on the ice in the frozen North. Canada is a long way from Hungary, but Lawrence's story corroborates and amplifies the results of Panyik and Komlós' research. Small arts festivals, conceived and organized by locals, and the involvement of networked community volunteers, can be a deliberate strategy in which small tourism is deployed to promote cultural sustainability. This idea was also voiced in our first set of chapters set in rural British Columbia and Maribor, Slovenia. And cultural sustainability is a way forward to a resilient future not only for local communities, but also, as we will see in the final study-story set, for tourism as a sustainable industry.

Small Tourism: Community Resilience and Agency

COVID-19 has highlighted the need for resilience in the tourism industry. In this section's study, Meng Qu and Simona Zollet argue that community-based tourism activities in small places have a huge impact on the quality of life, revitalization and resilience, and sustainability of local populations. Tourism is often seen as the last chance for challenged places. The power of small is that it is flexible and can generate great impacts. It can also offer unique, one-of-a-kind experiences based on place. Developing micro-tourism enterprises can be attractive for entrepreneurs who are not motivated purely by profit and who wish to contribute to their communities as well. These are lifestyle entrepreneurs, similar to those in our section on altruism and small tourism. Creative tourism in particular, which relies on meaningful participation in local intangible cultural knowledge, is often best offered in small places to small groups. In their chapter "The Power of Small: Creative In-Migrant Micro-Entrepreneurs in Peripheral Japanese Islands during COVID-19," Qu and Zollet's research on the island of Mitarai shows how the integration of various local and external networks developed in tourism micro-enterprises contributes to "individual and community-level resilience" on this island, on which two-thirds of the residents are over sixty-five, with half of those over eighty. The tourism enterprises in this already fragile peripheral community that depends on tourism for economic sustainability was especially challenged to help ensure the safety of this vulnerable local population during the pandemic. Qu and Zollet's work shows "how COVID-19, despite its initial negative impact on tourism, also served as the catalyst for creative adaptation and innovation processes both at the individual and network levels" (page 236). The authors further argue that their

> findings add to the literature on the role of creative micro-businesses in small declining communities as a major driving force in supporting tourism development in ways that are respectful of the local community, enhance its social resilience, and promote sustainable tourism development and regional revitalization (Fleming 2010; Jóhannesson and Lund 2018; Qu and McCormick, and Funck 2020; Yachin and Ioannides 2020). The examples presented in the chapter show the social innovation aspects of diversified micro-entrepreneurs and their networks and their involvement in community-engaged initiatives. Small-scale

businesses in small-scale destinations are more likely to develop their businesses through a creative enhancement approach (Mitchell 2013); in our examples, the crucial role played by their creative and relational attributes was demonstrated during the pandemic. The social role of micro-businesses can be described as the capacity to use innovative ideas to enhance community resilience. (237)

This case study took place from 2017 to 2021, so both before and during the pandemic. The author's findings echo a case study carried out from 2017 to 2019 in the small Central Appalachian community with the pseudonym Nolan, whose population of approximately two thousand has been decimated by the decline of the coal industry, authored by Neda Moayerian, Nancy G. McGehee, and Max O. Stephenson (2022). Although they do not broach COVID-19, Moayerian and her co-authors examine a community arts collective's work in small tourism, and ask

whether and how the interaction of community cultural development and community capacity were influencing the sustainability of tourism in the small community we studied. Those interviewed for this study contended that the Collective's work has contributed to more sustainable tourism in Nolan by increasing residents' participation in tourism decision-making processes, encouraging locals' partnership and ownership of tourism development projects, and providing space for more genuine guest-host relationships. Effective engagement manifested as more informed and inclusive decision-making processes. Those, along with engaged residents' capacity to collaborate and own tourism projects appeared to be leading to increased "fairness and equity in the distribution and use of tourism-related resources" (Dangi & Jamal, 2016, p. 457). Additionally, community cultural development's contributions to residents' balanced awareness of tourism development, along with their capacity to engage in authentic dialogue with tourists (i.e., the hospitality and stewardship of local culture) look set to support ongoing efforts to develop a more sustainable form of tourism in Nolan. (11–12)

These findings support those of Qu and Zollet. Both studies, carried out around the same time approximately sixty-seven hundred kilometres apart, show that integrated clusters of creative actors offering small tourism experiences contribute to the development, resilience, agency, cultural and social capacity, and sustainability of small places.

The emphasis on sustainable local development through community-based tourism is a trend identified by Ian Yeoman and Una McMahon-Beattie as one of their ten predictions offered in "Small Tourism and Ecotourism: Emerging Micro-Trends," our volume's final chapter. They contend that

> COVID-19 has changed the world, and from a tourism perspective, destinations have started to think about the values that are important to them. Therefore, tourists in general are thinking "local," "visiting friends and relatives," and "doing the right thing" (Carr 2020; Sharfuddin 2020; Sheldon 2021). Often, this means small trips to visit small groups. (243)

Two of the trends the authors point out, supporting local and an increased sense of community, mirror the findings of Qu and Zollet's case study. Yeoman and Mahon-Beattie, like Qu and Zollet, argue that the "ability of small tourism destinations to deliver rare, bespoke, local experiences provides the tourist with opportunities to acquire . . . the ultimate souvenir" (page 249). These visitors to small communities constitute another trend, the authenti-seeker: "small destinations with a clear sense of place, heritage, and culture are well positioned to deliver the unique experiences so keenly sought after by authenti-seekers" (page 246). Both chapters in this set also conclude that the impact of COVID-19 provides an opportunity for tourism to reimagine the future. Both sets of authors surmise, in the words of Yeoman and Mahon-Beattie, that

> small tourism allows communities to address issues of social inequality, to create a sense of place, to gain ownership of the tourism-development process, and, most importantly of all, to allow the development of entrepreneurship and innovation. (258)

Like all chapters in this book, this set points to the burgeoning interest in and implementation of community-based micro-enterprises in tourism futures.

Small communities with informed residents can be innovative when it comes to developing small tourism enterprises that reap all the benefits of creative tourism, including cultural resilience and participant agency.

Can Small Tourism Help Define the Path to Regenerative Tourism?

Throughout this introduction, I have sought to orient readers of this volume within the context of my earlier edited volume, *Creative Tourism in Smaller Communities*, as I conceive these two books very much as a complementary pair. Because I wanted in this book to provide as much content for students as for practitioners curious about case studies of small tourism in small places, I alerted the reader to the study-story structure as a device to express the common themes demonstrated in each set of chapters, emphasizing that the issues raised in tourism scholarship also exist for—in this case—small tourism entrepreneurs, consumers, and locations. None of the authors gathered here knew who the other authors would be, so I did not construct these mirroring concepts—they bubbled up in the work, and I merely noticed and arranged the sets to highlight these connections. By way of acquainting the reader with our authors and their chapters, I identified the conceptual constituents that led me to arrange the work into these particular sets, and further contextualized the sets with recent scholarship and pieces from the popular press that reflect similar ideas or findings. Finally, I endeavoured to connect each set of chapters to the definition of and conditions for creative tourism established in 2021's *Creative Tourism in Smaller Communities*.

Small tourism in small places with small numbers of visitors is not the catholicon for the problems generated by mass tourism or the obliteration caused by the pandemic. Nor will mass tourism likely disappear. But as a number of our authors—and others—have pointed out, this crisis provides a useful opportunity to rethink tourism, and perhaps a great chance for community-led and community-based micro-tourism to establish a foothold as waves of tourists begin to crest again. This rethinking includes a call for a more informed local community that engages actively and intelligently in the creation of tourism experiences. Local, community-led tourism practice is thus a topic of great interest. Books such as Nancy Duxbury, Sara Albino, and Cláudia Carvalho's *Creative Tourism: Activating Cultural Resources and Engaging Creative Travellers* (2021) offers perspectives for tourism providers.

Similarly, tourism journals are publishing articles about the rise in local community participation that create resident agency, taking a hand in their place's tourism. Quite recently, Dimitrios Stylidis and Ana Maria Dominguez Quintero (2022), in their study on resident knowledge of tourism and positive word-of-mouth endorsements in Seville, Spain, wrote,

> A tenable explanation offered by . . . researchers is that knowledge reinforces "critical citizens" who hold more critical attitudes towards further tourism development (Christensen & Laegreid, 2005). For Rua (2020) . . . these more knowledgeable residents can act as gatekeepers of sustainable tourism development in the area, with such knowledge elevating their notion of empowerment (Joo et al., 2020). For example, Joo et al. (2020) reported that the more knowledgeable about tourism local residents were, the more psychologically, socially, and politically empowered they felt. In contrast, lack of knowledge is reported as a main obstacle in residents' participation in decision making related to tourism (Weng & Peng, 2014).

But recent scholarship calls not only for informed residents, but also informed visitors who make tourism choices that benefit the destination community. Dianne Dredge has recently written that acting on this call requires a complete change of mindset, a paradigm shift she believes is currently underway in many fields. In her 2022 article "Regenerative Tourism: Transforming Mindsets, Systems and Practices," she establishes a case for regenerative tourism, which she says "seeks to ensure travel and tourism reinvest in people, places and nature and that it supports the long-term renewal and flourishing of our social-ecological systems." She further argues that "regenerative tourism requires a deeply engaged bottom-up approach that is place-based, community-centred and environment-focused."

These are also characteristic elements of small creative tourism experiences. Also writing in 2022, and in the context of the war in Ukraine, Sara Dolnicar and Scott McCabe published a piece in *Annals of Tourism Research* introducing the concept of "solidarity tourism," which they define as

> tourism-related action taken by governments, tourism businesses and tourists to help people suffering during and after crises,

driven by empathy towards people, a sense of unity, and a shared understanding of societal standards and responsibilities.

The tourism industry in Ukraine, they suggest, could rebuild its offerings with an emphasis on helping locals. This, too, sounds like one of the desirable tenets of small creative tourism enterprises. Perhaps small tourism has the ability to contribute to regenerative tourism.

In this introduction's survey of the chapters you are about to read, we see this theme of local empowerment through resident involvement in community-based tourism, and we recognize the benefits of an informed resident participation. We see elements of neolocalism, altruism, diversity, and ecology. We see the need to support and market tourism micro-enterprises. We see trends pulling tourists to smaller places. We see visitors and residents coming together to co-create place. We see walks and workshops. We see gastronomy and art. We see festivals. We see niche markets and niche experiences. We see authenticity. We see economic, ecological, social, and cultural sustainability. We observe the marked emphasis on local. But above all, we see small. And in my view, we see that small creative tourism initiatives can be part of the movement toward regenerative tourism.

Big tourism is not only unsustainable; it also does not address tourism trends such as those enumerated in Yeoman and McMahon-Beattie's chapter in this volume. Neither does it account for local tourism. I live part of the year in Mainz, an ancient city on the Rhine that has been my family's home for generations. There is plenty of traditional tourism available here, what with *die Altstadt*, the Romans, Gutenberg, the world wars, the museums, the Mainz Citadel, the river, cathedrals, old churches, the city's thrice-weekly open farmers market, and, of course, the wine. There is no end of city tours complete with guides holding colour-coded flags and tourists with headsets coming off the river cruises. I wanted to seek out some small tourism activities in the months I've been here working on this book, so that I could learn a bit more about my city's *Orte*—those points at which residents, visitors, and sense of place come together. I wondered if my hypotheses about small tourism and community are actually reflected in the place where I live. It took a while, but I eventually found a tourism micro-enterprise called Best of Mainz (founded by Stephanie Jung in 2016, with five employees).[7] I was able to tour and learn fascinating stories about neighbourhoods that are not of particular interest to typical tourists. I took two of the walks, and was interested to find not a single tourist among the ten guests that made up the tour of *die Neustadt*, nor in the sixteen that made up that of the Hauptfriedhof—the main cemetery. All were Mainz residents. I asked them why they were there, and they all thought they would like to know more about their town. One couple said they often walk by the main cemetery, but they did not know much about its history, and nothing about its cultural significance. As we stopped at places where our guides provided explanations, the Mainzers would often chime in with their own stories about that particular *Ort*, or would chat about the *Ort* and their experiences with it among themselves. Here, I saw real community development, real resident engagement with place, real social capital being built. The shared stories wove a tapestry of community perspectives. Small places, small groups, small provider. Frau Jung, when I interviewed her on 17 March 2022, said she did not have tourists in mind when she started her walking tours—they were at first a way to market her books on Mainz, also her family's hometown for generations. The walks proved very successful, even with tourists, but on the majority of her tours, which tend to attract people who are interested in the lived culture of Mainz, as opposed to those who merely want to check off items from a list, Frau Jung says she wants to provide an alternative perspective of Mainz: Mainz the way a local knows it. I share this story—and believe me, it is much abridged, and would be better discussed over a glass (or two) of nice crisp local Riesling—because isn't that just what we have been talking about in this introduction to small tourism? Someone exploring localhood as curated by its residents, with the ripples from these interactions nourishing the community's well-being. Such can be the effect of small.

NOTES

1   https://www.ricksteves.com.

2   The film is available on YouTube: https://www.youtube.com/watch?v=kdXcFChRpmI.

3   https://borntocookbarcelona.com.

4   https://localhood.wonderfulcopenhagen.dk.

5   Readers interested in pursuing other examples of micro-enterprises offering local, endogenous-knowledge workshops are well-advised to watch the fabulous documentary *CREATOUR—Creative Tourism in Portugal* directed by Nuno Barbosa, which showcases the creative tourism projects initiated by this groundbreaking creative tourism institution founded in Portugal by Nancy Duxbury at the Centre for Social

Studies at the University of Coimbra. The film is available on YouTube: https://www.
youtube.com/watch?v=JXVsGLGUaUs&ab_channel=NunoBarbosa.

6   https://burningman.org/about/10-principles/.

7   https://best-of-mainz.com/#!/cal-d/2021-08-28/cw/5f1986b5310e789b0678c29f2614d5af.

References

Baidin, Ivan. 2021. *Forbes*, 3 May 2021. https://www.forbes.com/sites/
forbesbusinesscouncil/2021/05/03/three-post-pandemic-travel-trends-to-watch-
this-year/?sh=37a5fa0a6a2e.

Bradby, Keith. 2016. "Biodiversity Restoration and Sustainable Tourism in South-Western
Australia." In *Life Cycle Approaches to Sustainable Regional Development*, edited
by Stefania Massari, Guido Sonnemann, and Fritz Balkau. New York: Taylor and
Francis.

Carr, Anna. 2020. "COVID-19, Indigenous Peoples and Tourism: A View from New
Zealand." *Tourism Geographies* 22, no. 3: 491–502. doi:10.1080/14616688.2020.176
8433.

Christensen, T., and P. Laegreid. 2005. "Trust in Government: The Relative Importance of
Service Satisfaction, Political Factors, and Demography." *Public Performance and
Management Review* 28, no. 4: 487–511.

Dangi, Tek B., and Tazim Jamal. 2016. "An Integrated Approach to 'Sustainable
Community-Based Tourism.'" Sustainability, 8(5), 475. https://doi.org/10.3390/
su8050475.

Derrett, Ros. 2020. "Community Festivals Reveal Tangible and Intangible Bounty." In
Neolocalism and Tourism: Understanding a Global Movement, edited by Linda J.
Ingram, Susan L. Slocum, and Christina T. Cavaliere, 100–22. Oxford: Goodfellow
Publishers.

Dolnicar, Sara, and Scott McCabe. 2022. "Solidarity Tourism: How Can Tourism Help the
Ukraine and Other War-Torn Countries?" *Annals of Tourism Research* 94 (May).
https://doi.org/10.1016/j.annals.2022.103386.

Dredge, Dianne. 2022. "Regenerative Tourism: Transforming Mindsets, Systems and
Practices." *Journal of Tourism Futures*, 31 May 2022. https://doi.org/10.1108/JTF-
01-2022-0015.

Duxbury, Nancy, Sara Albino, and Cláudia Carvalho, eds, *Creative Tourism: Activating
Cultural Resources and Engaging Creative Travellers*. London: CABI.

European Commission. 2015. *User Guide to the SME Definition*. Brussels: Publications
Office. https://ec.europa.eu/regional_policy/sources/conferences/stateaid/sme/
smedefinitionguide_en.pdf. Accessed 27 March 2022.

European Commission. 2016. Directorate-General for Internal Market, Industry, Entrepreneurship and SMEs, User guide to the SME definition, Publications Office, 2017, https://data.europa.eu/doi/10.2873/620234

Fleming, Rachel C. 2010. "Creative Economic Development, Sustainability, and Exclusion in Rural Areas." *Geographical Review* 99, no. 1: 61–80. https://doi.org/10.1111/j.1931-0846.2009.tb00418.x.

Hernández-Martín, Raúl, Moisés Ramón Simancas-Cruz, Jesús Alberto González-Yanes, Yurena Rodríguez-Rodríguez, Juan Israel García-Cruz, and Yenis Marisel González-Mora. 2016. "Identifying Micro-Destinations and Providing Statistical Information: A Pilot Study in the Canary Islands." *Current Issues in Tourism* 19, no. 8: 771–90. http://dx.doi.org/10.1080/13683500.2014.

Higgins-Desbiolles, Freya, and Bobbi Chew Bigby. 2022. "A Local Turn in Tourism Studies." *Annals of Tourism Research* 92 (January). https://doi.org/10.1016/j.annals.2021.103291.

Ingram, Linda J., Susan L. Slocum, and Christina T. Cavaliere, eds. 2020. *Neolocalism and Tourism: Understanding a Global Movement.* Oxford: Goodfellows Publishers.

Jóhannesson, Gunnar Thór, and Katrin Anna Lund. 2018. "Creative Connections? Tourists, Entrepreneurs and Destination Dynamics." *Scandinavian Journal of Hospitality and Tourism* 18, no. 1: 60–74. https://doi.org/10.1080/15022250.2017.1340549.

Joo, D., K. M. Woosnam, M. Strzelecka, and B. B. Boley. 2020. "Knowledge, Empowerment, and Action: Testing the Empowerment Theory in a Tourism Context." *Journal of Sustainable Tourism* 28, no. 1: 69–85.

Lobrano, Alexander. 2021. "Making Discovery, Not Distance, Travel's Point." *New York Times*, 22 July 2021. https://www.nytimes.com/2021/07/21/travel/small-travel-france.html?smtyp=cur&smid=tw-nytimestravel.

McCormick, A.D., and Meng Qu. 2021. "Community Resourcefulness under Pandemic Pressure: A Japanese Island's Creative Network." *Geographical Sciences* 76, no. 2: 74–86.

Mitchell, Clare J. A. 2013. "Creative Destruction or Creative Enhancement? Understanding the Transformation of Rural Spaces." *Journal of Rural Studies* 32 (October): 375–87. https://doi.org/10.1016/j.jrurstud.2013.09.005.

Moayerian, Neda, Nancy G. McGehee, and Max O. Stephenson. 2022. "Community Cultural Development: Exploring the Connections between Collective Art Making, Capacity Building and Sustainable Community-Based Tourism." *Annals of Tourism Research* 93 (March): 103335. https://doi.org/10.1016/j.annals.2022.103355.

Rua, S. V. 2020. "Perceptions of tourism: A Study of Residents' Attitudes towards Tourism in the City of Girona." *Journal of Tourism Analysis* 27, no. 2: 165–84.

Russo, Antonio Paolo, and Greg Richards, eds. 2016. *Reinventing the Local in Tourism: Producing, Consuming and Negotiating Place.* Buffalo, NY: Channel View Publications.

Sharfuddin, Syed. 2020. "The World after Covid-19." *The Round Table: The Commonwealth Journal of International Affairs* 109, no. 3: 247–57. doi:10.1080/00358533.2020.1760 498.

Scherf, Kathleen, ed. 2021. *Creative Tourism in Smaller Communities: Place, Culture, and Local Representation.* Calgary: University of Calgary Press.

Sheldon, Pauline J. 2021. "The Coming-of-Age of Tourism: Embracing New Economic Models." *Journal of Tourism Futures*, 23 June 2021. doi:10.1108/JTF-03-2021-0057.

Slocum, Susan L. 2020. "Governance and Neolocalism: Guiding the Creative Process." In *Neolocalism and Tourism: Understanding a Global Movement*, edited by Linda J. Ingram, Susan L. Slocum, and Christina T. Cavaliere, 208–26. Oxford: Goodfellow Publishers.

Stylidis, Dimitrios, and Ana Maria Dominguez Quintero. 2022. "Understanding the Effect of Place Image and Knowledge of Tourism on Residents' Attitudes towards Tourism and Their Word-of-Mouth Intentions: Evidence from Seville, Spain." *Tourism Planning and Development*, 11 March 2022. https://doi.org/10.1080/21568 316.2022.2049859.

Peng, Guanhua, Solène Prince, and Marianna Strzelecka. 2020. "Neolocalism and Social Sustainability: The Case of Öland's Harvest Festival, Sweden." In *Neolocalism and Tourism: Understanding a Global Movement*, edited by Linda J. Ingram, Susan L. Slocum, and Christina T. Cavaliere, 164–84. Oxford: Goodfellow Publishers.

Qu, Meng, A. D. McCormick, and Carolin Funck. 2020. "Community Resourcefulness and Partnerships in Rural Tourism." *Journal of Sustainable Tourism* 30, no. 10: 2371–90. https://doi.org/10.1080/09669582.2020.1849233.

UNWTO (United Nations World Tourism Organization). 2022. Tourism Grows 4% in 2021 but Remains Far below Pre-pandemic Levels." UNWTO, 18 January 2022. https://www.unwto.org/news/tourism-grows-4-in-2021-but-remains-far-below-pre-pandemic-levels.

Weng, S., and H. Peng. 2014. "Tourism Development, Rights Consciousness and the Empowerment of Chinese Historical Village Communities." *Tourism Geographies* 16, no. 5: 772–84.

Yachnin, Jonathan Moshe. 2020. "Alters and Functions: Exploring the Ego-Networks of Tourism Micro-Firms." *Tourism Recreation Research* 46, no. 3: 319–32, https://doi.org/10.1080/02508281.2020.1808933.

Yachin, Jonathan Moshe, and Dimitri Ioannides. 2020. "'Making Do' in Rural Tourism: The Resourcing Behaviour of Tourism Micro-Firms." *Journal of Sustainable Tourism* 28, no. 7: 1003–21. https://doi.org/10.1080/09669582.2020.1715993.

1

The Development of Inclusive Small Rural Destinations for Gay Tourists in Canada

Spencer J. Toth, Josie V. Vayro, and Courtney W. Mason

The typical image of rural regions in British Columbia (BC) is a scene of rugged wilderness and abundant nature. However, these perceptions of rurality cannot be generalized to all people. For those comprising the lesbian, gay, bisexual, transgender, queer and two-spirit (LGBTQ2+) community, rural areas are commonly viewed as constraining environments that foster repression and conformity (Gottschalk and Newton 2009; Bell and Valentine 1995; Fenge and Jones 2012; D'Augelli 2006). Outward expressions of homosexuality in rural environments can result in overt discrimination against LGBTQ2+ people, as such acts are often considered taboo in contrast to hegemonic expectations of family and masculinity in rural settings (Swank, Frost, and Fahs 2012; Gottschalk and Newton 2009; Bell 2000; Fellows 1996). This can be partly attributed to the traditional view of rural areas as a haven for people holding socially conservative values regarding marriage, sexuality, and lifestyle (Bell and Valentine 1995). Gay men have avoided tourism in small rural areas in large part due to this perception. The primary focus of this study is on the rural travel experiences of gay men as opposed to the entire LGBTQ2+ community.

Gay tourism can be defined as the development and marketing of tourism products and services to LGBTQ2+ people (UNWTO and IGLTA 2017). Gay travellers visit predominantly urban gay spaces that provide a welcoming environment and allow the establishment of connections to locals and travellers of the same sexual orientation (Herrera and Scott 2005; Cox 2002; Gottschalk and Newton 2009). Urban areas have been particularly important to gay men because they allow them to connect with their community (Hughes 1997). Consequently, the majority of research on gay tourism focuses on urban areas (Johnston 2005; Hughes 2006; Guaracino 2007; Hughes 2003; Visser 2014) or on coastal beach resort towns (Melián-González, Moreno-Gil, and Araña 2011; Hughes, Monterrubio, and Miller 2010; Vorobjovas-Pinta and Robards 2017). Event tourism for gay men also receives significant attention, including in studies on gay pride parades (Johnston 2005), gay sporting events like the Gay Games (Guaracino 2007; Hughes 2006), and even events that are not explicitly associated with gay tourism but that embrace alternative sexualities and encourage attendance by gay tourists (Baker 2017). In direct contrast, rural gay tourism has not been extensively studied (Vorobjovas-Pinta and Hardy 2016).

In this chapter we explore gay tourism in rural areas of BC, Canada. We investigate the motivations, behaviours, and preferences of gay tourists who reside in BC and travel intra-provincially. To understand if the gay travel market is an area of interest for small rural destinations, we analyze how rural BC destination marketing organizations (DMOs) approach gay tourism and what actions these DMOs are taking to attract LGBTQ2+ people. Because research on gay tourism has centred on urban destinations, we aim to broaden our understandings of gay tourism by focusing on smaller, rural regions.

For the purpose of this research, we define rural destinations as parts of the province that are situated outside of BC's four census metropolitan areas (CMAs): Vancouver, Victoria, Kelowna, and Abbotsford-Mission (Statistics Canada 2019). Based on 2019 population estimates, the four CMAs have a total population of 3,710,300, or 69.75 per cent of BC's total population of 5,319,324 (BC Stats 2023). The province as a whole is over 944,000 square kilometres in size (Ministry of Forests, Lands, Natural Resource Operations and Rural Development, n.d.). By comparison, the four CMAs in BC comprise just 7,090.82 square kilometres, or 0.75 per cent of BC's total land area. With 30.25 per cent of BC's population living outside of its four major urban metropolises and distributed throughout the remaining 99.25 per cent of BC's land area, the majority of the province is rural and not densely populated, with destination centres being correspondingly small. This vast rural space increases opportunities for rural tourism throughout the province. This study can thus help tourism researchers and professionals better understand how rural destinations can attract gay visitors and develop inclusive communities that welcome diverse audiences.

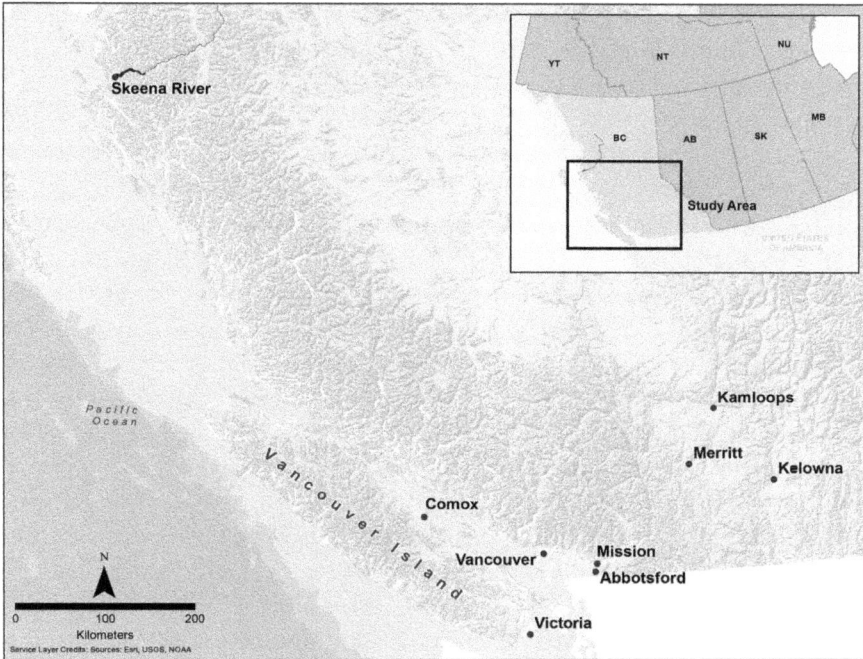

Figure 1.1: Map of Southern British Columbia.

Map created by Olea Vandermale.

Dimensions of Gay Travel and Tourism

Gay tourism has slowly become more mainstream as attitudes toward homosexuality improve in the Global North. Gay travel rose in visibility when advertisements targeting gay travellers started to appear in the late 1960s. This brought to the forefront a form of tourism that was usually hidden to protect the identity of gay travellers (Waitt and Markwell 2006). During this same period, gay villages emerged as trendy urban destinations that provided outlets for LGBTQ2+ people to escape homophobia in their daily lives and enter environments that were openly gay (Clift, Luongo, and Callister 2002). It was in these types of spaces that gay men were able to safely express their homosexuality. With the acceptance of homosexuality increasing substantially in the Global North, the expression of sexual freedom may appear to be less contentious. However, that is not necessarily the case in many regions. One study in Britain found that only 5 per cent of queer couples felt comfortable expressing open affection with their partner while travelling overseas, in sharp contrast to 84 per cent of heterosexual couples (Clarkson 2017). Such findings suggest that gay men experience varying levels of trepidation about openly expressing their sexuality while travelling in unfamiliar environments.

Gay travel is often seen as a form of identity tourism (Cox 2002; Hughes 1997; Monterrubio 2009), and sometimes as a way for gay men to explore spaces that foster self-discovery related to their sexuality (Waitt and Markwell 2006). Many rural-dwelling members of the LGBTQ2+ community do not feel comfortable expressing their queer identity until they visit gay spaces, typically in urban areas, where they feel accepted for who they are (Gottschalk and Newton 2009; Herrera and Scott 2005). Therefore, gay men living in rural areas or small towns undertake travel to traditionally gay destinations to access environments that do not exist in their hometowns (Clift and Forrest 1999), and as a way of escaping the constraints of these heteronormative environments (Herrera and Scott 2005). Gay tourism can also benefit local gay men in host destinations by providing opportunities for them to interact with other gay men and embrace their sexuality (Monterrubio 2018). Travel thus allows gay men to escape daily constraints, be they social, religious, or otherwise, that prevent them from openly embracing their gay identities (Roth and Luongo 2002).

Gay travellers are sometimes defined homogeneously as a group of high-spending individuals with a great propensity to travel because they often visit similar destinations (Golding 2003). This perception is in part due to researchers focusing heavily on the perspectives of younger gay men and neglecting to explore how travel needs and motivations differ among the entire gay population (Hughes 2005). This gap in research means that the diversity in the gay travel market is not recognized. Similar to the broader tourism market, age, race, occupation, socio-economic status, and marital status are factors that influence the desires and abilities of gay travellers (Hughes 2003). There is, however, a growing body of literature showing that the gay travel market is very heterogeneous (Ro, Olson, and Choi 2017; Vorobjovas-Pinta and Hardy 2016). In fact, destination selection and travel interests among gay men are very similar to those of heterosexual tourists (Blichfeldt, Chor, and Milan 2011; Clift and Forrest 1999; Weeden, Lester, and Jarvis 2016), with the added requirement of gay-friendliness (Hughes and Deutsch 2010). Despite this, the profile of gay travellers varies from that of the average tourist in some respects. One study conducted in the Canary Islands found gay tourists were more highly educated, stayed longer in the destinations, were more likely to travel alone, and had an average daily expenditure that was substantially higher than that of the general tourist (Melián-González, Moreno-Gil, and Araña 2011). While research specific to gay travellers' preferences needs further research, the most critical consideration for queer travellers is the gay-friendliness of a destination (Hughes 2005; Herrera and Scott 2005).

Gay-friendliness of a destination, which correlates directly with safety, is a central consideration for many gay travellers (Want 2002; Pritchard et al. 2000). Destination selection is often viewed through a risk-avoidance lens to reduce the chance of encountering homophobia and unsafe environments when travelling (Hughes 2002). Many LGBTQ2+ tourists feel they do not receive the same treatment on holiday as heterosexual tourists. Research indicates that queer people often change how they act and conceal their queer identity while on vacation (UNWTO and IGLTA 2017). In this way, gay tourists have fundamentally different concerns when travelling compared to their heterosexual counterparts. Most queer people refuse to travel to destinations that are socially, culturally, or legally unwelcoming to homosexuality. With gay tourism frequently undertaken to escape the constraints of a generally heteronormative society, the safety and acceptance of individuals who wish to express their queer identities while on vacation is an important consideration for destinations looking to attract an LGBTQ2+ market (Pritchard et al. 2000). Small destinations may be especially challenged in this regard.

Major urban centres and beach resort towns in North America and Europe have historically been quintessential gay travel destinations, as they frequently have large LGBTQ2+ communities that attract additional LGBTQ2+ people from other places (UNWTO and IGLTA 2017). As a result, many gay resort towns are situated in close proximity to urban metropolises, particularly in the United States (US), to ensure easy access for urban-dwelling gay men. North America and western Europe are the biggest gay destinations, with large urban capitals like Berlin and San Francisco the most prominent hot spots, alongside a few gay-coded beach resort towns like Key West and Provincetown (Waitt and Markwell 2006). However, increasing acceptance of homosexuality, combined with a growing desire by gay men to expand their travel beyond the walls of traditional gay utopias, means small rural destinations have a new opportunity to market themselves to gay travellers

(Roth and Luongo 2002). Rural communities are increasingly embracing the LGBTQ2+ community, as is the case in the US state of Arkansas, where Eureka Springs' Spring Diversity Weekend and Fayetteville Pride attract a significant number of gay visitors (Kesslen 2019). Currently, large-scale events for the LGBTQ2+ community in rural areas are uncommon, but some exist and can act as a means of promoting rural gay tourism. The rural ChillOut Festival in Daylesford, Australia, which is located roughly a hundred kilometres north of Melbourne, attracts over fifteen thousand visitors annually, including an international contingent (Gorman-Murray, Waitt, and Gibson 2012; Gorman-Murray 2009). Similarly, the former Michigan Womyn's Music Festival attracted a considerable lesbian audience to a women's-only event in rural Michigan (Browne 2011). Even traditionally conservative spaces are starting to provide distinctly gay event offerings, with the gay rodeo circuit as one example that actively subverts the hyper-masculine rodeo scene (Hanvelt 2004). Events marketed to the LGBTQ2+ community, combined with a growing acceptance of homosexuality, can all help grow the tourism industry in rural areas.

Research Methods

This qualitative research explores rural gay tourism in BC based on in-depth interviews with DMOs and self-identified gay travellers. The choice to centre this research on the perspectives of gay men was made as a result of the challenges of representing the diversity of the LGBTQ2+ communities in one study (Gottschalk and Newton 2009; Toth and Mason 2021). BC was used as the focus due to the diversity of rural tourism opportunities within the province. DMOs that promote rural BC destinations are responsible for marketing these areas both within Canada and internationally. Each DMO's perspective on gay tourism are presented from one or more staff member from each organization. We used a semi-structured approach for interviews with rural DMOs. The interview guide was provided to the interviewee at least one week in advance to provide adequate time to consult their team on current practices and future plans related to gay tourism. We used convenience sampling to reach possible participants, utilizing the researchers' existing connections. In total, five DMOs participated in this study: one provincial DMO, located in Vancouver, and four other DMOs representing different regions of the province's interior.

The second aspect of this research involved self-identified gay men living in BC as a significant, if smaller, segment of BC's intra-provincial travel market. Intra-provincial travel comprises 52.4 per cent of total visitation in BC (Destination British Columbia 2019). As a result of the identified gaps in research related to rural gay tourism, we considered this aspect critical to our study. While we also used a semi-structured approach for interviews, we did not provide participants with the guide in advance. To recruit participants, we invited some personal acquaintances of the first author, as he is an active member of the gay community in BC, to participate in the study. We used snowball sampling to recruit additional participants, along with referrals from two LGBTQ2+ community organizations based in rural BC. Ultimately, twenty individuals from eight municipalities across the province participated in this study. The average age of the gay men participating in the study was 33.4, with an age range between 25 and 50.

We developed interview guides separately for both research groups. For rural DMOs, the goal was to understand each organization's perceptions about gay tourists and determine how gay tourists are considered as a segment of the travel market. The interviews with gay men explored pull factors for travel, perceptions of rural destinations in BC, the impact of this perception on travel decision making, and how past rural travel experiences in the province have shaped future intentions to visit small rural regions. We primarily conducted in-person interviews, with phone or Skype used for only two interviews conducted after COVID-19-related public-health orders were instituted in March 2020. Each interview was voice-recorded and transcribed verbatim by the researchers. The interview transcripts were then analyzed using thematic analysis, with themes established using open coding. The researchers then collaboratively discussed this coding to determine appropriate sub-themes and collectively reviewed the data analysis and validated the results. Each participant was emailed a copy of their verbatim interview transcript to review and edit. All of the gay men interviewed for the study are identified by pseudonyms.

Gay Men's Perspectives of Rural Travel

Research participants held generally positive perceptions of rural BC as a travel destination. Every interviewee spoke about the province's natural beauty and the wealth of outdoor activities as a core tourism offering. Participants were unanimous in their belief that rural BC has a unique mix of nature and local culture that contribute to a one-of-a-kind tourism experience.

> I think the likes [of visiting rural BC] would be . . . meeting people and having experiences that I've never had in [urban] BC. You know, I've ate fresh seafood straight out of the ocean with some First Nations friends of mine at the mouth of the Skeena River, and we went on a little boat ride around the islands with them and saw dolphins jumping up alongside the boat, playing with us. It was just unreal. (Preston, interview with authors, 14 March 2020)

Participants also highlighted the welcoming nature of rural BC residents, and how this adds to the unique experiences they have had in rural areas.

> You start talking to people at . . . a pub or a bar and everyone's like, "Come on over here gentlemen!" And you get to know, I guess, a little bit more of the flavour of the town, and I kind of like that community vibe. (Edward, interview with authors, 25 February 2020)

In addition to offering a great tourism experience and welcoming residents, participants living in urban communities talked about rural travel as a means to get away from the hectic nature of city life. Going from dense urban living to slower-paced, small-town vacations was one appealing aspect of travel to rural BC.

> [Rural towns] are quiet; I would say they're relaxing, and they're quite remote if you want to get away from the hustle and bustle. (Ken, interview with authors, 3 March 2020)

In general, outdoor activities, events, food, nightlife, arts, and cultural offerings were some of the most popular attractions and amenities highlighted by participants. Outdoor activities and camping were the most commonly mentioned travel interests specific to rural BC.

> Predominantly one of the driving forces for the types of vacations that we're looking for have to do with outdoor experiences—that has lent itself toward looking at rural places. Because

they're traditionally located in spaces that provide easy access to those types of experiences of hiking, mountain biking, kayaking, camping. (Connor, interview with authors, 26 February 2020)

In spite of a desire for more remote experiences, accessibility was a distinct concern for several participants. The remote nature of many parts of rural BC made visiting difficult, particularly for urbanites without a vehicle.

It's just hard to get to the [rural] places. I was torn with the idea of going north for some small trip in the summer, and it just takes time to get up there. So I would say the remoteness can be a negative . . . and we lost the Greyhound [bus transportation], so there's not really many options for travel within rural BC unless you own a car. (Dorian, interview with authors, 13 March 2020)

While there is a desire to visit rural areas in BC, participants also pointed out that gay spaces and events are limited. The majority of participants could not recall a single gay space in their past rural travels in BC. At least two participants indicated that travelling to visit gay spaces and events is an urban pursuit, and therefore not an interest of theirs when visiting rural areas.

Even with some gay events taking place in smaller cities and rural towns throughout the province, participants had mixed opinions of rural communities in BC. They noted that rural BC still presents a challenging environment for openly gay people, in part due to perceptions about how accepting rural BC communities are of homosexuality.

The only other dislike [about travelling in rural BC] is that feeling of not being able to necessarily be open with expressing my sexuality in some of these small communities because of—really, only my perception—that people in those areas may be less welcoming toward that. . . . I would say [there's] acceptance, yes; I wouldn't necessarily say that I think rural BC is gay-friendly. I think there's not a lot of folks that would dislike you or turn you away from their business if you were gay . . . but at the same time I think people just don't know a lot of gay people in rural communities, and are either curious, or they don't know how to act, or think it's odd or strange. So I get that in rural communities sometimes, where I might mention my partner and people kind of give me a weird look. But I don't think it's homophobia, per se; it's just not something that they're used to as much there. (Preston, interview with authors, 14 March 2020)

Another participant mentioned that their perception that rural communities in BC are less welcoming of LGBTQ2+ people compared to urban centres is tied to their belief that rural residents of BC lack exposure to diversity.

Vancouver Island [is gay-friendly] for sure, and Vancouver downtown proper. I wouldn't go, honestly, past [Vancouver's suburbs]. . . . I only say that because, from what I understand, there's not as many people, population-wise, therefore the lack of representation means a lack of diversity . . . and people understanding. (Linden, interview with authors, 13 March 2020)

Perceived intolerance resulted in a tangible concern for personal safety among participants, and several participants noted that they changed their behaviour if they felt unsafe in an effort to decrease the potential risks of travelling in rural areas. This can manifest itself as avoidance behaviour, such as preferring to remain in urban areas to assuage any safety concerns or discomfort associated with rural travel.

I think that I'm more cautious. Maybe, in those communities, they're smaller, you're more apt to find people that are going to be prejudicial in those circumstances, and so no PDA [public displays of affection]. . . . I certainly think that I'm more cautious in those spaces. I think for that reason we gravitate toward urban travel a bit more. (David, interview with authors, 19 February 2020)

Research indicates that safety is important for gay tourists when deciding their travel plans (Pritchard et al. 2000). This is particularly relevant to rural BC due to the circulating perceptions of these regions as less gay-friendly than urban areas. Yet, while many participants felt that rural BC is less welcoming to LGBTQ2+ people compared to urban BC, this perception is not always warranted. Demystifying small rural communities in BC is a critical consideration for tourism businesses wishing to develop more welcoming and inclusive destinations.

> I think gay people also have a stereotype of rural communities, which isn't necessarily always true. And, you know, my experiences in rural communities have definitely been positive, and there's a way for rural communities to actively try and dismantle that. (Preston, interview with authors, 14 March 2020)

Half of the participants indicated an interest in connecting with the local gay community when travelling, and some participants worked around the safety concerns related to travel in rural areas by finding local gay community members with which to interact. Due to the changing nature of gay spaces, the work of making these connections has largely moved online.

> When we go [to rural areas], we'll totally try to meet with some of the people there and try to chat. . . . I'll use Grindr and I'll try to find some of the locals, not in a sexual way but more so in . . . [terms of] friendship, we're looking for a tour guide kind of thing. We want to meet someone there, to tell us what it's like living there and get that experience, so I appreciate that. (Edward, interview with authors, 25 February 2020)

As mentioned in the previous quote, some participants used mobile technologies, like Grindr or other gay-oriented mobile apps, to connect with local queer people. The benefits of these connections are twofold: they allow gay tourists to quickly and easily determine a destination's safety, and they encourage a more nuanced understanding of the local area that may not be shared in other forms of online media.

> I think what the apps give you, how they can influence gay rural travel, is you can go onto an app to actually gauge the sense of the safety of the community. Grindr . . . is also a way to connect with a community virtually that might be underground, to learn how safe it is or what there is available to do as well. So I think that has, in many respects, changed the perception of rural travel because of the access to information. . . . The apps now allow you to go into a rural situation and know that there is

this community here. They're like, "Don't go to that bar because you might not be safe there." (Keith, interview with authors, 13 March 2020)

Connecting with local gay men was important for participants not only for the opportunities such connections provide to learn about a place, but also because they allow them to assess the safety of a destination before their arrival. Using this type of technology to make those connections is a novel approach to learning about destinations and an important consideration for DMOs working to attract a more diverse tourist base as they seek to appeal to smaller "niche" communities.

Rural travel held a lot of appeal for the gay men participating in this research, particularly those living in urban areas. There still exists a pervasive belief that rural BC is less accepting of LGBTQ2+ people; however, in spite of this perception, participants did not avoid travelling in rural BC. Nevertheless, many gay tourists change their behaviour to avoid inadvertently outing themselves, and some avoid rural travel altogether. Based on the perspectives of gay travellers in this study, attracting gay tourists to small rural areas requires an active and ongoing effort. With this in mind, we now examine how rural DMOs in BC approach gay tourism so as to understand how rural gay tourism in the province can be further supported.

Destination Marketing Approaches and Responses to Gay Tourism in Rural BC

Community and provincial DMOs are crucial to understanding the current state of rural tourism to rural and small community destinations in BC, and how these destinations view and attract gay tourists. Although many DMOs lack proper resources and act more as information offices than managers and marketers for their particular destination (Adeyinka-Ojo, Khoo-Lattimore, and Nair 2014), DMOs in this study proved to be hands-on champions for their local tourism industry. There was an overall interest in creating inclusive tourism experiences to attract LGBTQ2+ travellers, but there is clearly a need for increased resources in order to realize that objective. The provincial DMO noted that its approach to inclusive tourism is not direct, but instead focuses on supporting individual DMOs across the province wishing to address the LGBTQ2+ market. Offering a province-wide perspective, the provincial DMO explained its process as follows:

[Our organization] partners on the premise of leading where we can lead best, such as at the inspirational level, and then [we] support our partners to do specific marketing that attracts specific consumer segments to our [BC] destination. (Provincial DMO, interview with authors, 26 May 2020)

Similarly, from a local perspective, most community DMOs focus their marketing efforts on visitor interests and passions, rather than marketing to specific demographics. Depending on what a given community has to offer, different activities are targeted, but most activities in rural BC revolve around the outdoors, nature, sports, and events. One participant explained that targeting interests over demographics is a core strategy for many BC DMOs.

There's quite a few of these DMO professionals [in rural BC] that are actually openly LGBTQ2+, that are actually sitting in these executive positions. . . . They are smart marketers, brilliant marketers, but I never saw them openly going after that [the LGBTQ2+ travel market] ever. Even though they were part of that community, they never targeted that community, they just went after the activity and the interests. (Former DMO employee in northern BC, interview with authors, 18 March 2020)

As stated by this former DMO employee, most DMOs target tourists broadly rather than focusing specifically on welcoming LGBTQ2+ tourists. This is particularly the case in small, isolated cities, due to personnel and financial constraints. DMO representatives did explain, however, that while advertising campaigns are not usually aimed directly at prospective LGBTQ2+ visitors, it is still important to many destinations to promote themselves as inclusive and welcoming of all people.

Our tagline right now is "[our community], where you belong," so we're always looking to promote an inclusive, welcoming atmosphere. And so that's something that's important to us, [but] we haven't specifically worked out any part of our campaign that would be specific to gay travel. (Community DMO 3, interview with authors, 6 April 2020)

Even though they are not creating marketing campaigns aimed directly at the LGBTQ2+ community, DMOs actively welcome LGBTQ2+ tourists while at the same time marketing activities and events that are relevant to the LGBTQ2+ community.

> [Our community DMO] welcomes gay tourists with open arms. We have a page on our website, we have hosted influencers to help tell our story, blog posts, we support the pride festivals, and we are working with [a national DMO] on the LGBTQ2+ campaign to [attract] gay and lesbian American tourists. . . . We target by both passion and demographics. (Community DMO 2, interview with authors, 9 June 2020)

A major component of the participating DMOs' support for the LGBTQ2+ community is to always list pride events on the events pages of their websites and communicate with event organizers regularly. This support for local pride associations and their events is seen as a way to help connect with the LGBTQ2+ community and advertise that they are a welcoming destination.

In addition to participant DMOs, there was ample discussion by gay travellers about marketing destinations and attractions to gay men or the wider LGBTQ2+ community. While specific efforts to entice gay consumers can be met with skepticism (Stuber 2002), LGBTQ2+ community members' decision making can be impacted by an organization or destination choosing to give back to the queer community (Roth and Luongo 2002). Some gay participants noted that they are more inclined to financially support destinations and businesses that are outwardly supportive of the LGBTQ2+ community.

> Every crosswalk in the city should be a rainbow, not just to make me feel happier but because everyone loves a rainbow—rainbows are fantastic! For me, with a business, it definitely is a nice thing to see, coming from a place of little visibility to knowing that something as simple as Starbucks or a bank are welcoming. I understand I'm being pandered to, to a degree, because it's in the [gay] village, but it's still a nice gesture to see, and it does encourage me to go to the business or appreciate the business. (Martin, interview with authors, 3 March 2020)

While the majority of participants appreciated such efforts to reach out specifically to the gay community, they were weary of perceived "pinkwashing" by businesses. Pinkwashing is the act of advertising to the LGBTQ2+ community so as to appear gay-friendly, in an attempt to leverage the benefits of increased spending and goodwill on the part of LGBTQ2+ customers (Stark 2015).

A number of participants felt it was easy to tell when an organization was advertising to the gay community in an inauthentic manner. And while pinkwashing in an urban centre is sometimes derided, many participants felt differently about the same actions in a rural context. This hints at greater acceptance of marketing to gay audiences in rural areas, as such acts help to deconstruct common perceptions of small rural communities as less welcoming of queer individuals.

> [At] the Vancouver Pride Parade, I'm very . . . questioning of [corporate sponsorship]. That's kind of like everyone's getting involved because they want the gay dollar. . . . But if you're dealing with a smaller town, the context of that is very different, so that's one or two individuals trying to make more visibility and trying to support the community. I see that more and I appreciate that more, in that sense. (Edward, interview with authors, 25 February 2020)

According to participants, advertising also needs to be more inclusive of different types of gay men. Marketing of circuit parties and other gay events can project the image of exclusionary spaces aimed primarily at affluent Caucasian gay men with toned, muscular bodies (Waitt and Markwell 2006). Marketing to gay audiences should include more diverse imagery that includes people of different ages, racial backgrounds, and body types.

> I think the one thing I'd add . . . this might open up a can of worms . . . is just there's a huge opportunity for gay spaces to be body-positive as well. . . . If I were to be piqued to take a look at gay promotions or anything, I would also want to be reassured that there's space for body positivity. (Xavier, interview with authors, 12 November 2020)

For destinations and tourism businesses interested in attracting gay visitors, it is important to actively speak to LGBTQ2+ people in marketing efforts and community initiatives. With some indications that mainstream tourism-marketing efforts actively exclude queer individuals by focusing on heterosexual subjects (Stuber 2002), a number of participants wished to see more direct marketing efforts to their community.

> Marketing specifically to the community and making a real effort to attract gay tourists [is important], because we are a very small community and word of mouth travels fast. And so the latest thing I've heard is that all the gays are moving to [a small rural town] . . . and so now I'm thinking of, "Oh, well maybe a year or two down the road I would visit there because it's a place that is attracting members of my community." (Preston, interview with authors, 14 March 2020)

Attracting gay tourists to small rural areas should be an active process driven by DMOs. Gay men are keen to travel to rural areas; however, there is still an uncertainty about the extent to which rural areas in BC welcome LGBTQ2+ people.

In general, BC is widely perceived as a gay-friendly place to live, work, and travel, but there is still a need to actively market rural areas to LGBTQ2+ travellers. Several DMOs talked about this need while highlighting that insufficient resources can make marketing directly to one audience a challenge.

> I think this depends on the destination. I would expect that each DMO should have a pulse on their community and decide on which target demographics they think make sense. Many DMOs are operating at capacity and may not have capacity to add to their plates. I do think that LGBTQ2+ tourism is a big opportunity, which is why we are putting effort into this space. (Community DMO 2, interview with authors, 9 June 2020)

DMOs are balancing personnel and financial constraints with the goal of expanding their marketing goals. There is a need for additional funding if DMOs are to introduce new marketing strategies, including marketing specifically to the LGBTQ2+ community. Every participating DMO indicated they would consider actively pursuing the LGBTQ2+ travel market if they had the additional resources and information needed to develop inclusive, well-rounded marketing communications and events.

> Yeah, I think support in general would be needed. . . . The resources, the information, the data side is very important. But also, the funding side. . . . We have lots of facilities here and we're looking to bring in more festivals and events and things like that, so that can be something that we're partnering with other organizations to bring in those. And if there's a pride event that is looking to find a new home, then we'd definitely be open for that. We've had some other festivals relocate to the community because they feel welcomed here. (Community DMO 1, interview with authors, 4 March 2020)

Several participating DMOs communicated that budgetary constraints limit their ability to market to LGBTQ2+ travellers. A number of participants explained that their funding is usually tied to the Municipal and Regional District Tax (MRDT), which was introduced by the BC government in 1987. Its purpose is to help fund tourism marketing and associated programs through a tax of up to 3 per cent applied to short-term accommodation stays (Destination British Columbia, n.d.).

When discussing their current challenges, DMO representatives stressed funding as one of their most significant issues. For those DMOs that were not primarily funded by the MRDT, getting buy-in for tourism from the local community and municipal government is a critical barrier.

> One of the biggest challenges was proving, in an oil and gas community and a farming community, that tourism has the value to be part of the municipal budget. (Former DMO employee in northern BC, interview with authors, 18 March 2020)

Limited funding means limited marketing budgets. Participants said this was one of the main reasons they marketed to prospective visitors' interests instead of specific demographics.

> [A considerable challenge is] the funding and the market return, the return on value. With marketing directly to that specific group. . . . I had so little funding, as it was, to really reach out

and leverage . . . so I needed to hit as many people as I could with the money that I had. . . . . So we're going to go after that activity, as opposed to that demographic. (Former DMO employee in northern BC, interview with authors, 18 March 2020)

With sufficient funding for tourism development a necessity, external funding and programs are extremely important. However, tourism grant applications are very competitive (Wilson et al. 2001). When asked to identify possible support programs they would like to see introduced to enhance efforts to target LGBTQ2+ travellers, funding was emphasized. At least one participating DMO indicated that they would also appreciate programs or initiatives that would help them use their marketing dollars more efficiently, such as through collaborative campaigns with other DMOs.

One thing I would say is that [our local tourism organization] always looks for opportunities for our marketing and event dollars to go further, so we keep a grasp on any co-operative programs that fit with our goals of attracting visitors. . . . So if something like that were to become available, whether it's a co-op or something where we could join in so that our marketing dollars go further, then that would be something that we would likely look into, as long as it's matching with our goals. (Community DMO 3, interview with authors, 6 April 2020)

Ultimately, participating DMOs struggled to undertake all of their desired marketing activities with the limited resources at their disposal. Rural DMOs focused heavily on dealing with the challenges around using a small marketing budget to attract sustainable numbers of visitors. Marketing their destinations to LGBTQ2+ tourists, while widely desired and seen as worthwhile, could not be easily justified due to this demographic's perceived niche nature; it is doubtful that limited resources will be spent on smaller market shares. Without additional funding and other resources, rural DMOs in BC are unlikely to be able to market their destinations to LGBTQ2+ travellers. Short of government funding, or an increase to the MRDT tax on short-term accommodation stays, DMOs will need to develop innovative partnerships with LGBTQ2+ event producers as one means of attracting queer events and festivals to their rural communities.

Understanding who is travelling to which destinations is an important first step in demonstrating the need for marketing that targets the LGBTQ2+ community. Every DMO participant indicated that research and data collection are crucial parts of their operations and help determine marketing strategies and which demographics to target. However, none of the participating DMOs directly indicated that their research or data collection centred on LGBTQ2+ visitors.

> We do not have unlimited budgets and therefore we must choose the markets, channels, and target consumers we focus on. These decisions are based on data, [like] economic factors, product match, tourism industry infrastructure, . . . [whether] they [can] get here, . . . [or if] we have the product they have. If we see that a consumer segment in a market is one we should focus on, then we will pivot, based on budget, to undertake target marketing. (Provincial DMO, interview with authors, 18 March 2020)

Some rural BC communities do not take an in-depth approach to data collection due to stakeholders' singular interest in the value of tourism for the local economy. This reduced the importance of more targeted marketing initiatives to smaller groups and underlined the use of broader targeting for rural destination marketing campaigns.

> The numbers that really mattered for us at the time were visitors . . . so the number of visitors that were tracking through the door to our visitor centre, essentially, was critical to our survival, it was critical for funding from the city. It was a very conservative approach to tourism, but not uncommon in the region. (Former DMO employee in northern BC, interview with authors, 18 March 2020)

The primary reason given for not gathering more information or conducting research about LGBTQ2+ travellers to their destination was the sensitivity surrounding asking visitors about their sexual orientation, which is an important ethical concern. Participants explained that demographic information and other data, including some related to LGBTQ2+ travel, is often obtained from regional and provincial tourism bodies, but that these resources are lacking. Easier access to data about LGBTQ2+ travellers could help DMOs justify using their marketing budget to attract gay tourists and encourage further investment for this type of research.

Destination marketing plays a key role in welcoming gay travellers to a destination, and destination image contributes to perceptions of value and increases the likelihood of repeat visits (Phillips et al. 2013). In light of historic discrimination against LGBTQ2+ people, it is crucial for marketers to actively encourage gay travellers to visit their destinations, and to do so they must demonstrate that they are safe spaces (Guaracino 2007). Marketing activities that specifically target LGBTQ2+ people, like advertisements that include photographs of same-sex couples, can help build loyalty (Hughes 2005). Destination marketers and developers need to increase their use of gay-friendly symbolism (like the rainbow flag), add more mainstream travel media focusing on LGBTQ2+ travellers, and encourage greater corporate investment in queer events (Guaracino 2007). Ultimately, marketing directly to LGBTQ2+ visitors can be beneficial to destinations as they pursue new markets. It is vital that DMOs and other tourism marketers ensure they are forthright about attracting the queer community.

Inclusive Destination Development Approaches to Gay Tourism in Rural BC

While most participating rural DMOs do not directly target LGBTQ2+ visitors, several brought up the importance of creating inclusive and welcoming communities to ensure that LGBTQ2+ visitors have a good experience. While DMOs are not able to directly control attitudes toward homosexuality in their rural communities, they can help steward a more inclusive and welcoming environment. Many discussed public initiatives, including the use of gay symbols like rainbow flags and rainbow crosswalks to publicly indicate support for and inclusion of the LGBTQ2+ community.

> Two years ago there was a pride bumper sticker campaign that occurred in [a small rural community in the interior of the province], and there was around eight hundred bumper stickers that went out just in the first week to the community to make sure that community members are sharing that they're LGBTQ supporters, and they were available at multiple stores and they continue to be distributed there. . . . Businesses [also] got behind

that [initiative]. (Community DMO 1, interview with authors, 4 March 2020)

Such symbolic gestures, like supporting the installation of a rainbow cross-walk or working with the local government and other organizations to support pride initiatives, were one way participating DMOs helped to shape a more inclusive destination for LGBTQ2+ visitors. Some DMOs spoke about the positive results of programming they developed.

> While I was there they actually put in a rainbow sidewalk right near [a major local attraction]. Without that [attraction], nobody would stop in that town. And to them, a conservative town in [northern] BC, in the centre of oil and gas country, to put down a rainbow sidewalk? Big deal. Huge deal. (Former DMO employee in northern BC, interview with authors, 18 March 2020)

Actions that demonstrate support for the LGBTQ2+ community can have a palpable impact on a queer person's decision to visit a destination. Every participating DMO perceived their local community to be welcoming and inclusive.

> [Our destination] is known, in general, to be an accepting, welcoming community. When the pride workshop [around diversity and inclusion] was offered, several businesses participated and took immediate action to be more inclusive in their messaging. (Community DMO 3, interview with authors, 6 April 2020)

Creating inclusive communities also involves diversity and inclusion training related to the LGBTQ2+ community. Participating DMOs affirmed that they pursued tangible actions to support these efforts.

> Yes, under the SuperHost training provided by [our organization] there are a few programs that have a section on LGBTQ2+. These programs could benefit from some additional and updated content. All visitor-servicing staff or volunteers must take Service For All, and it talks about mindfulness with LGBTQ2+, Indigenous groups, new Canadians, seniors, etc. (Community DMO 2, interview with authors, 9 June 2020)

DMOs in this study are making every effort to foster a welcoming environment for visitors. However, the visitor experience will ultimately come down to whether local attitudes toward homosexuality line up with a DMO's vision for developing an inclusive destination. Despite the conception that all destinations are welcoming, there can still be barriers as it is impossible to ensure that the majority of local residents feel the same way.

Overall, DMO representatives in this study appeared interested in creating inclusive tourism experiences to attract LGBTQ2+ travellers. Development efforts to support inclusive community building are taking place in destinations across rural BC, but more resources are needed to increase destination marketing efforts. Budgetary constraints were the primary barrier to marketing rural BC to gay men, as most rural DMOs operate as non-profits with limited resources to spend on advertising their destination. Given this constraint, broader marketing initiatives that advertise the community's unique local attractions and activities seems the most effective way to maximize marketing resources, particularly given the limited number of gay spaces and events in rural BC. There is a need for governmental bodies, as well as provincial and national DMOs, to support community-level or regional leadership to expand the scope of their destination marketing efforts through the provision of funding, programming, research, and other supports for gay tourism.

Discussion and Conclusion

Destinations that have a supportive and accepting cultural and legal climate have an advantage in attracting LGBTQ2+ visitors. While tourism alone cannot change homophobia or socially conservative policies within a destination (Hughes 2002), DMOs and tourism and hospitality businesses can contribute to the construction of safe and welcoming communities for all visitors, including LGBTQ2+ people. However, more planning is needed to ensure a welcoming destination for gay travellers in rural BC. Our interviews established that gay men, and the broader LGBTQ2+ community, are rarely the focus of DMOs' efforts to attract visitors. For a destination like BC, which has an existing image as a gay-friendly place to live, work, and travel, growing rural gay tourism remains a complicated process.

The gay tourism landscape is shifting. While some tourism products and services are created exclusively for LGBTQ2+ visitors, including gay-only resorts or tours designed for queer travellers, these do not interest all members of the LGBTQ2+ community. DMOs are increasingly focused on providing comfortable, welcoming, and respectful destinations to LGBTQ2+ travellers, but without catering to them specifically (UNWTO and IGLTA 2017). Our study found that gay tourists often do not view gay-specific activities and spaces as a required feature for a prospective destination unless the purpose of the trip is to attend a gay event. Consequently, rethinking gay tourism is a necessary step in small rural communities that do not have the gay population to support venues and events, or the resources to develop gay travel marketing. Our evidence suggests that fostering an inclusive and welcoming community, while aiming to attract gay events and festivals where possible, is the best option for rural destinations.

DMOs should view gay men as an additional market segment and not an enigmatic group with complicated needs. While gay men undoubtedly have unique requirements as travellers, including an interest in gay spaces and events, the gay travel market is not fundamentally different from the wider tourism market, and gay men's travel interests are similar to those of non-queer travellers (Blichfeldt, Chor, and Milan 2011). While many destinations that are popular with the LGBTQ2+ community will likely continue to position themselves as queer sanctuaries for travellers, some rural locations with limited resources are better off focusing their efforts on broader initiatives to improve LGBTQ2+ inclusion. In addition to developing queer-specific programming like LGBTQ2+ events and festivals, destinations can attract members of the LGBTQ2+ community by working to ensure their regions are as inclusive and welcoming of diversity as possible. Our results suggest that the adoption of inclusive imagery and messaging in marketing efforts can make queer visitors feel welcome and dispel some concerns among gay men about safety in rural BC.

Ultimately, this study has demonstrated that welcoming gay visitors to rural BC is no simple process. While the majority of participants enjoy visiting rural BC and its small towns, and plan to continue travelling to those regions, it is evident that there is a widespread perception of rural areas as being less welcoming of LGBTQ2+ visitors, which impacts these travellers' behaviour and destination choices. Insights into this market encourages community DMOs in western Canada, and in similarly rural and/or socially conservative regions internationally, to design more-inclusive communities that will attract the gay market and foster meaningful change to better support gay travellers to diverse rural regions.

References

Adeyinka-Ojo, Samuel Folorunso, Catheryn Khoo-Lattimore, and Vikneswaran Nair. 2014. "A Framework for Rural Tourism Destination Management and Marketing Organisations." *Procedia—Social and Behavioral Sciences* 144 (August): 151–63. https://doi.org/10.1016/j.sbspro.2014.07.284.

Baker, Catherine. 2017. "The 'Gay Olympics'? The Eurovision Song Contest and the Politics of LGBT/European Belonging." *European Journal of International Relations* 23, no. 1: 97–121. https://doi.org/10.1177/1354066116633278.

BC Stats. 2023. "Municipal and Sub-provincial Areas Population, 2011 to 2022 (XLSX)." Government of British Columbia, January 2023. https://www2.gov.bc.ca/assets/gov/data/statistics/people-population-community/population/pop_municipial_subprov_areas.xlsx.

Bell, David. 2000. "Farm Boys and Wild Men: Rurality, Masculinity, and Homosexuality." *Rural Sociology* 65, no. 4: 547–61. https://doi.org/10.1111/j.1549-0831.2000.tb00043.x.

———. 2006. "Variations on the Rural Idyll." In *The Handbook of Rural Studies*, edited by Paul Cloke, Terry Marsden, and Patrick Mooney, 149–60. London: SAGE Publications. https://doi.org/10.4135/9781848608016.n10.

Bell, David, and Gill Valentine. 1995. "Queer Country: Rural Lesbian and Gay Lives." *Journal of Rural Studies* 11, no. 2: 113–22. https://doi.org/10.1016/0743-0167(95)00013-D.

Blichfeldt, Bodil Stilling, Jane Chor, and Nina Ballegaard Milan. 2011. "'It Really Depends on Whether You Are in a Relationship': A Study of 'Gay Destinations' from a Tourist Perspective." *Tourism Today* 11 (Autumn): 7–26.

Browne, Kath. 2011. "Beyond Rural Idylls: Imperfect Lesbian Utopias at Michigan Womyn's Music Festival." *Journal of Rural Studies* 27, no. 1: 13–23. https://doi.org/10.1016/j.jrurstud.2010.08.001.

Clarkson, Natalie. 2017. "Virgin Holidays Reveals LGBT+ Couples' Experiences on Holidays." Virgin, 5 October 2017. https://web.archive.org/web/20200727061542/https://www.virgin.com/news/virgin-holidays-reveals-lgbt-couples-experiences-holiday.

Clift, Stephen, and Simon Forrest. 1999. "Gay Men and Tourism: Destinations and Holiday Motivations." *Tourism Management* 20, no. 5: 615–25. https://doi.org/10.1016/S0261-5177(99)00032-1.

Clift, Stephen, Michael Luongo, and Carry Callister, eds. 2002. *Gay Tourism: Culture, Identity and Sex*. London: Continuum.

Cox, Martin. 2002. "The Long-Haul Out of the Closet: The Journey from Smalltown to Boystown." In *Gay Tourism: Culture, Identity and Sex*, edited by Stephen Clift, Michael Luongo, and Carry Callister, 151–73. London: Continuum.

D'Augelli, Anthony R. 2006. "Coming Out, Visibility, and Creating Change: Empowering Lesbian, Gay, and Bisexual People in a Rural University Community." *American Journal of Community Psychology* 37, nos. 3–4: 203–10. https://doi.org/10.1007/s10464-006-9043-6.

Destination British Columbia. 2019. *Value of Tourism: Trends from 2007–2017.* Vancouver: Destination British Columbia, June 2019. https://www.destinationbc.ca/content/uploads/2019/10/2017-Value-of-Tourism_FINAL.pdf.

———. n.d. "Municipal & Regional District Tax Program (MRDT)." Destination British Columbia, accessed 22 march 2023. https://www.destinationbc.ca/what-we-do/funding-sources/mrdt/.

Fellows, Will. 1996. *Farm Boys: Lives of Gay Men from the Rural Midwest.* Madison: University of Wisconsin Press.

Fenge, Lee-Ann, and Kip Jones. 2012. "Gay and Pleasant Land? Exploring Sexuality, Ageing and Rurality in a Multi-method, Performative Project." *British Journal of Social Work* 42, no. 2: 300–17. https://doi.org/10.1093/bjsw/bcr058.

Golding, Christina. 2003. "The Pink Pound." *The Caterer*, 1 May 2003. https://www.thecaterer.com/archive/the-pink-pound.

Gorman-Murray, Andrew. 2009. "What's the Meaning of ChillOut? Rural/Urban Difference and the Cultural Significance of Australia's Largest Rural GLBTQ Festival." *Rural Society* 19, no. 1: 71–86. https://doi.org/10.5172/rsj.351.19.1.71.

Gorman-Murray, Andrew, Gordon Waitt, and Chris Gibson. 2012. "Chilling Out in 'Cosmopolitan Country': Urban/Rural Hybridity and the Construction of Daylesford as a 'Lesbian and Gay Rural Idyll.'" *Journal of Rural Studies* 28, no. 1: 69–79. https://doi.org/10.1016/j.jrurstud.2011.07.001.

Gottschalk, Lorene, and Janice Newton. 2009. "Rural Homophobia: Not Really Gay." *Gay and Lesbian Issues and Psychology* 5, no. 3: 153–9.

Guaracino, Jeff. 2007. *Gay and Lesbian Tourism: The Essential Guide for Marketing.* Oxford: Elsevier.

Hanvelt, Jonathan. 2004. "Cowboy Up: Gender and Sexuality in Calgary's 'Gay' and 'Straight' Rodeo." Master's thesis, University of British Columbia. https://open.library.ubc.ca/cIRcle/collections/ubctheses/831/items/1.0091802.

Herrera, Sergio L., and David Scott. 2005. "'We Gotta Get Out of This Place!': Leisure Travel among Gay Men Living in a Small City." *Tourism Review International* 8, no. 3: 249–62. https://doi.org/10.3727/154427205774791564.

Hughes, Howard L. 1997. "Holidays and Homosexual Identity." *Tourism Management* 18, no. 1: 3–7.

———. 2002. "Gay Men's Holidays: Identity and Inhibitors." In *Gay Tourism: Culture, Identity and Sex*, edited by Stephen Clift, Michael Luongo, and Carry Callister, 174–90. London: Continuum.

———. 2003. "Marketing Gay Tourism in Manchester: New Market for Urban Tourism or Destruction of 'Gay Space'?" *Journal of Vacation Marketing* 9, no. 2: 152–63. https://doi.org/10.1177/135676670300900204.

———. 2005. "A Gay Tourism Market." *Journal of Quality Assurance in Hospitality & Tourism* 5, nos. 2–4: 57–74. https://doi.org/10.1300/J162v05n02_04.

———. 2006. *Pink Tourism: Holidays of Gay Men and Lesbians.* Wallingford, UK: CABI.

Hughes, Howard L., and Richard Deutsch. 2010. "Holidays of Older Gay Men: Age or Sexual Orientation as Decisive Factors?" *Tourism Management* 31, no. 4: 454–63. https://doi.org/10.1016/j.tourman.2009.04.012.

Hughes, Howard L., Juan Carlos Monterrubio, and Amanda Miller. 2010. "'Gay' Tourists and Host Community Attitudes." *International Journal of Tourism Research* 12, no. 6: 774–86. https://doi.org/10.1002/jtr.792.

Johnston, Lynda. 2005. *Queering Tourism: Paradoxical Performances at Gay Pride Parades.* Abingdon-on-Thames, UK: Routledge.

Kesslen, Ben. 2019. "Gay-Friendly Towns in Red States Draw LGBTQ Tourists: 'We're Here to Be Normal for a Weekend.'" NBC, 26 April 2019. https://www.nbcnews.com/feature/nbc-out/gay-friendly-towns-red-states-draw-lgbtq-tourists-we-re-n998541.

Melián-González, Arturo, Sergio Moreno-Gil, and Jorge E. Araña. 2011. "Gay Tourism in a Sun and Beach Destination." *Tourism Management* 32, no. 5: 1027–37. https://doi.org/10.1016/j.tourman.2010.08.015.

Ministry of Forests, Lands, Natural Resource Operations and Rural Development. n.d. "Forests." Government of British Columbia, accessed 12 March 2023. https://www.for.gov.bc.ca/hfd/pubs/docs/mr/mr113/forests.htm.

Monterrubio, Juan Carlos. 2009. "Identity and Sex: Concurrent Aspects of Gay Tourism." *Tourismos: An International Multidisciplinary Journal of Tourism* 4, no. 2: 155–167.

———. 2018. "Tourism and Male Homosexual Identities: Directions for Sociocultural Research." *Tourism Review* 74, no. 5. https://doi.org/10.1108/TR-08-2017-0125.

Movement Advancement Project. 2019. *Where We Call Home: LGBT People in Rural America.* Boulder, CO: Movement Advancement Project. https://www.lgbtmap.org/file/lgbt-rural-report.pdf.

Phillips, WooMi Jo, Kara Wolfe, Nancy Hodur, and F. Larry Leistritz. 2013. "Tourist Word of Mouth and Revisit Intentions to Rural Tourism Destinations: A Case of North Dakota, USA." *International Journal of Tourism Research* 15, no. 1: 93–104. https://doi.org/10.1002/jtr.879.

Pritchard, Annette, Nigel J. Morgan, Diane Sedgley, Elizabeth Khan, and Andrew Jenkins. 2000. "Sexuality and Holiday Choices: Conversations with Gay and Lesbian Tourists." *Leisure Studies* 19, no. 4: 267–82. https://doi.org/10.1080/02614360050118832.

Ro, Heejung, Eric D. Olson, and Youngsoo Choi. 2017. "An Exploratory Study of Gay Travelers: Socio-demographic Analysis." *Tourism Review* 72, no. 1: 15–27. https://doi.org/10.1108/TR-05-2016-0011.

Roth, Thomas, and Michael Luongo. 2002. "A Place for Us 2001: Tourism Industry Opportunities in the Gay and Lesbian Market (an Interview with Thomas Roth of Community Marketing)." In *Gay Tourism: Culture, Identity and Sex*, edited by Stephen Clift, Michael Luongo, and Carry Callister, 125–46. London: Continuum.

Stark, Jill. 2015. "'Pink Washing': Marketing Stunt or Corporate Revolution?" *Sydney Morning Herald*, 6 June 2015. https://www.smh.com.au/national/pink-washing-marketing-stunt-or-corporate-revolution-20150605-ghhthh.html.

Statistics Canada. 2019. "Focus on Geography Series, 2016 Census: Province of British Columbia." Statistics Canada, last modified 10 April 2019. https://www12.statcan.gc.ca/census-recensement/2016/as-sa/fogs-spg/Facts-pr-eng.cfm?Lang=Eng&GK=PR&GC=59&TOPIC=1.

Stuber, Michael. 2002. "Tourism Marketing Aimed at Gay Men and Lesbians: A Business Perspective." In *Gay Tourism: Culture, Identity and Sex*, edited by Stephen Clift, Michael Luongo, and Carry Callister, 88–124. London: Continuum.

Swank, Eric, David M. Frost, and Breanne Fahs. 2012. "Rural Location and Exposure to Minority Stress among Sexual Minorities in the United States." *Psychology & Sexuality* 3, no. 3: 226–43. https://doi.org/10.1080/19419899.2012.700026.

Toth, Spencer J., Courtney W. Mason. 2021. "'Out' in the Countryside: Gay Tourist Perspectives on Rural Travel in British Columbia, Canada." *Journal of Rural and Community Development* 16, no. 3: 84–107.

UNWTO (United Nations World Tourism Organization) and IGLTA (International Gay and Lesbian Travel Association). 2017. *Affiliate Members Global Reports, Volume 15—Second Global Report on LGBT Tourism*. Madrid: UNWTO. https://doi.org/10.18111/9789284418619.

Visser, Gustav. 2014. "Urban Tourism and the De-gaying of Cape Town's De Waterkant." *Urban Forum* 25, no. 4: 469–82. https://doi.org/10.1007/s12132-014-9237-1.

Vorobjovas-Pinta, Oskaras, and Anne Hardy. 2016. "The Evolution of Gay Travel Research." *International Journal of Tourism Research* 18, no. 4: 409–16. https://doi.org/10.1002/jtr.2059.

Vorobjovas-Pinta, Oskaras, and Brady Robards. 2017. "The Shared Oasis: An Insider Ethnographic Account of a Gay Resort." *Tourist Studies* 17, no. 4: 369–87. https://doi.org/10.1177/1468797616687561.

Waitt, Gordon, and Kevin Markwell. 2006. *Gay Tourism: Culture and Context*. Binghamton, NY: Haworth Hospitality Press.

Want, Philip. 2002. "Trouble in Paradise: Homophobia and Resistance to Gay Tourism." In *Gay Tourism: Culture, Identity and Sex*, edited by Stephen Clift, Michael Luongo, and Carry Callister, 191–213. London: Continuum.

Weeden, Clare, Jo-Anne Lester, and Nigel Jarvis. 2016. "Lesbians and Gay Men's Vacation Motivations, Perceptions, and Constraints: A Study of Cruise Vacation Choice." *Journal of Homosexuality* 63, no. 8: 1068–85. https://doi.org/10.1080/00918369.2016.1150045.

Wilson, Suzanne, Daniel R. Fesenmaier, Julie Fesenmaier, and John C. Van Es. 2001. "Factors for Success in Rural Tourism Development." *Journal of Travel Research* 40, no. 2: 132–8. https://doi.org/10.1177/004728750104000203.

Rajzefiber: A Community Hub for Small Tourism in the Small City of Maribor, Slovenia

Katja Beck Kos, Mateja Meh, and Vid Kmetič

After decades of a booming tourism industry with wide impact on territories and economies all over the world, are there smaller-scale, non-intrusive ways of promoting tourism experience?

(Boelen and Sacchetti 2014, 333)

Slovenia, a Hidden Gem

Slovenia, a small European country of 1.2 million inhabitants, is situated between Italy, Austria, Hungary, Croatia, and the Adriatic Sea. Tourism in Slovenia has typically been noted for its winter sport destinations such as Bovec, its political and vibrant cultural capital Ljubljana, Lake Bled and its iconic island, the wild nature of Lake Bohinj, the emerald-coloured Soča River valley, the Postojna karst cave system, and the coastal resort town of Piran.

A mountain hiking route and multistage cycle trail give good reason to visit the country in the run-up to its stint as next year's

European Region for Gastronomy. . . . Beginning on the Italian border, it traces a fiercely beautiful route that incorporates many of the destination's established highlights—including, yes, the lovely Lake Bled—as well as lesser-known parts of the country. No less enticing is the Bike Slovenia Green project, a diverse, 150-mile, multistage cycle route which launched in November. And you won't have to look far for a good meal. Slovenia will spend 2021 as the official European Region for Gastronomy, in recognition of its quality local produce. (*National Geographic Traveller* 2020)

The main touristic attractions in Slovenia are in the central and western parts of the country, which, in such a small place, even before COVID-19, were already experiencing symptoms of over-tourism; dispersing the flow of tourists has therefore become of interest:

Excessive tourism is becoming one of the hottest debates in the modern age of travel. More and more destinations are wondering how to deal with this problem, without magic formulas and uniform solutions that would be suitable for all destinations. In Slovenian tourism, we are tackling this challenge in the long run and with a strategic approach based on sustainability. We are aware that quality is more important than quantity, so our attention is focused on long-term values such as interpersonal relationships and authenticity, and we involve the local community in the processes. (Pak 2019)

Even so, the annual study tours to which the Slovenian Tourism Board invites foreign tour operators via the "Slovenian Incoming Workshop" are still—even as recently as September 2021—highlighting typical sights such as Lake Bled, the Postojna cave system, and Piran, while the eastern part Slovenia receives minimal focus. So, untypical, small-scale tourism places and enterprises must try to help themselves, without support from the Slovenian Tourism Board and with only scarce marketing funds, making it difficult to attract an international audience.

The COVID-19 pandemic may actually have offered an opportunity for small-scale tourism, pushing visitor interest in less-crowded venues and nature destinations even further. And thus tourists, searching for nature, peace, and quiet, are now discovering eastern Slovenia, including the small city of Maribor, home to 110,000 people. Maribor has been receiving more attention from visitors who are seeking a way out of the crowds, hoping to discover places off the beaten track. Maribor is, however, still in the touristic shade of Ljubljana, the capital city, despite Maribor's numerous positive characteristics (near nature, small but urban, good weather, handy geographical position). It lacks not only recognition from the main Slovene tourist organizations, but also self-confidence. In Maribor, therefore, there has been a tendency to copy tourism products that work in other similar towns, resulting in the proliferation of inauthentic mass-tourism offerings and a lack of support for local experiences. Sustainable tourism processes, and not only for small cities, lie elsewhere: supporting local providers and developing authentic, small-scale content that arises from the local living and historic heritage and culture. And so, Maribor can be a good example for our small tourism in small cities case study. But let us first look into the history of Maribor.

Maribor's Historical Context

After the end of the First World War, new states and state formations began to emerge from the ashes of the former monarchies of Europe. On 29 October 1918, the territories of present-day Slovenia, Croatia, and Bosnia-Herzegovina, which previously belonged to the Austro-Hungarian Empire, merged into the State of Slovenes, Croats, and Serbs. This confederation of the former southern Austro-Hungarian territories was short-lived, however, lasting only a little over a month. In December 1918, it merged with the Kingdom of Serbia to form the Kingdom of SHS (Kingdom of Serbs, Croats, and Slovenes), and later the Kingdom of Yugoslavia.

The Kingdom of Yugoslavia, with a predominantly rural and underdeveloped south, and a much more industrially developed north, represented a bridge between Asia and Europe. This country of differing languages, religions, and customs represented a combination of five hundred years of co-existence between the Ottoman Empire and the Habsburg monarchs. The Second World War resulted in chaos among the various peoples, but they were ultimately united under the command of Marshal Tito in a partisan struggle that finally ended in 1945—without substantial Allied aid—with a liberated Yugoslavia.

Although the Socialist Federal Republic of Yugoslavia was a one-party system under the Communist Party of Yugoslavia, the state itself did not follow the path taken by other countries with communist rule. Yugoslavia was never a member of the so-called Eastern Bloc. In the bipolar world divided between NATO on the one hand and the Warsaw Pact on the other, Yugoslavia took a third path and, together with India and Egypt, founded the Non-Aligned Movement. This placed Yugoslavia in an exceptional geo-strategic position, as it represented a kind of buffer zone between the Eastern and Western Blocs. Moreover, the regime, albeit under communist ideology, was far from the hard communism of the Soviet Union and its satellites, as the country always had open borders, and Yugoslav citizens were able to travel virtually unrestricted all over the world. But after Tito's death in 1980, trouble began to bubble beneath the surface of this multinational state. The Yugoslav ideal of brotherhood and the unity of nations and ethnic groups was largely kept alive by the figure of Tito. Only he managed to hold together the state of six nations, five languages, and three religions, a state that had swept all the divisions of the Second World War under the carpet, or even rudely silenced them. Shortly after 1980, various nationalisms began to emerge, culminating in 1991 with the disintegration of the state and bloody wars of succession, especially in Croatia and Bosnia-Herzegovina.

This walk through the history of the territory of Slovenia until 1991 and the beginning of an independent state is necessary to facilitate an understanding of the extraordinary diversity present in this small part of central Europe. Slovenia's location is almost ideal for tourism, both in terms of natural resources and cultural diversity, which together make the country attractive to visitors. On its territory—only a mere 20,271 square kilometres sandwiched between the Alps, the Adriatic Sea, the Slovak Karst, and the Pannonian Plain—we can find almost everything. In a singe day, we can climb almost 3,000 metres into the mountains and swim in the sea the same evening, as well as explore the mysterious underworld of the Karst. In addition to natural resources and fortunately still quite unspoiled landscape, perhaps the even greater wealth of Slovenia is its cultural heritage and diversity of customs, local dialects, and cuisines. And in the northeast of this small country we find the city we want to present to you: Maribor.

Maribor has always been at crossroads or borders of one kind or another. Already during the Roman Empire, roads connecting Celeia (near today's Celje), Flavia Solva (near today's Lipnica), Poetovio (today's Ptuj), and Virunum (on the Gosposvetsko Polje), crossed near the territory where the city was formed much later. The name Marchburch first appears in a deed of gift dated 20 October 1164. Marchburch was a castle that stood on a hill, which today we call the Piramida. However, below the hill and especially along the Drava River, a city started to form at that time, which was named after the castle: "Marchburch" means "a castle in marka" (a border landscape).

The predominantly rural and artisan city gained real impetus only after 1846, when it was connected to the railway line between Vienna and Trieste. This opened a window to the world in Maribor, and at the same time brought the world to the city. Soon the first industrial plants began to appear, and the industrialization of the city continued after the Second World War, so that Maribor was always considered an industrial city, this description failing only with the collapse of the great industrial giants. The consequences of decline are still partially felt by the city today. It was known by the German name Marbug until the end of the First World War. During the disintegration of the Austro-Hungarian Empire, a small military coup, led by General Maister, resulted in Maribor landing in the newly formed Kingdom of Yugoslavia instead of Austria.

Maribor has always sat along one or another border: the extreme edge of the Alps and the beginning of the great Pannonian Plain; the Slavic and Germanic languages; ancient crossroads leading in all four directions. Maribor has had its share of historical moments as well. Nikola Tesla lived in Maribor for a few months in 1878–79; Marshal Tito was imprisoned here in 1931; Adolf Hitler visited in 1941; Pope John Paul II presided over a beatification in 1999; the Dalai Lama stopped at Maribor twice, in 2010 and 2012. And of course, the "Žametovka" or "Modra Kavčina," the world's oldest producing grape vine at over four hundred years old, is an indelible part of our history.

Maribor's Small Tourism Context

Our historical journey through Maribor has demonstrated the cultural and outdoor tourism opportunities even such a small city can offer.

The formal start of tourism in Maribor can be traced to the establishment of Beautifying Society (Marburger Stadtverschönerungsverein) in 1869. Its main task was to design and lay the big park in the north of the city. Even before, in the times of Habsburg Empire, Maribor and its natural surroundings were the preserve of spas or summer residences for wealthy Austrians. Theatre has existed in Maribor since the late eighteenth century. When the train connection between Triest and Vienna came through Maribor in the late nineteenth century, the city grew in industrial importance, and also gained even more in terms of social life: the National House for Culture, a puppet theatre, museums, and art galleries all opened. The members of the new bourgeoisie were keen to attend balls and festivities. Because of the massive industrialization that supplied Hitler's army, Maribor was bombed by the Allies several times during the Second World War.

When Yugoslavia was established, Maribor grew into one of the federation's biggest industrial towns, mainly for the automobile, textile, and rail industries. During the 1970s and '80s, the town engaged in economic diversification, including tourism. And the most important tourism product in Maribor was skiing on Pohorje, easily reached by city bus. Since 1964, Maribor has hosted an International Ski Federation Women's World Cup event, the Golden Fox. The world's oldest producing grape vine and its wine provide another popular tourism attraction, marketed beginning in the 1980s.

Maribor's status as an industrial power collapsed with Yugoslavia's dissolution, and with the absence of former markets, unemployment grew, a problem from which the city has not yet recovered. One therefore wouldn't tend to think of Maribor in terms of cultural tourism. Although its cultural scene has been vibrant throughout the decades, providing recognized Slovene artists, festivals, and works, the existing tour operators in the city were still mostly outgoing. Slovenia's national destination organization didn't include the city in its new promotional actions or products; indeed, it tends to focus only on Ljubljana or on nature and adventure tourism.

Even though it was designated a European Capital of Culture in 2012, and a European Region of Gastronomy in 2021, Maribor has not yet fully taken up the possibilities offered by small, creative tourism enterprises that would address the authenticity sought by visitors who want to immerse themselves in the everyday life and sense of a particular place. This is not to say, however, that improvements in tourism products have not occurred.

Since 2010, we can see a rise in the quantity of cultural industries providing activities of interest for potential tourists. The Maribor Slovene National Theatre, which includes drama, opera, and ballet performances, has established a system of buses bringing tourists from Austria. The museums and galleries are developing high-quality tours for schools and kindergartens, which can easily be adjusted for tourists. The Museum of National Liberation even provides a live role-playing exercise for schoolchildren, with the director of the museum, Dr. Aleksandra Berberih Slana, taking the role of a historical figure, Franziska Scherbaum, who was the wife of Karl Scherbaum, a Maribor businessman who owned a steam mill and who brought to Maribor its first thirty-six lightbulbs, lit on 4 April 1883, just four years after the Edison's patent—an important part of the industrial history of the town. The Scherbaums lived in the villa that currently houses the Museum of National Liberation.

The new Maribor Puppet Theatre is an important regional institution providing high-quality puppet theatre for children and adults, while also offering great production spaces for artists from all over Slovenia. Maribor has many festivals that are more popular domestically than abroad, but they are also gaining a profile in other countries thanks to such events as the international theatre festival Borštnikovo Srečanje, the summer music and theatre series Festival Lent, and the celebration of classical music that is Festival Maribor. All of them host many international artists, especially Festival Lent, which fills all big hotels with visiting companies in its best years. And those artists are very pleased with the renowned local hosting culture, ensuring return visits. And last but definitely not least: local NGOs are very responsive to trends and are endeavouring to provide content of interest to the urban tourist. While fabulous, these activities do not generally exploit the opportunities of micro-tourism.

A noteworthy NGO in the area of small, creative tourism is the Living Courtyards Initiative, which since 2010 has been working to revive and highlight one of Maribor's unique urban features: the courtyards in the medieval city centre, using them to provide artistic, social, and cultural programs that suit these special intimate spaces, which in many cases have regrettably become parking lots or have simply been abandoned. The programs invite locals and visitors to look behind the facades of the city and to discover its hidden dimensions, providing direct insight into both the current lives of Maribor's people and a perfect illustration of life in centuries past, when the courtyards provided gardens, livestock sheds, public washing spaces and laundries, artisan workshops, gathering places, and facilities for communal child care. This ingenious enterprise led directly to the establishment of our initiative.

Rajzefiber

In this chapter, we would like to share our experience, our aims, and our good (and not so good) practices in order to encourage similar processes in other small cities where the existing touristic ecosystem remains very shallow and unable to connect the dots between creative locals and creative visitors, or where tourism just reproduces, rather than regenerates, a locality's tired assets.

We established Rajzefiber[1] in 2014 in order to develop attractive creative walks in the city, to design unique souvenirs by local creatives, and to build social capital among stakeholders in Maribor.

> A nanotourist agency, Rajzefiber Biro was strategically established in an abandoned shop within the old city of Maribor. The collectively self-renovated project space operates as a multipurpose arena for exchange, performance, education, and production. It provides and produces co-creative memorabilia—ART-FACTS—made by special local artists and craftsman, redefining the typical souvenir. It is a melting pot, a platform that constantly researches and follows the needs of co-creators of touristic/ cultural/artistic activities. The agency avoids formality, yet provides and collects an endless all sensual experience of Maribor. (Boelen and Sacchetti 2014, 356)

This is the first description of Rajzefiber, an idea, a term, a concept that was formed in a workshop on nano-tourism in the Design Biennale, Design 50, held in Ljubljana in 2014, and the quotation still aptly describes our mission. It was intended to describe the opposite of mass tourism—so it focuses on providing authentic, small-scale (i.e., nano) tourism experiences in which both visitors and locals participate. And Rajzefiber is a trial of this idea/concept that we hope will promote local heritage in small contexts and support development of new contents/products in the creative tourism space. We started as, and indeed still are, a program of our existing NGO, House! Society for People and Spaces, which has approximately 25 members, residents of Maribor and its surroundings, all with very different backgrounds but all keen to promote local heritage. Every two years, we elect a new executive board. The NGO has been publicly funded and has complementary programs such as Living Courtyards. We benefited from unemployment funding measures for Rajzefiber, which allowed us to hire four employees. Now, our team varies between 2 and 3 permanent employees, plus an additional 10–60 co-workers from outside Rajzefiber during the Festival of Walks. Since we were addressing social issues through sustainable economic and cultural development, we received social enterprise status, which allows us some benefits. Rajzefiber is still receives around 40 per cent of its funded through different funding programs (for the Festival of Walks, for the PAKT, etc.) and the rest we develop from our sales.

Arising from Maribor's cultural and artistic scene, Rajzefiber faced a challenge, as the established tourism infrastructure was ill-equipped, or perhaps even unwilling, to support our goal to promote local cultural engagement in small contexts. For guidance, we looked to the principles of creative tourism, which values place-based intangible cultural heritage, and individual or small group immersive experiences. In 2020, our walks were described as follows:

> Stories can be told, danced, sung and painted. Many walks offer various experiences, such as photographing, painting, printing, singing or dancing. Walkers are encouraged to use other methods of expressing the way they see or feel the city and the whole intangible heritage experience. Media, or the way the stories will be told, are also part of the creative process. This way, participants start to care for the stories and recognise them as their own heritage. They also get a new and different experience of their city. Through the Festival of Walks, lots of new stories find their own media. Moreover, the stories that haven't been written yet find their place in the realm of the intangible heritage of Maribor. (Ratković and Tolić 2020, 39)

Curiosity Leads to Creativity

The team at Rajzefiber is curious about people, untold stories, everyday paths, and hidden spaces. This curiosity has led us to be innovative in approaching subjects and developing formats. We use creative strategies to bring stories alive: we might dress up as historical figures, or we might ask walk participants to cover their eyes and discover the city using their other senses. We try to evoke curiosity and creativity in visitors.

Authenticity Based on Facts

While we are creative in our approaches to intangible cultural assets, we believe that authenticity must also recognize factual data. Our team member Vid Kmetič is responsible for examining the archives, and for finding stories in historical newspapers. All our local experts as well as our walkers are required to verify the information used in their walks.

Collaboration and Co-creation

Rajzefiber would not have achieved the success it has without the strategic and systematic methodology of collaboration and co-creation, which is written into its DNA. We have always worked closely with local and regional stakeholders, small enterprises, artists, shop owners, guesthouses, Airbnbs, with public institutes of art and culture and cultural heritage, and with public institutes of tourism, as well as with governmental bodies, private agencies, and finally with universities and schools. We connect a network of stakeholders in the town with those in the wider region in order to gain more presence in the tourism market, to exchange knowledge, and to advocate for common issues. We invite young people to work with us, and we offer older people a space for their creativity.

Above all, we connect cultural heritage—both tangible and intangible—and creative industries and culture with tourism. We must often persuade creatives that their processes and behind-the-scenes work can be even more interesting for the visitors than their formal performances or products. We must also convince the tourism industry that tourists are definitely open to some hands-on work during their visits. We are all about connection and collaboration in co-creating small tourism experiences.

Small and Agile

Rajzefiber is one of the four main programs, along with Living Courtyards, Lumina, and the Center for Graphic Arts, in House! Society for People and Spaces. House! has been a social enterprise since 2016. The team is small—currently five people—and we are very connected with others, as we have described. In addition, we have a strong system of volunteer workers who helps us execute our events, such as the Festival of Walks.

Our primary team members come from the fields of cultural management, cultural studies, media communication, visual art pedagogy, and organizational sciences and cover the roles of researcher, programmer, executive producer, public relations person, and administrator. We use any digital tools that enhance our productivity and ease our workload.

Financing

The four prime tenants of House! are financed from different European Union, national, and local funding agencies and gain approximately 15 per cent of their funds from revenue, principally from Rajzefiber activities. Through Rajzefiber's first five years, the municipality provided us with a rent-free space in the city centre; as a result of Maribor's very high unemployment rate, we also received funding from the national employment agency to hire unemployed people as our main personnel.

About Our Walks

Our "walks" are the curated individual experiences that our local guides provide for visitors. We call these guides "walkers." Walkers are people who live in and with the city, and who know its stories; some of them are also professional tour guides or experts in a given field. Walks allow visitors to feel, smell, taste, hear, and touch the cultural heritage in real time and space. The format of these walks comprises community-led content offered by locals, including students, professors, chefs, writers, former factory workers, and artists. Walks are reasonably priced and open to the public, whether visitors or locals.

In Rajzefiber, we avoid the term "guided tour," as we are of the opinion that the walks we offer are a departure from standard "guided" ways of presenting the city to visitors. We believe that in the time of the Internet, when a person can find any information they seek with a few clicks on a mobile device, "classic" guided tours are outdated and stale, offering only the serial reproduction of culture. If we are visiting a place, why would we pay for someone to tell us something that we can find by ourselves by directly consulting our devices?

Rajzefiber walks express the various senses of place in Maribor by exploring the stories written behind the walls of city buildings, on the streets, and in the squares. These stories "creep under the skin" of participants much more deeply than they would if they had simply ingested the dry data typically provided by tourist guides. Of course, accurate data is also vital, but we believe that information can be presented in a different way, often with humour, and sometimes with an ironic self-deprecation. Rajzefiber walks are generally themed, and the topics we tackle are as unique as the different impressions of a city its citizens may have. Although walks can reference rumours or myths, walkers must indicate when these references occur; information offered as facts must be verified through credible sources. We check.

Some walkers take on the task of "role-playing": this is when the walker takes, with the help of a particular wardrobe, a personage from the past and presents the city through that character's eyes. This can happen, for example, in our series of Cool:Tours, and of course during our popular (In)tolerant walk. In the latter, we learn about Maribor's former brothels through the eyes of a conservative city dweller, a young sex worker, and a madam; in this way visitors get a sense of the various attitude toward brothels in the past, and whether public opinion about prostitution is any different today.

Many visitors prefer not to get to know the city in groups, but rather individually or with their particular travelling companions. We reserve our best stories for them! With the help of some simple instructions, they perform tasks at their own pace: in the Electric Story Hunt they learn about the electrification of the city, and in the Wine Story Hunt about the wine that is closely connected with Maribor. In Crown Hunting, children look for crowns on the facades of buildings and thus, by the way, also learn something new and interesting, while in ParkPlac Hunt, they get to know the city park. Our Hunt series of walks is very popular.

Perhaps our most unusual walk is the Deklajca, in which we direct our attention to the ground and to objects that we don't typically notice at all, but which are present at every step: for example, the covers on sewer shafts, an unspoken but integral part of everyday life, and surprisingly interesting. At Deklajca, visitors also play an active role, as they can imprint their choice of sewer cover on a T-shirt, canvas bag, or any other piece of fabric. In this way, they also take home a piece of the city that they themselves have created.

Rajzefiber walks are a going concern, constantly being made and remade, just as a city is active, writing and living its new stories every day, 24 hours a day, 7 days a week, 365 days a year.

About Souvenirs and Memorabilia

Rajzefiber also offers a range of local products in its space in the city centre; we attempt to move beyond the classic tourist souvenirs that can otherwise be seen in all cities. Through social networks and personal contacts, we are constantly looking for new, young creatives and designers. We help young people to create an idea, develop a product, and place the final product in our sales program. In this way, we contribute to cultural and economic sustainability. For example, since 2018, we have been co-operating with Štajerski Argo, the linguistic project of a young woman from Maribor, which has grown from pure entertainment into one of the city's more recognizable brands, exposing and nurturing the Styrian dialect. In addition to the products of local artists,

Rajzefiber also offers its own production of objects that we design and print at the Center for Graphic Arts, co-located in our space. Both ours and the products of other designers draw inspiration from local stories and the cultural heritage of the city.

The Annual Festival of Walks

To gain more media recognition for local heritage and culture, to promote local heritage and creative tourism among locals and visitors from Slovenia and abroad, to address local issues, to showcase great heritage projects developed by pupils of local schools, and, finally, to provide a community focus for residents, Rajzefiber has since 2018 organized an annual Festival of Walks (FW): at least once annually it presents more than fifty different thematic walks that lead the visitors through untold city stories, those that aren't typically given space in museums, through architectural landscapes or the places that once existed but are not there anymore, and about historical figures that lived in the city. These thematic walks engage all senses and are veritable photographic safaris. The walks are curated every year with the help of a public open call. Anyone can apply to curate and lead a walk, so we get very different views on the same city, assuring a living and lively reflection of Maribor's cultural assets. In 2021, the FW was recognized as a best practice by the European Association for Heritage Interpretation (Koritnik Trepel 2021, 21). All walks during the festival are free. By employing and then subverting the more traditional "festival" tourism structure, the FW brings direct attention to the city's lack of a cultural tourism strategy to highlight intangible heritage. Moreover, it offers space and time to bring together stakeholders to discuss current issues and trends.

> Maribor city has numerous untold and unheard stories that remain in the archives, books and people's memories. It is an intangible heritage that can easily vanish with time. The FW presents more than 40 of these stories each year through walks around the city and storytelling. Stories are designed and presented by the local inhabitants that are in love with small or big, every-day or a superhero type of stories of the city. (Ratković and Tolić 2020, 37)

In the time since the first Rajzefiber FW was held in 2018, the event has grown from the initial three-day affair into a ten-day festival with more than sixty different themed walks, as well as evening talks on topics related to tourism, cultural heritage, and culture in general. It is here that we can directly address current issues.

Cities are of course physical entities; they are compact settlements with buildings, streets, and all other necessary infrastructure. And yet, they are defined as much by their inhabitants and the stories they have written over decades and centuries, on the same streets and in the same buildings. Without these stories, cities would be mere clusters of architecture, grey streets, and cold walls, more or less colorful facades, intersections, parks and squares, spaces. Big and very important stories are indeed captured in history books, but cities also comprise small, seemingly insignificant stories: the everyday stories of individuals. These are stories that perhaps only a handful of residents know, but such stories have over time built the city and its identity. And it is these stories that the FW seeks to tell. We are looking at the people in these tales; we are most interested in them, we want as many people as possible to meet them.

The festival occurs at the end of March, which symbolically marks the beginning of spring and the awakening of nature and the city (this is also, frankly, the beginning of the tourist season). For the last two years, we have been forced to postpone the festival to the beginning of autumn due to public health measures related to the pandemic, but we will return to a spring start as soon as conditions allow.

> Based on the principle of co-creation, local people tell their stories during daytime walks while evenings are reserved for contemplation and discussions about different topics of heritage and creative tourism. Thus, walkers who are heritage bearers themselves become active heritage interpreters. (Ratković and Tolić 2020, 38)

Preparations for the festival, including the composition of the program, begin about two months before the start date. We start with an open call to local residents: anyone who knows an interesting story related to the city, and who would like to present it as a walk, is invited to contact us. We are open to all topics, but the walk must be carried out at a sufficient level of quality, and it must not falsify historical facts.

We can proudly say that the response has been exceptional, and that every year we enjoy the entirely pleasant stress of having to find a way to program and place all the registered walks and walkers. It is noteworthy that public institutes and institutions related to tourism, culture, and cultural heritage also apply to offer walks, confirming that our approach to small tourism is gaining traction. Through their participation, the FW can access and share with our participants the knowledge of experts, which is usually reserved for museums, galleries, theatres, and archives.

The FW is intended for both visitors and residents. We are particularly interested in the latter; when locals know their city well, all its hidden corners and stories, written over the centuries, a collaborative sense of place is developed, and sustainable cultural capital is created. The communal sense of place is perhaps easier to achieve and share with others in a small destination; we dare to claim that the FW contributes—from the bottom up—to this process. We highlight and encourage our community's engagement by awarding three FW prizes annually:

- Rajzefirbčni Špancirštok, or Rajzefiber Walking Stick: awarded to the visitor who takes part in the most festival walks.

- Rajzefirbčni Šuh, or Rajzefiber Shoe: awarded to the walker who is most appreciated by walk participants.

- Rajzefirbčni Šniranc, or Rajzefiber Shoelace: awarded to the part of the city that receives the most criticism from walk participants, in the hopes that the award will call attention to locations that require improvement in Maribor.

Generally, the festival days end with evening talks on topics related to tourism, especially cultural and creative tourism, and culture in general. We like to tackle innovative topics like creative tourism by small enterprises, or industrial heritage tourism, and potentially uncomfortable local topics such as the denigration of the Piramida. In many cases, a joint conversation with experts in a given topic is enough to identify and address problems, or at least to start solving them. Such community collaboration is a hallmark of the FW, and indeed of Rajzefiber itself.

The festival is gaining profile and has been well-received not only in locally, but also more widely.

- FW is a part of the European Cultural Heritage Days program, a joint initiative by many European countries under the auspices of the Council of Europe and the European Commission, run in Slovenia by the Institute for the Protection of Cultural Heritage.

- FW is recognized by *Interpret Europe* as an example of good practice in the western Balkans and thus, together with twenty-two other good practices, was included in the publication *Fostering Communities through Heritage Interpretation* in 2020.

PAKT for Developing the Community in the Region and Beyond

To enhance the development of regional creative touristic products, Rajzefiber established Potujočo Akademijo Kreativnega Turizma (Travel Academy of Creative Tourism), or PAKT, which is steadily growing to be the first regional, bottom-up educational platform for small tourist providers who live and work in the rural outskirts. PAKT offers training through shared experience and peer learning, as well as discussions of theories and trends in small tourism.

PAKT is a subprogram of Rajzefiber/House! in co-operation with Center for Creativity, and so is a member of the partner network Center for Creativity Platform. The Center for Creativity project is co-financed by the European Union from the European Regional Development Fund (from 2017 to 2022) and the Republic of Slovenia. PAKT currently has more than ten regional partners from Murska Sobota, Ptuj, Novo Mesto, Lovrenc na Pohorju, Trbovlje, and elsewhere, as well as from public institutes and local societies. Together, they co-create the PAKT program in order to address the needs of the stakeholders in their own communities.

The educational content is devised and offered by Dr. Dejan Križaj, of the Faculty of Tourism Studies at the University of Primorska, along with his team of assistants and postgraduates, as well as Ana Osredkar, an expert on service design, and others. PAKT uses formats that enhance creativity, allow peer-to-peer learning and collaboration, and boost confidence for providers:

- Laboratory: a half-day lecture plus workshop in which the participants work on their own and/or common products.

- Clinic: a half-day workshop that focus on a specific tourism case that exemplifies best practices.

- Incubator: an individual coaching program, generally several months long, that supports providers in enhancing their products.

Discussion: The Three Main Challenges of Smallness

Being small and agile, we were able to quickly overcome the everyday challenges of our work, such as programming and execution of events. However, we have faced some recurring challenges.

Like other small tourism enterprises, the biggest challenge we have faced is the wider marketing and sales profile. Our products are high-quality, authentic, innovative, and in demand from local and regional guests, but we do not have established channels to address foreign markets. Our team members are all producers at heart; we are so busy creating and producing our tourism products, that we do not have the time to invest in marketing. And to be honest, we do not possess the expertise to effectively market our products, nor do we have the money to pay for people with that expertise.

Moreover, our destination management organization (DMO) and the national tourist organization, which are mainly responsible for promotion abroad, do not see how to fit our innovative products into their more conservative campaigns. It is revealing that Maribor's tourist information centre has not yet agreed to sell any of our souvenir products. However, since 2021, there has been a positive development: the local DMO has decided to include our popular Story Hunts in their sales program. Also, we are sensing more demand from tour agencies. However, creatives do not feel encouraged to participate in creative tourism. As one told us,

> The main challenges that prevent me from engaging even more intensively in creative tourism are: no funds for promotion; no common platform for promoting such products; lack of insights into the needs and interests of urban cultural tourists visiting Maribor; ignorance of promotional and sales channels and their specifics; lack of time and finances for product development

and upgrades; disconnection of tourism from existing local creatives; and the lack of related tourist-products. (Tanja Cvitko, art worker in Maribor, interview with authors, 24 April 2021)

Additionally, we still are not coping with the vast amount of digital channels of sale and promotion.

> In recent years (especially during the pandemic), technology and digitalization has advanced at an unimaginable pace that is hard to keep up with. People (especially the young) are getting more and more used to it and it accompanies them at every turn (shopping, booking, searching, sharing, networking, etc.). Surely, its presence will only increase in the future. On the other hand, online absence, the improper use of the internet and the lack of online promotion on the supply side lead to invisibility, unattractiveness, loss of opportunities and revenue streams (Cai et al. 2019; Nugroho et al. 2017). According to our findings (we have conducted more than 20 workshops with local stakeholders all across Slovenia in the last year) this is especially true for smaller local providers mostly working in crafts sector and other creative industries (artisans, associations, clubs, etc.), as they lack financial resources, ICT skills/knowledge, time and support but still want to become part of the tourism market, get in touch with tourists, become bookable and generate additional income from their unique activities. Such actors are often overlooked, even though they contribute greatly to the preservation of local (past and present) traditions, cultures and environments, both in rural and urban areas. Normally, DMOs should take care of them, but they too often lack the resources, staff and time to take care all in the best possible way. (Rogelja et al. 2021)

The next biggest challenge for us is that we are working across two fields: culture and tourism. In Slovenia, there are separate legislative requirements in each area. For instance, while often producers of cultural artifacts, our walkers must also provide a local or national tour guide licence, or we must provide (and pay for) a silent guide to accompany them during their walks. The system and content of national tour guide licences is a bit out of date and does not incorporate newer approaches such as live role-playing, and it is focused, yet again, on central Slovenia, where you must also go to take your practical exam. In order to provide interesting walks, though, we search for walkers who mostly come from other fields, such as, for example, cultural workers, historians, artists, cooks, ethnologists, or writers, who hold expertise on the theme they want to discuss. And to accord with the formal requirements of tourism legislation, we must then provide a national licensed tour guide, which eventually makes our tours more expensive.

Finally, the last main challenge for us is the fluctuation of co-workers and walkers. Maribor experiences huge waves of employment and unemployment; these transitions affect our walkers, as many are not otherwise employed, so we sometimes lose them when they do find regular employment, or when they move to another place for work. Our core team has also fluctuated since 2014, resulting in the loss of experience, personal knowledge, and contacts. Since 2018, however, the core team has more or less stabilized, and already we can see positive developments in sales and profile.

Summary and Ways Forward

Maribor is the second-largest city in Slovenia, with a very diverse cultural history, a well-preserved medieval city centre, a vibrant creative scene, a storied industrial heritage, great wines, wonderful gastronomy, a gorgeous river, the largest ski resort in the country, and a veritable jungle of the forests and meadows, all reachable by foot from the city centre. It is a fabulous small destination.

Rajzefiber and its stories can help develop green, creative, innovative, sustainable, low-key tourism products that attract individuals and small groups. Working together with the new initiative Tourism from Zero,[2] a virtual organization dedicated to healing tourism from the devasting dual wounds of the pandemic and over-tourism, and its community (Ideas from Zero),[3] we see vast possibilities and potential in those local stories, which we believe could bring Maribor back from the pandemic, serving the curious and demanding tourist who prefers to interact with the local culture, who wants to learn new things, and who is therefore prepared to pay for the experience, helping to sustain the economic, ecological, social, and cultural aspects of our city. According to Dr. Dejan Križaj in his role with the Alliance for Innovators and Researchers in Tourism and Hospitality,

Modern tourists are looking for authentic experiences in the environments they visit, interested in authentic local heritage and locals. They are often closer to local events that reflect the pulse of the place than artificially developed and environmentally friendly experiences that primarily follow only business logic and imitation of global short-term trends. (interview with authors, 29 July 2021)

If we strategically support small tourism providers by encouraging locally executed, tailor-made educational programs, clearly defining roles of stakeholders, coaching and mentoring tourism providers, and offering strategic marketing assistance with creative and cultural heritage content in small towns and rural regions, we at Rajzefiber believe we can achieve a wonderous diversity of regionally/locally authentic content, and put our small towns offering small tourism experiences on the tourism map.

NOTES

1   *Rajzefiber* is an expression in the local German dialect, meaning "travel fever."

2   https://www.tourismfromzero.org/en/insights.

3   https://www.tourismfromzero.org/en/about/.

References

Boelen, Jan, and Vera Sacchetti, eds. 2014. *Designing Everyday Life*. Ljubljana, SI: Park Books.

Koritnik Trepel, Dominika. 2021. "International Day of Tourist Guides celebrated in Slovenia." Interpret Europe Newsletter 1-2021, https://interpret-europe.net/home-news/2021/international-day-of-tourist-guides-celebrated-in-slovenia/.

National Geographic Traveller. 2020. "The Cool List: Celebrating the Reasons to Travel in 2020." *National Geographic Traveller*, 4 February 2020. https://www.nationalgeographic.co.uk/travel/2020/01/cool-list-celebrating-reasons-travel-2020.

Pak, Maja. 2019. "Tourism for All Destinations: Dispersal Over Place and Time." Paper presented at Bled Strategic Forum, Bled, Slovenia, 3 September 2019.

Ratković, Dragana Lucija, and Aydemir Helena Tolić. 2020. *Fostering Communities through Heritage Interpretation: Case Studies from the Western Balkan Region*.

Witzenhausen, DE: Interpret Europe. https://www.interpret-europe.net/fileadmin/ Documents/publications/interpret_europe_fostering_communities_through_ heritage_interpretation_v28-05-2020.pdf.

Rogelja, Tadej, Dejan Križaj, Miha Bratec, and Peter Kopič. 2021. "A Step Closer to Empower Everyone in the Tourism Market." Smartdest, 27 January 2021. https:// smartdest.eu/a-step-closer-to-empower-everyone-in-the-tourism-market/.

3

Sustaining Castello Sonnino: Small Tourism in a Tuscan Village

John S. Hull, Donna Senese, and Darcen Esau

Introduction

Tuscany is one of the most popular tourism destinations in Italy, with 6 World Heritage Sites, 120 protected nature reserves, and a reputation for outstanding wine and cuisine. At the heart of that cuisine is the *cucina povera*, a culinary tradition developed out of necessity to feed poor farm workers during the eight hundred years of the *mezzadria*, or sharecropping system, which so profoundly influenced the iconic Tuscan countryside that remains today. Castello Sonnino is a 150-hectare Tuscan estate and working farm dating back to the thirteenth century, located in the heart of the village of Montespertoli, home to approximately thirteen hundred residents and located twenty kilometres outside of Florence, on the ancient Volterrana Road linking the region to Siena in the southern Tuscany. Historically, the estate served as a customs post between the Florentine and Sienese territories, and since the fourteenth century it has been passed down through powerful local families. The Sonnino family has owned the estate for generations, building a model for sustainability through agricultural and social innovation, balancing tradition and experimentation. They produce wines, grains, and extra virgin olive oils reflective of a new Tuscan generation of agrarians who are conservators of tradition, but who employ appropriate modernization in creating internationally recognized products (Camuto 2016). Today, the entire region is marketed as a territory of small villages, attracting explorers of slow travel interested in adventure, who want to escape the city and enjoy nature, culture and local cuisine (VisitMontespertoli 2021). In Montespertoli, small is the way forward.

Using a mixed qualitative methodology, this chapter provides an exploratory case study of small-scale tourism to focus on the role of altruism in the development of slow tourism through international education to sustain a historic estate. The data collected through interviews, focus groups, and autoethnography describe how the estate, encompassing vineyards, olive groves, grain fields, and patches of woodlot, adopted slow tourism that includes the commonplace rural Tuscan offerings of estate tours, tastings, retail, restaurant, and overnight accommodations to remain economically sustainable. Recently, Castello Sonnino has diversified the sort of tourism offering usually found in Tuscany with the development of experiential educational programs that highlight the circular economy that has existed between the village and the estate for centuries. For visiting tourists and students, there are workshops, lectures with local experts, and experiential course fieldwork that focuses on sustainable culture, agriculture, and environmental issues. In the twenty-first century, Castello Sonnino also serves as the residence of the Baronessa Caterina de Renzis Sonnino and her family; they are descendants of Sidney Sonnino, a prime minister of Italy in the early twentieth century.

The main purpose of this exploratory case study is to understand how and why the small-scale educational tourism developed at Castello Sonnino by the Sonnino family has transformed the estate into an economically viable and internationally recognized rural centre for sustainable development. The objectives of the study are to identify the role of altruism in promoting slow tourism that provides experiential programs and authentic tourism experiences for students and visitors, and to understand the role of the Sonnino family in implementing innovative, multi-functional, and sustainable development strategies that are preserving the environment and cultural heritage in the village of Montespertoli and in the larger region of Tuscany.

Literature Review

The following review of literature provides our context for understanding the role of altruism, slow tourism, and sustainable development in supporting the evolution of small-scale, educational tourism at Castello Sonnino.

Altruism and Tourism

Altruism is defined by Wilson (2015, 141) as "motives that cause people to help others." Altruism also is the principle or practice of concern for others (Beer and Watson 2009). Kim, Lee, and Bonn (2016) suggest that altruism occurs between individuals who have a common-bond attachment. Paraskevaidis and Andriotis (2017) in their review of literature exploring the concept of altruism in tourism, found that the majority of articles addressed the motives and behaviours of volunteer tourists, who visit a destination to offer their services, gain work experience, and increase welfare in host societies (Weaver 2015; Wearing and McGehee 2013; Zahra and McGehee 2013; Tomazos and Butler 2012). A second group of articles addressed altruism in host communities and host-tourist encounters (Fennell 2006; Uriely et al. 2002). Smith and Holmes (2012) argue that host volunteering involves residents as volunteers in their own community at visitor attractions such as museums and heritage sites, at events, or in destination service organizations. Researchers point out (Paraskevaidis and Andriotis 2017; Alonso and Liu 2013; Smith and Holmes 2012) that host volunteers often contribute to the social capital of their community, being motivated by place attachment, civic pride, and the emotional ties within their community.

In general, acts of altruism result in social exchange between individuals that can be categorized as either direct or indirect (Paraskevaidis and Andriotis 2017; Molm, Collett, and Schaefer 2007). There are two forms of direct social exchange. The first is defined as a reciprocal exchange, which refers to resource exchanges between two actors, when contributions are "separately performed, non-negotiated, and initiated by performing beneficial acts for another" (Paraskevaidis and Andriotis 2017, 27). The second is defined as negotiated exchanges where two actors negotiate to reach a mutually beneficial agreement (Andriotis and Agiomirgianakis 2014). In the case of indirect exchanges, the recipient does not reciprocate the giver directly, but they receive benefit as a result of multi-party interactions in the community (Paraskevaidis and Andriotis 2017; Fennell 2006).

Paraskevaidis and Andriotis (2017) have adapted the concept of reciprocal altruism to direct and indirect forms of social exchange, arguing that altruistic acts can be either direct, benefiting two actors (host/host, host/guest), or indirect, in which individuals help those who help others, for example, in the broader tourism community (Kim, Lee, and Bonn 2015; Fennell 2006).

Researchers (Osiński 2009; Fennell 2006; Trivers 1971; Hamilton 1964) also point out that reciprocal altruism can exist both between non-kin individuals and individuals biologically related as a result of mutual co-operation that promotes new levels of societal organization and a beneficial return over time. Fennell (2006) found that promoting a co-operative environment for tourism development at a destination requires altruistic behaviour from both the giver and the recipient that should be recognized and rewarded by local authorities. Paraskevaidis and Andriotis (2017) argue that only a few studies address altruism as a motivational factor influencing host-host and host-guest relationships in tourism development, and that the concept of altruism in tourism studies lacks precise criteria and requires more clarity (Wright 2013; Lockstone-Binney et al. 2010; Holmes and Smith 2009; Anderson and Cairncross 2005). The Castello Sonnino case study will help us understand what types of altruism are playing a role in promoting slow tourism, benefiting the estate itself, the small village of Montespertoli, and the broader region of Tuscany.

Slow Tourism

Another important theme identified by the Castello Sonnino case study is the role of slow food in supporting the sustainability of small tourism. Incensed by the proposed development of a McDonald's restaurant at the foot of the Spanish Steps in Rome, Carlo Petrini in 1986 began a collective retaliation against the consumption of fast food and its culture that would quickly have global reach into a variety of consumptive industries, including tourism. Slow food raised public awareness of and respect for food, natural lifecycles, the dignity of farmers, and biodiversity; it is encapsulated in the term "eco-gastronomy" (Croce and Perri 2008, 4). Slow tourism is conceptualized as tourism that respects local cultures, history, and environment. It also values social responsibility that celebrates diversity and connects people (Clancy 2017; Heitmann, Robinson, and Povey 2011); that it finds a natural alliance in food and wine destinations where slow oeno-gastronomic consumption that is good, fair, and local, has been well-documented (Fullagar, Markwell, and Wilson 2012; Dickinson and Lumsdon 2010). Slow tourism embodies mobility and the spatio-temporal practices and immersive modes of travel that consider rhythm, pace, tempo, and velocity produced in the relationships between the traveller and the world (Cresswell 2010). Slow food travellers seek shared culinary experiences, where travel is deliberate and there is a greater sense of self-awareness (McGrath and Sharpley 2017).

In central Italy, the appeal of slow food and travel has drawn both tourists and amenity migrants to small rural communities, including Montespertoli, where a way of life associated with agricultural work, food and wine products, and family relationships (Williams, King, and Warnes 1997) is prominently marketed. Slow food, wine, and agri-tourism in Tuscany remains focused on traditional and typical gastronomic production and lifestyles. In 1999, the Slow Food Presidia project was created to bring the traditional gastronomic products of Tuscany to a global audience, and the *Slow Wine Guide* quickly followed by marketing Italian wineries to present to consumers a sense of place and eco-sustainability of the cellar (Gariglio and Giavedoni 2015). The imprint of the slow movement on rural tourism in Tuscany is based in the gastronomic sector but is entwined with agri-tourism through the construction of social and cultural networks that enable the development of local traditions, art forms, celebrations, experiences, entrepreneurship, and knowledge (Saxena and Ilbery 2008).

Tourism remains a stable driver of the rural economy in Tuscany as the pioneering wave of slow food and wine tourists with demands for good, fair, and local food and wine have become mainstream; food, wine, and tourism production are now inseparable in Tuscany. The Slow Food Manifesto, which defends local production and the culture of farm life, family, and lifestyle, remains central to both the tourism and the agriculture industries. The principles for good community governance and the slow movement coalesce here under the broader umbrella of an eco-gastronomic lifestyle that values authenticity, quality, education, conservation, and the protection of partnerships between local agents (Saxena et al. 2007). Slow gastronomy and oeno-gastronomic tourism thus captures the political and ethical discourse of sustainable values based in territory, landscape, and culture, manifesting an outgrowth of the sustainable development movement and the more recent focus on the circular economy summarized in the next section (UNWTO 2016).

Sustainable Development

The sustainable development debate, popularized in the 1980s (IUCN, UNEP, and WWF 1980; WCED 1987) and defined as "development that meets the needs of the present without compromising the future," was operationalized globally through integrated economic, social, and environmental strategies with the participation of local stakeholders (UNEP and UNWTO 2005). These strategies increased awareness of the global nature of environmental problems, identified the significance of the environment-economic development relationship, and provided a basis for government and private-sector response to encourage more sustainable forms of development. To advance sustainable futures, researchers agree the process by which change occurs is of increasing concern. Identification of the adaptive capacities of rural areas such as Montespertoli reveals a need to understand the changing nature of the local economic, social, and environmental conditions as part of a co-operative process in which businesses (Smit and Skinner 2002), member organizations, and scientists encourage ecosystem and socio-economic resilience as a pathway to sustainability (Brouder 2017). Now, however, there is an urgent need to consider transformation of the global tourism system aligned with the UN's Sustainable Development Goals. The challenge is to accelerate the transformation of sustainable tourism, putting people and their well-being first (Gossling, Scott, and Hall 2020; UNWTO 2020). Fusté-Forné and Jamal (2020) argue that slow food experiences reflect the need for responsible, mindful relationships and practices among guests and hosts that foster resilience, sustainability, and social plus ecological well-being. Slow experiences produce a "terroir of holistic relationships" that are a conduit to sense of place, emphasizing artisanal, handmade, and quality local foods (Fusté-Forné and Jamal 2020). In this way, slow tourism contributes to sustainable livelihoods and social well-being, while also empowering visitors and residents to help one another and be active rather than passive consumers as a form of altruistic partnership as part of a circular economy.

Circular economy theory proposes a business and solutions-oriented approach to sustainability, referring to the production and consumption of tourism services through a "circular" system that limits use of non-renewable resources, promotes recycling, and produces almost no waste (Sørensen and Baerenholdt 2020; Andersen 2007). The concept of the circular economy emerged in the 1990s to promote innovation and the transition toward a regenerative and restorative economy (MacArthur 2013). A review of the literature reveals a focus on how producers are adopting circular economy production principles through innovation and transformations in tourism products, such as through reductions of CO_2 emissions, cruise ship and air pollution, and hotel waste (Pamfilie et al. 2018; Manniche et al. 2017). In these cases, supply chain sustainability occurs as a result of the introduction of new production methods, for new markets (Bianchi 2011). It can also occur by returning to traditional supply chains. For instance, in the Montespertoli DOCG (Denominazione di Origine Controllata Garantita), wineries source their glass from nearby Empoli, creating unique, local bottles (Chianti Fiasco), and also enabling consumers to bring their own bottle to a *Vino Sfuso* to establish a relationship and familiarity with local producers. These types of short, local, small supply chains result in changes that can have long-term sustainable benefits to the wine destination, supporting the economic, the socio-cultural, and the environmental elements of a region (Sigala 2020). The changes developed through the supply side of a wine region also foster symbiotic relationships between the destination and the tourist that can result in transformation (Ateljevic 2020; Senese 2016).

Sørensen and Baerenholdt (2020) have addressed the circular economy in a context marked not only by the importance of changes in the supply side of production, but also the importance of consumption and the role of the tourist through a three-step model focusing on (1) the providers' production/service activities, (2) tourism opportunities focused on new ownership and sharing models, and (3) tourist practices in consuming experiences and engaging in practices that reduce environmental footprints, thereby encouraging resource-intensive production as part of a sustainable future. Researchers argue that these strategies require building tourism products and services focused on new business-user relations supporting de-marketed or de-commodified tourist practices that facilitate change as part of a circular economy (Sorensen and Baerenholdt 2020; MacArthur 2013).

Summary of Literature Review

Our review of literature has identified that there are research gaps in the field of educational tourism that the Castello Sonnino case study will help to clarify. First, researchers identify that there are only a few studies that address altruism as a motivational factor influencing host-host and host-guest relationships applied to an educational setting in a slow food destination. Second, we require more research on the role of slow food in supporting the sustainability of small-scale tourism through educational centres such as Castello Sonnino. Finally, there is also a need to identify how industry practices can, if they aren't already, contributing to environmental, economic, social, and cultural sustainability.

Exploratory Case Study and Qualitative Methodologies

To achieve the objectives of this case study on small-scale tourism, we focused on participatory, co-transformative learning, and mindful sustainability (Pritchard et al. 2011). Our three themes of altruism, slow tourism, and sustainable development are explored through the socio-cultural context of educational tourism at Castello Sonnino. Case studies are useful for understanding people, events, experiences, and organizations in their social and historical context (Veal 2017; Singh, Milne, and Hull 2012). As a result, place-specific insights that represent the participants' perspective are generated to provide a holistic and meaningful understanding of real-life events (Yin 2018).

Qualitative analysis, including focus groups and in-depth interviews in particular, allow for co-creation of transdisciplinary knowledge, which is particularly important in sustainability research (Mauser et al. 2013). A mixed-methods research strategy included ten semi-structured interviews conducted with experts in the wine and wine tourism industries in the study area. The semi-structured, open-ended interviews enabled industry experts to share their unique perspective on how reciprocal altruism can influence sustainable tourism development and contribute to the social capital of a community. These semi-structured interviews took a fluid conversational approach that lasted approximately one hour, depending on the expertise and interest of each subject. Five topic areas were used to guide each conversation: wine region environment; short and long-term sustainability; organic/bio-dynamic farming practices; food and tourism within the context of local culture; and the process and impact of the wine label. All ten industry participants also participated in the educational experiences of the educational field course as guest lecturers, workshop facilitators, or hospitality managers and hosts.

Nineteen university students participated in an experiential course, living and working at the Castello Sonnino estate between 29 April and 20 May 2018. The students participated in focus groups at the end of their trip to reflect on their experiences and summarize the key conceptualization of food and wine sustainability experienced during the course. Auto-ethnographies of experiential educational tourism by the field school instructor and a student followed an approach outlined by Chang (2016, 46) that combines cultural analysis and interpretation with narrative details of experience and stories that are reflected upon, analyzed, and interpreted within a broad socio-cultural context. Additionally, a detailed daily journal kept by a co-investigator records impressions of repeated topics, emerging themes, and salient patterns (Chang 2016, 131). All interviews and focus groups were transcribed and coded in NVivo 12.7.0 qualitative analysis software (QSR 2018), along with the outcomes from the reflective observations and auto-ethnographies. This qualitative analysis generated three key themes and narratives representing small altruistic tourism, and these are described in the results of this case study.

Case Study: Castello Sonnino—Caring for Place

Background

Florence, like other large regional cities in Italy, may be the nerve centre of international educational tourism in the country (De La Pierre and Bracci 2021); however, it is the interest and interplay between wine and food production from landscapes that are healthy, environmentally sound, and sustainable (Saxena et. al 2007) that drives experiential educational tourism in many parts of Tuscany. Globally, the demand for experiential forms of travel encouraged farmers and wine makers outside of their primary industries into the world of hospitality, tourism, and education (Knowd 2006; Sonnino 2004). Educational programs in regions of wine and food production that provide an opportunity for experiential and transformative tourism has its roots in Mezirow's (1991) theory of transformative learning and is believed to satisfy a growing need to learn and consume in a manner that is fulfilling and highly personalized (Soulard et al. 2021). Wine and food are among the most salient and defining markers of place, profoundly rooted as they are in historical, cultural, and environmental origins. The experiential opportunities for educational tourism in wine and food destinations that are small-scale, and values-based, works toward ethical ideals that promote reciprocal partnerships for co-learning among hosts, students, and educators.

When Caterina and Alessandro de Renzis Sonnino inherited the historic estate from their ancestors and began restoration of the villa at Castello Sonnino in the 1980s, the importance of kin and family lineage assumed a central place in their intentions to restore the estate. During the restoration they came across the personal documents of their ancestor, Sidney Sonnino.

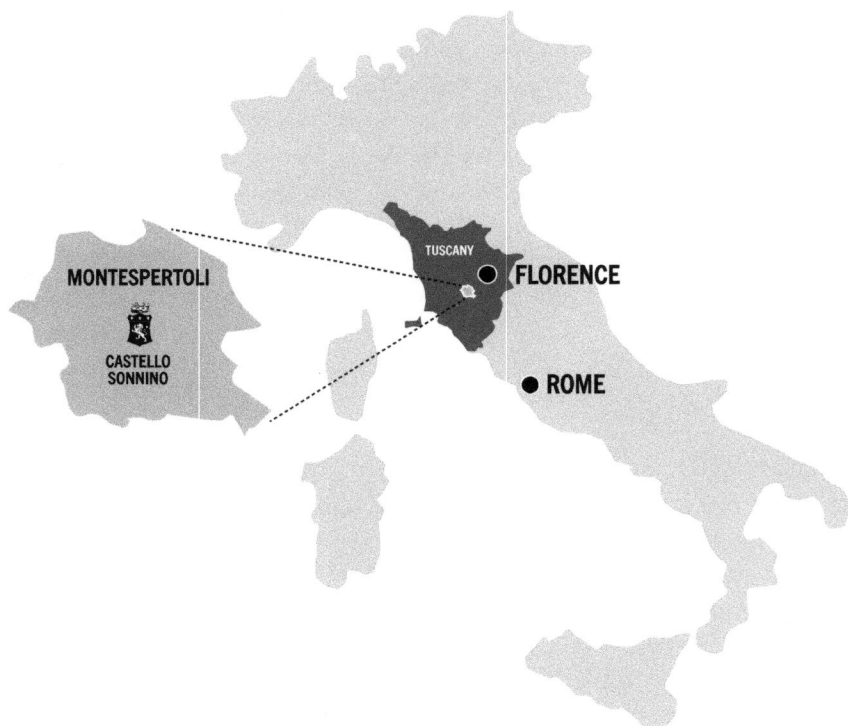

Figure 3.1: Map of Castello Sonnino, located within Chianti DOCG, Montespertoli, Italy.
Map source: Darcen Esau, Donna Senese, and John Hull. All rights reserved.

The documents detailed Sidney Sonnino's time in politics as prime minister, minister of foreign affairs, and secretary treasurer of Italy between 1889 and 1910. Sidney Sonnino was also a prolific writer, and inspired by the writings of they uncovered, the couple used his personal library to create a historical archive, the Sidney Sonnino Study Centre, with the support of academics from the Universities of Florence and Pisa. Their work drew attention to Sonnino's liberal thought and work in relation to the issues of a rural renaissance in modern times. Continuing to recognize the estate as a valuable witness of the past, some years later, the de Renzis Sonnino family also created the Sonnino International Education Centre (SIEC), envisioned to encourage educated thought about a sustainable future for rural communities and agrarian life and landscape. In 2013, SIEC began hosting university educators, researchers, and students with interests in preserving the natural environment and the cultural heritage of this place for future generations. SIEC opened as one of the only operating farms, wineries, and historic sites in Tuscany, offering the university community on-site experiential learning and research opportunities together with formal academic instruction. A network of scholars from Italian and international universities, local practitioners, entrepreneurs, and leaders from the local community began to use the Castello's unique character as a preserved but functioning family-run agricultural and viticultural operation to provide both educational opportunities and support for the local community.

The Italian *mezzadria* left a living landscape handed down through kin relationships of large ruling landowners and the peasant families who produced the food. In the late 1980s the current occupants of Castello Sonnino, Barone and Baronessa de Renzis Sonnino, moved to the abandoned estate in a quest for refuge from the city and a pleasant home in which to start a family. Their desire to return to the roots and traditions of the ancestors who have owned the property for centuries led them through a journey of historical discovery of the long line of famous Italian families that have resided in the estate since the thirteenth century, including the Macchiavelli and Gucciardini families. It was, however, their homage to kin, especially Sidney Sonnino, who in his time proposed major changes to rural life, economy, and landscape for families of peasant farmers in Italy, that formalized their vision for a restored and sustainable Castello Sonnino. Their forward-looking projects have never lost sight of the past, and they continue on in the work of their children, Virginia and Leone, who have played a central role in running the estate farm, winery, and education centre since their father Alessandro's tragic loss to the COVID-19 epidemic in March of 2021.

The geographical position and scale of the estate, adjacent to the village of Montespertoli, provides opportunities for students and scholars to experience farm life, sustainable agricultural production, as well as the quotidian pattern of life among members of a Tuscan village. Montespertoli, a market town and historical trading hub, lies at the gates of Castello Sonnino, which has served as the heart and engine of the cultural and socio-economic life of the village for centuries. The close relationship between village and estate provides students and researchers with the opportunity for immersion in the environment, culture, history, and circular economy, not simply the study of it. The landscape of the ancient *mezzadria* provides the foundation of the classroom at SIEC, with access to the remnants of a reciprocal agricultural system based on small-lot mixed farming and woodlot management, with whatever processing industry was required of the community. At Sonnino this meant a grain mill that still operates in the village, a brick-making facility, and the production of power. The complete economy of the *mezzadria* has left a living landscape that has remained relatively unchanged as a fortunate result of the EU Landscape Convention, and in particular the Florence Conventions of 2000 and 2004, which demarcated the agricultural landscape as a public good or asset. In keeping with the Florence Conventions, which emphasize the importance of landscape to the social well-being and quality of life for people everywhere, walking paths and community or social gardens for those in the village are maintained for public access at the estate, and students at SIEC are encouraged through volunteerism and organized workshops to maintain and care for these assets.

In the midst of the Tuscan hills, the Sonnino family and SIEC envision an innovative, interactive, post-disciplinary model that demonstrates how historical places can be transformed into sustainable entities in modern times, while still respecting their traditions. The post-disciplinary nature of courses at SIEC varies; however, they all share a fundamental appreciation for the value of hands-on experience to impart an understanding of how best to use traditional local knowledge to care, account, and show respect for the places and cultures of food systems in circular community relationships. Community-based learning at SIEC has ranged in focus, but has been concentrated, therefore, on the preservation of ecosystems services, biodiversity, and connections between agricultural production, rural life, history, social and cultural fabric, health, and the environment (De La Pierre and Bracci 2021, 111). SIEC maintains a small-scale setting for courses, and limits accommodation to a maximum of twenty students in four restored farmhouse apartments on the estate, each complete with traditional Tuscan kitchens. The historical archive and private library are made available to researchers, instructors, and students, but the bulk of instructional time takes place in the estate learning garden, or *orto*, as well as in the olive orchards, grain fields, woodlots, and vineyards, where students, instructors, and researchers are welcome to work during organized workshops, or as volunteers. On request, experiential workshops are also arranged on a variety of topics, including the social, economic, and political history of the region; Tuscan language and culture; vineyard and orchard management; geology and terroir; wine-making, cellaring, and marketing; sustainable tourism; agricultural and food security; ancient grain preservation; and traditional trade, restoration, and culinary practices. There are a number of important archaeological sites in the territory available for exploration. The estate also boasts a small lake, available for hydrological study. University courses at SIEC range in length from three weeks to full fourteen-week semesters. Coursework completed at SIEC has come from programs in sustainability, geography, geology, business management, hospitality and tourism, sociology, and agriculture and food systems.

Student practicums in a variety of local businesses are also a part of coursework at SIEC. The practicums serve to link students to the local community, provide experiential field work and training, and promote opportunities for a community-based flipped classroom (De La Pierre and Bracci 2021). The practicums offer students a unique opportunity to identify, connect, analyze, and apply useful theories and concepts highlighted in their coursework on, and their experiences related to, sustainable agriculture, food security, and food systems, all in the context of the local circular economy. Such pedagogy enhances the capacity for lifelong learning, reflective practice, and professional development. In practicum, students intern and volunteer with a local farmer, experience sustainable farming practices in Tuscany, and learn directly the challenges that local farmers encounter in the face of an international agri-business market dominated by multinational companies.

Like other Canadian universities, the University of British Columbia—Okanagan Campus encourages students to engage with both local and global communities. While university mission statements contain a wealth of good intentions regarding community-based learning, global citizenship, and internationalization, less attention is paid to ensuring these experiences are transformative for the student and the host community. Our auto-ethnographic reflections are derived from the experiences of the authors during the course Rural Sustainability: Wine, Food and Tourism in Tuscany held at Castello Sonnino. The learning objectives of the course include student reflection on the lived meaning of sustainability in the overlapping industries of wine and tourism, and on the methods and means of resilience to vulnerabilities in wine and wine tourism regions.

Results

Our Castello Sonnino small-scale educational tourism case study reveals three interwoven themes that demonstrate how altruism plays a critical role in host-host and host-guest relationships that benefit slow tourism and the sustainability of the Castello Sonnino estate, the small village of Montespertoli, and the broader region of Tuscany. The first theme to emerge is that the promotion of small tourism through typical cuisine results in mutual benefits for hosts. The second emergent theme is the importance of tourists experiencing the processes of small tourism and sustainable development for themselves. The final theme reveals the benefits of reciprocal altruism between educational tourists and their hosts that are achieved through participatory agri-tourism.

Promoting Distinctiveness through Typical Cuisine: Small Villages, Sense of Place, Mutual Benefits

Promoting "typical" styles of cuisine and wine create a unique experience for tourists and helps define a sense of place. To establish a perception among consumers that they will have a unique sensory experience they cannot have anywhere else, a sense of place needs to be emphasized through the promotion of a specific terroir, which gives food and wine a "somewhere-ness" (Easingwood, Lockshin, and Spawton 2011). While globalization pushed many farmers to engage in homogenized, low-cost mass production, creating undifferentiated foods, farmers throughout Italy are focusing more on traditional items that reflect their areas (Bianchi 2011), which provide exclusive experiences through locally identified production (Overton and Murray 2011).

Tourists want to connect to the culture and places they travel to, and local food traditions are an effective way of doing this (Everett and Aitchison 2008) by establishing unique associations with the destination (Kah, Shin, and Lee 2020). By creating an association between a specific culinary heritage and a small village, a region can form a unique identity. This process requires each town to focus on what they believe is "typical" so that they can work together to promote this uniqueness. This host-to-host co-operation results in reciprocal altruistic behaviour with the aim of gaining future benefits (Paraskevaidis and Andriotis 2017). A student working for one of the local producer offered the following observation:

There's no [acting independently] for my brand. . . . It's less about that and I think more about the story behind it. I guess it is more about the co-operation. I think it's really cool if one winery is doing something, not to make their wine better than everyone else, but they do it because there is a social responsibility between one another. (Student focus group)

When traveling between the small village of Montespertoli and neighbouring towns, producers promote tourism by emphasizing the typical cuisine. This collective focus on the symbolic power of food has the ability to establish a culinary heritage in a given area (Bessière 1998). In this way, the host-to-host co-operatives not only enhanced the benefits for each small village, but also for the entire region, as consumers were seeking to experience the cuisine that made each place unique (Colombini 2015). Individual wineries and food producers have a history and story they can communicate to build a connection with consumers, and through reciprocal altruistic behaviour, typical cuisine can be promoted to create small tourism that benefits the villages and the larger image of the area (Timothy and Ron 2013). Mutual success can be amplified by working together to share knowledge, develop typical products, and create marketing together, so as to develop a more robust local industry (Fennell 2006). Importantly, it is these local foodways that provide a distinctiveness to the region (Long 2004) and support the needs of a local economy by encouraging slower, smaller, and more interconnected food systems. As one of our industry interviewees noted, each town has "typical sausage, typical pecorino, and even typical jokes."

Experiencing Local Culture: Nose to the Olive and Grain Grindstone

Living in a small village in Montespertoli enabled the student tourists to interact with the producers and residents of the community, not only to observe the circular socio-economy, but also to interact and participate in it. When tourists insert themselves temporarily into communities, it opens the door for relationships that can result in co-operation and altruistic partnerships (Fennell 2006). Students made daily trips into the village to procure food and supplies from the local butcher, markets, pizzerias, and shops, affording the opportunity to establish relationships with the store owners and locals. There is a strong incentive for the host producers and visiting guests to perform altruistic acts and establish reciprocity because the visitors will be spending money daily within the village, and they will gravitate to a positive local experience. In this way, our students became "cultural creatives," who travel to find connection and meaningful experiences that allow them to develop personally (Ateljevic, Sheldon, and Tomljenović 2016). Cultural creatives value what is slow, small, and local—especially food (Ateljevic 2020).

> The business makes a difference. . . . Supporting an underdog makes me feel good. Something I like to do. If there's no person . . . it's very kind of, like, ambiguous. And my money is basically just going to a company. Then I'm not supporting the underdog. (Student focus group)

A common way of strengthening this connection was for producers to appear small and without large commercial interests. This can often be achieved by emphasizing that the product was created by hand in a genuine way (Beverland and Luxton 2005). Cultural creatives value small and local, so downplaying the commercial aspect by making the production sound more like craftmanship is an effective way of creating a memorable experience (Alexander 2009).

> I think one of the most important things for me was just learning what goes behind a bottle of wine because . . . when you learn the history . . . you learn to like the way it's changed the socio-economics behind it, and the culture and the production and everything that goes into one single glass. I think it gives a lot more appreciation for what you're drinking. (Student focus group)

Students did acknowledge the modernization and technology being used by producers, specifically wineries. However, they appreciated when these commercial processes were downplayed, and the tradition and heritage of the production emphasized.

> When I think of traditional knowledge . . . they [Tuscan wineries] really take that and apply it to modern ways of winemaking, but they still try to maintain the integrity of the traditional knowledge as well. (Student focus group)

One way for cultural creatives to have meaningful experiences is to have their local connections demonstrate the traditional art of producing the food and allow them to experience the process for themselves. Students in this study were able to do this at the local grist mill known as Paciscopi. This mill in Montespertoli has traditionally acted as an important point in the local supply chain for the village. There are eleven ancient grains that have been historically grown at farm estates in the region, including at Sonnino. The grain from these estates is milled into a local traditional flour exclusively at Paciscopi, and the flour is then used by local bakeries to make products for the community, including the local elementary school—as well as the bread and pizza that was regularly consumed by the students.

By visiting the local grist mill, students were able to appreciate the circular economy, where the basic ingredients of daily food are found in surrounding farms, processed in place, and sold down the street in local stores.

> I don't know, like just being here, I realized all the ingredients are a lot . . . less processed. I feel like their tomato sauces taste a lot better. I understand that the grains are a lot better for us. So . . . if you think about that aspect, then you would assume the wines are organic, or better quality than what we would have back in North America. (Student focus group)

Another student offered a similar opinion:

> The way they did the things that they've accomplished, like using the old grain and the biscuits . . . I found it was very, very innovative, and I'm thinking . . . it was kind of much more . . . traditional since there's still a very luxurious feeling to it, which is what I think a lot of tourists come looking for. (Student focus group)

Importantly, students not only toured the facility, but were able to experience and interact with the mill. They were taught about traditional knowledge like the old grindstone that grinds the grains into flour, and then were given the opportunity to pick up the tools and use the grindstone themselves, producing flour that could be bagged and used to make food. This experiential tourism helped build a connection to place and reinforce the reciprocal relationship that the tourists have with local producers, especially in small villages like Montespertoli.

Slow Educational Tourism: Reciprocity and the Mutual Benefits of Participatory Agri-tourism

Tourists are interested in learning about and interacting with ancient traditions, and this type of educational tourism can be experienced on a working farm like Castello Sonnino. When tourists live and work at a host producer, an altruistic partnership can be created (Fennell 2006). This relationship is centred around reciprocal altruism, which is motivated by a common vision aimed at providing community benefits, while also expecting personal benefits (Paraskevaidis and Andriotis 2017). Specifically, our students were motivated to help the host produce food and wine, all while benefiting from the hands-on learning experience. Conversely, the host is motivated to provide a meaningful educational experience, while expecting the benefit of having students work on the property and purchase goods from their store.

Agri-tourism has three common features that provide a successful participatory tourism experience: a working farm, contact with agricultural activity, and an authentic agricultural experience for tourists (Di Gregorio 2017). Such authentic farm experiences can be achieved by staying the night in a traditional country home, walking among farm animals, touring the vineyards, riding a tractor, stomping the grapes, or drinking wine directly from a barrel (Randelli and Martellozzo 2018).

> They provided an effective agri-tourism experience. They brought you to the field, showed you the crops . . . then they did the same with the wine. (Student focus group)

During our field course, students had the opportunity to volunteer in many aspects of the working farm and winery. Many students highlighted working in an experimental bio-dynamic vineyard as memorable. Castello Sonnino has planted bio-dynamic plots to understand how this practice can be used to develop more sustainable vineyards, and to teach students about the impacts of this farming technique. The process of using ancient techniques to hand till the land, create compost, and prune the vines is laborious, so having students work the land is advantageous for the farm. For their part the students, who were instructed by a charismatic teacher on the spiritual significance of their work and the long-term sustainability of these practices, were able to better appreciate the taste of the wine.

Students also visited an organic winery, Tenuta di Valgiano, which operates as a host to Willing Workers on Organic Farms (WWOOF), an organization that offers volunteer workers the opportunity to experience life on an organic farm by becoming fully immersed in the day-to-day activities of organic growing methods (McIntosh and Bonnemann 2006). Accommodation and food are provided for visitors in exchange for volunteer work on the farm property (McIntosh and Campbell 2001). Students in this case study were provided with an in-depth tour of Tenuta di Valgiano's bio-dynamic farming practices, which are used to grow different varietals within the same plot; these are then blended to produce a wine that expresses its unique terroir. This experience taught students the importance of place in the production process, as well as the importance of sustainable best practices in the production of quality wine and food products that protect local environments. On this interactive tour, students were allowed to syphon wine out of a barrel and pass it around to experience how bio-dynamic wine tasted and felt.

> We want to maintain traditional methods through modern technology. Grow natural grains with the vines. Maintain organic even as we grow. (Industry interview)

> And then we went there, and he literally takes the wine out of the barrel and just hands around a glass. So, you see . . . the difference in how they want to present the wine, who they're directing it toward. (Student focus group)

In this way, the students developed reciprocal relationships with their hosts by volunteering at the farms, providing clear community benefits that supported sustainable farming practices in the bio-dynamic vineyards that protect local environments. Students experienced the personal benefits of learning about these methods through participatory agri-tourism.

Discussion

The two main objectives of this research have been, first, to understand the role of altruism in promoting slow tourism. Students through their courses were volunteer tourists whose altruism vis-à-vis Sonnino, Montespertcli, and Tuscany increased over time. They developed motives that caused them to want to help their hosts in the region. As volunteer tourists, they visited a destination to offer their services, gain work experience, and increase welfare in the host society (Weaver 2015; Wearing and McGehee 2013; Zahra and McGehee 2013; Tomazos and Butler 2012). Over their three-week course, they contributed to the social capital of the community, becoming motivated by an attachment to the place and emotional ties within the community (Paraskevaidis and Andriotis 2017; Alonso and Liu 2013; Smith and Holmes 2012). As one student commented, "when you learn the history behind [the wine], you learn the culture and production and develop a relationship with more of a connection to it" (student focus group). These experiences resulted in a type of altruism that encourages direct social exchanges between hosts and guests, when contributions are "separately performed, non-negotiated, and initiated by performing beneficial acts for another" (Paraskevaidis and Andriotis 2017, 27). Participation in the production and consumption of agricultural products through experiential education allowed the students to immerse themselves in authentic experiences to develop relationships with place and the people of that place that resonated through the longer-term connections characteristic of slow tourism. Slow tourism values authenticity, quality, education, conservation, and the protection of partnerships between local agents (Saxena et al. 2007). Slow tourism also supports sustainable values based in territory, landscape, and culture, through an outgrowth of the sustainable development movement that is fostered through the Sonnino educational centre.

Secondly, this research has sought to understand the role of the Sonnino family in implementing innovative, multi-functional, and sustainable development strategies that are preserving the environment and cultural heritage in the village of Montespertoli and in the larger region of Tuscany. Even though the educational centre has provided educational experiences of three to twelve weeks for students, these relatively brief relationships between hosts and guests have grown into a longer-term "terroir of holistic relationships" as a result of slow tourism experiences (Fusté-Forné and Jamal, 2020). The residual and altruistic sense of caring for place is well illustrated by the desire of students to return to Castello Sonnino in order to sustain the Sonnino family's dream of keeping the farm alive and supporting the production and sale of artisanal agricultural products. Several students have now returned to the estate as volunteer educators to assist and guide other educational programs in the years since their own field experience. During a 2022 field course at Castello Sonnino, the group was visited by two sets of parents of former Sonnino students from Canada who needed to explore the place that "had so profoundly influenced" the career paths and land-food relationships of their children. As one of those family members explained in an industry interview, "wine must be welcoming—you know, to make a toast bigger, giving it a bit of food, something which you know brings people together, having fun and staying together, that's a beautiful thing." These types of reciprocal relationships, as demonstrated by the hospitality extended to returning students, their parents, and instructors by family members of the Sonnino estate and their employees, is sustaining a small-scale tourism industry that is grounded in slow tourism.

Conclusion

This case study focusing on a small-scale educational tourism enterprise illustrates the important role of host-host and host-guest relationships in small tourism that embraces altruism, slow tourism, and sustainable development. Specifically, the study suggests that direct reciprocal altruism is a motivating factor influencing sustainable tourism development, and that these altruistic acts support the sustainability of small-scale tourism programs at educational centres such as Castello Sonnino. Direct reciprocal altruism between hosts can contribute to the social capital of a community (Paraskevaidis and Andriotis 2017; Alonso and Liu 2013; Smith and Holmes 2012) by establishing unique associations with the destination. By working together to focus more on traditional items that reflect the area (Bianchi 2011) and emphasizing the typical styles of cuisine and wine, hosts can define a sense of place that promotes the distinctiveness of their region (Long 2004). Tourists desire exclusive experiences through locally identified production (Overton and Murray 2011), and study confirms that small sustainable tourism can be achieved by host-to-host reciprocal altruistic behaviour that creates a sense of place.

Small tourism that embraces slow tourism and a circular social economy has existed between the village and the Castello Sonnino estate for centuries, and the demand for experiences that are slow, small, and local is, along with the host-guest relationship, essential to providing this. Tourists, especially cultural creatives, are looking for meaning and transformation, and altruistic partnerships can play a significant role in developing small sustainable tourism. Experiential tourism helps tourists build a connection to a place and demonstrates the importance of hosts establishing reciprocity with their guests, who are willing to spend money in exchange for a positive local experience. Enabling tourists to interact in the circular economy for themselves is an effective strategy to engage visitors in the everyday life of a destination.

Estates like Castello Sonnino provide a place for slow, small tourism deeply embedded in the local experience. Inspired by Sidney Sonnino's goals of universal suffrage, literacy, and long-term sustainable leases for farming families, the Sonnino family, through kin relationships, have set out to restore and improve the estate. Students in this case study benefited from the hands-on learning experiences provided by their hosts, showing them the sustainable best practices that produce local food and wine, while also protecting and preserving the local environments. These participatory tourism experiences developed at Castello Sonnino have helped diversify small-scale tourism offerings in the region, and have transformed the estate into an economically viable and internationally recognized rural centre for sustainable development. Importantly, this case study has demonstrated that altruism——in this case, between hosts and students at the SEIC—plays an important motivating role in small tourism and shows how it can help preserve the environment and cultural heritage for future generations.

Limitations and Future Research

Our case study revealed two areas of limitation that could be explored in further research. First, our study explored the impact of a host-guest altruistic relationship in one three-week course. This was done by examining the experiences of students who participated in an experiential course and who lived and worked at the Castello Sonnino estate between 29 April and 20 May 2018. Further research, however, could explore the altruistic relationships resulting from longer-term educational experiences via longitudinal analysis. This could include more long-term educational experiential programs at Castello Sonnino, or at WWOOF organizations. Second, our study looked briefly at kin relationships at the Castello Sonnino. There is an opportunity to go into more detail about how kin relationships can be a motivating factor for small tourism, and a driving force for long-term sustainability.

References

Alexander, Nicholas. 2009. "Brand Authentication: Creating and Maintaining Brand Auras." *European Journal of Marketing* 43, nos. 3–4: 551–62.

Alonso, Abel Duarte, and Yi Liu. 2013. "Local Community, Volunteering and Tourism Development: The Case of the Blackwood River Valley, Western Australia." *Current Issues in Tourism* 16, no. 1: 47–62.

Andersen, Mikael Skou. 2007. "An Introductory Note on the Environmental Economics of the Circular Economy." *Sustainability Science* 2, no. 1: 133–40.

Anderson, Emma, and Grant Cairncross. 2005. "Understanding and Managing Volunteer Motivation: Two Regional Tourism Cases." *Australian Journal on Volunteering* 10, no. 2: 7.

Andriotis, Konstantinos, and George Agiomirgianakis. 2014. "Market Escape through Exchange: Home Swap as a Form of Non-commercial Hospitality." *Current Issues in Tourism* 17, no. 7: 576–91.

Ateljevic, Irena. 2020. "Transforming the (Tourism) World for Good And (Re)Generating the Potential 'New Normal.'" *Tourism Geographies* 22, no. 3: 467–75.

Ateljevic, Irena, Pauline Sheldon, and Renata Tomljenović. 2016. "The New Paradigm of the 21st Century, 'Silent Revolution' of Cultural Creatives and Transformative Tourism of and for the Future." In *Affiliate Members Global Reports*, vol. 14, *The Transformative Power of Tourism: A Paradigm Shift towards a More Responsible Traveller*, 12–20. Madrid: UNWTO. https://doi.org/10.18111/9789284417834.

Beer, Andrew, and David Watson. 2009. "The Individual and Group Loyalty Scales (IGLS): Construction and Preliminary Validation." *Journal of Personality Assessment* 91, no. 3: 277–87.

Bessière, Jacinthe. 1998. "Local Development and Heritage: Traditional Food and Cuisine as Tourist Attractions in Rural Areas." *Sociologia ruralis* 38, no. 1: 21–34.

Beverland, Michael, and Sandra Luxton. 2005. "Managing Integrated Marketing Communication (IMC) through Strategic Decoupling: How Luxury Wine Firms Retain Brand Leadership while Appearing to Be Wedded to the Past." *Journal of Advertising* 34, no. 4: 103–16.

Bianchi, Rossella. 2011. "From Agricultural to Rural: Agritourism as a Productive Option." In *Food, Agri-culture and Tourism*, edited by Katia Laura Sidali, Achim Spiller, and Birgit Schulze, 56–71. Berlin: Springer.

Brouder, Patrick. 2017. "Evolutionary Economic Geography: Reflections from a Sustainable Tourism Perspective." *Tourism Geographies* 19, no. 3: 438–47.

Camuto, Robert. 2016. "The Prodigal Antinori: Decades after Selling Ornellaia, the Black Sheep of One of Italy's Leading Wine Families Performs an Encore." *Wine Spectator* 41, no. 9: 36–49.

Chang, Heewon. 2016. *Autoethnography as Method*. London: Routledge.

Clancy, Michael, ed. 2017. *Slow Tourism, Food and Cities: Pace and the Search for the "Good Life."* Abingdon, UK: Routledge.

Colombini, Donatella Cineli. 2015. "Wine Tourism in Italy." *International Journal of Wine Research* 7:29–35.

Cresswell, Tim. 2010. "Towards a Politics of Mobility." *Environment and Planning D: Society and Space* 28, no. 1: 17–31.

Croce, Erica, and Giovanni Perri. 2008. "Il turismo enogastronomico." In *Progettare, gestire, vivere*, 1–21. Scienze e professioni del turismo. Milano: Franco Angeli.

De La Pierre, Marco, and Marco Bracci. 2021. *Study Abroad in Italy: Fra economia della conoscenza, turismo e soft power*. Firenze: Autopubblicato.

Dickinson, Janet, and Les Lumsdon. 2010. *Slow Travel and Tourism*. London: Earthscan.

Di Gregorio, Dante. 2017. "Place-Based Business Models for Resilient Local Economies." *Journal of Enterprising Communities: People and Places in the Global Economy* 11, no. 1: 113–28.

Easingwood, Chris, Larry Lockshin, and Anthony Spawton. 2011. "The Drivers of Wine Regionality." *Journal of Wine Research* 22, no. 1: 19–33.

Everett, Sally, and Cara Aitchison. 2008. "The Role of Food Tourism in Sustaining Regional Identity: A Case Study of Cornwall, South West England." *Journal of Sustainable Tourism* 16, no. 2: 150–67.

Fennell, David A. 2006. "Evolution in Tourism: The Theory of Reciprocal Altruism and Tourist-Host Interactions." *Current Issues in Tourism* 9, no. 2: 105–24.

Fullagar, Simone, Kevin Markwell, and Erica Wilson, eds. 2012. *Slow Tourism: Experiences and Mobilities*. Bristol: Channel View Publications.

Fusté-Forné, Francesc, and Tazim Jamal. 2020. "Slow Food Tourism: An Ethical Microtrend for the Anthropocene." *Journal of Tourism Futures* 6, no. 3: 227–32. https://doi.org/10.1108/JTF-10-2019-0120.

Gariglio, G., and F. Giavedoni. 2015. *Slow Wine Guide 2015*. Turin: Slow Food Editore.

Gossling, S., D. Scott, and C.M Hall. 2020. "Pandemics, Tourism and Global Change: A Rapid Assessment of COVID-19." *Journal of Sustainable Tourism* 29, no 1: 1–20.

Hamilton, William D. 1964. "The Genetical Evolution of Social Behaviour. II." *Journal of Theoretical Biology* 7, no. 1: 17–52,

Heitmann, Sine, Peter Robinson, and Ghislaine Povey. 2011. "Slow Foo d, Slow Cities and Slow Tourism." In *Research Themes for Tourism*, 114–27. Wallingford, UK: CABI.

IUCN (International Union for Conservation of Nature and Natural Resources), UNEP (United Nations Environment Programme), and WWF (World Wildlife Fund). 1980. *World Conservation Strategy. Living Resource Conservation for Sustainable Development*. Gland, CH: IUCN, UNEP, WWF.

Kah, Junghye Angela, Hye Jin Shin, and Seong-Hoon Lee. 2020. "Traveler Sensoryscape Experiences and the Formation of Destination Identity." *Tourism Geographies* 24, nos. 2–3: 475–94.

Kim, Myung Ja, Choong-Ki Lee, and Mark Bonn. 2016. "The Effect of Social Capital and Altruism on Seniors' Revisit Intention to Social Network Sites for Tourism-Related Purposes." *Tourism Management* 53:96–107.

Lockstone-Binney, Leonie, Kirsten Holmes, Karen Smith, and Tom Baum. 2010. "Volunteers and Volunteering in Leisure: Social Science Perspectives." *Leisure Studies* 29, no. 4: 435–55.

Long, Lucy M. 2004. "A Folkloristic Perspective on Eating and Otherness." In *Culinary Tourism*, 20–50. Lexington: University Press of Kentucky.

MacArthur, Ellen. 2013. "Towards the Circular Economy." *Journal of Industrial Ecology* 2:23–44.

Manniche, Jesper, Karin Topsø Larsen, Rikke Brandt Broegaard, and Emil Holland. 2017. *Destination: A Circular Tourism Economy: A Handbook for Transitioning toward a Circular Economy within the Tourism and Hospitality Sectors in the South Baltic Region.* Stenbrudsvej, DK: Centre for Regional & Tourism Research.

Mauser, Wolfram, Gernot Klepper, Martin Rice, Bettina Susanne Schmalzbauer, Heide Hackmann, Rik Leemans, and Howard Moore. 2013. "Transdisciplinary Global Change Research: The Co-creation of Knowledge for Sustainability." *Current Opinion in Environmental Sustainability* 5, nos. 3–4: 420–31.

McGrath, Peter, and Richard Sharpley. 2017. "Slow Travel and Tourism: New Concept or New Label?" In *Slow Tourism, Food and Cities: Pace and the Search for the "Good Life,"* edited by Michael Clancy, 49–62. New York: Routledge.

McIntosh, Alison J., and Susanne M. Bonnemann. 2006. "Willing Workers on Organic Farms (WWOOF): The Alternative Farm Stay Experience?" *Journal of Sustainable Tourism* 14, no. 1: 82–99.

McIntosh, Alison, and Tamara Campbell. 2001. "Willing Workers on Organic Farms (WWOOF): A Neglected Aspect of Farm Tourism in New Zealand." *Journal of Sustainable Tourism* 9, no. 2: 111–27.

Molm, Linda D., Jessica L. Collett, and David R. Schaefer. 2007. "Building Solidarity through Generalized Exchange: A Theory of Reciprocity." *American Journal of Sociology* 113, no. 1: 205–42.

Osiński, Jerzy. 2009. "Kin Altruism, Reciprocal Altruism and Social Discounting." *Personality and Individual Differences* 47, no. 4: 374–8.

Overton, John, and Warwick E. Murray. 2011. "Playing the Scales: Regional Transformations and the Differentiation of Rural Space in the Chilean Wine Industry." *Journal of Rural Studies* 27, no. 1: 63–72.

Pamfilie, Rodica, Daniela Firoiu, Adina-Gabriela Croitoru, and George Horia Ioan Ionescu. 2018. "Circular Economy—A New Direction for the Sustainability of the Hotel Industry in Romania." *Amfiteatru Economic* 20, no. 48: 388–404.

Paraskevaidis, Pavlos, and Konstantinos Andriotis. 2017. "Altruism in Tourism: Social Exchange Theory vs. Altruistic Surplus Phenomenon in Host Volunteering." *Annals of Tourism Research* 62:26–37.

Pritchard, Annette, Nigel Morgan, and Irena Ateljevic. 2011. "Hopeful Tourism: A New Transformative Perspective." *Annals of Tourism Research* 38, no. 3: 941–63.

QSR International Pty Ltd. NVivo Version 12. 2018. Available online: https://www.qsrinternational.com/nvivo-qualitative-data-analysis-software/home (accessed on 1 March 2022).

Randelli, Filippo, and Federico Martellozzo. 2018. "The Impact of Rural Tourism on Land Use. The Case of Tuscany." Working Papers—Economics wp2018_02.rdf, Universita' degli Studi di Firenze, Dipartimento di Scienze per l'Economia e l'Impresa.

Saxena, Gunjan, Gordon Clark, Tove Oliver, and Brian Ilbery. 2007. "Conceptualizing Integrated Rural Tourism." *Tourism Geographies* 9, no. 4: 347–70.

Saxena, Gunjan, and Brian Ilbery. 2008. "Integrated Rural Tourism: A Border Case Study." *Annals of Tourism Research* 35, no. 1: 233–54.

Senese, Donna M. 2016. "Transformative Wine Tourism in Mountain Communities." In *Mountain Tourism: Experiences, Communities, Environments and Sustainable Futures*, edited by H. Richins and J.S. Hull, 121–30. Boston: Cabi.

Sigala, Marianna. 2020. "Tourism and COVID-19: Impacts and Implications for Advancing and Resetting Industry and Research." *Journal of Business Research* 117:312–21.

Singh, E., S. Milne, and J. Hull. 2012. "Use of Mixed-Methods Case Study to Research Sustainable Tourism Development in South Pacific SIDS." In *Field Guide to Case Study Research in Tourism, Hospitality and Leisure*, vol. 6, edited by K. F. Hyde, C. Ryan, A. G. Woodside, 457–78. Bingley, UK: Emerald Group Publishing.

Smit, Barry, and Mark W. Skinner. 2002. "Adaptation Options in Agriculture to Climate Change: A Typology." *Mitigation and Adaptation Strategies for Global Change* 7, no. 1: 85–114.

Smith, Karen A., and Kirsten Holmes. 2012. "Visitor Centre Staffing: Involving Volunteers." *Tourism Management* 33, no. 3: 562–8.

Sørensen, Flemming, and Jørgen Ole Bærenholdt. 2020. "Tourist Practices in the Circular Economy." *Annals of Tourism Research* 85:103027. https://doi.org/10.1016/j.annals.2020.103027.

Soulard, J., N McGehee, M. Stern and K. Lamoureux. "Transformative tourism: Tourists' drawings, symbols and narratives of change." *Annals of Tourism Research* 87:103141

Timothy, Dallen J., and Amos S. Ron. 2013. "Understanding Heritage Cuisines and Tourism: Identity, Image, Authenticity, and Change." *Journal of Heritage Tourism* 8, nos. 2–3: 99–104.

Tomazos, Kostas, and Richard Butler. 2012. "Volunteer Tourists in the Field: A Question of Balance?" *Tourism Management* 33, no. 1: 177–87.

Trivers, Robert L. 1971. "The Evolution of Reciprocal Altruism." *Quarterly Review of Biology* 46, no. 1: 35–57.

UNEP (United Nations Environmental Programme) and UNWTO (United Nations World Tourism Organization). 2005. *Making Tourism More Sustainable: A Guide for Policy Makers*. Paris. UNEP.

UNWTO (United Nations World Tourism Organization). 2020. *Tourism and COVID-19*. Madrid. UNWTO.

Uriely, Natan, Zvi Schwartz, Eli Cohen, and Arie Reichel. 2002. "Rescuing Hikers in Israel's Deserts: Community Altruism or an Extension of Adventure Tourism?" *Journal of Leisure Research* 34, no. 1: 25–36.

Veal, Anthony James. 2017. *Research Methods for Leisure and Tourism*. London: Pearson Publishing.

VisitMontespertoli. "A land of parish churches and small villages." Comune di Montespertoli, accessed 27 March 2023. https://visitmontespertoli.it/a-territory-of-small-villages/?lang=en.

WCED Special Working Session. 1987. "World Commission on Environment and Development." *Our Common Future* 17, no. 1: 1–91.

Wearing, Stephen, and Nancy Gard McGehee. 2013. "Volunteer Tourism: A Review." *Tourism Management* 38:120–30.

Weaver, David. 2015. "Volunteer Tourism and Beyond: Motivations and Barriers to Participation in Protected Area Enhancement." *Journal of Sustainable Tourism* 23, no. 5: 683–705.

Williams, Allan M., Russell King, and Tony Warnes. 1997. "A Place in the Sun: International Retirement Migration from Northern to Southern Europe." *European Urban and Regional Studies* 4, no. 2: 115–34.

Wilson, David Sloan. 2015. *Does Altruism Exist? Culture, Genes and the Welfare of Others*. New Haven, CT: Yale University Press.

Wright, Hayley. 2013. "Volunteer Tourism and Its (Mis)Perceptions: A Comparative Analysis of Tourist/Host Perceptions." *Tourism and Hospitality Research* 13, no. 4: 239–50.

Yin, Robert K. 2018. *Case Study Research and Applications*. Newbury Park, CA: Sage.

Zahra, Anne, and Nancy Gard McGehee. 2013. "Volunteer Tourism: A Host Community Capital Perspective." *Annals of Tourism Research* 42:22–45.

Revealing the Restorers: Small Tourism in Restored Lands of the Noongar Traditional Area of the Fitz-Stirling in Southwestern Australia

Moira A. L. Maley, Sylvia M. Leighton, Alison Lullfitz, Johannes E. Wajon, M. Jane Thompson, Carol Pettersen, Mohammadreza Gohari, and Keith Bradby

Introduction

Key elements of creative tourism are activities that culminate in the co-creation of the experience by tourists and hosts (Richards 2011, 1236). Yet creativity manifests in many ways. The restoration of cleared landscapes back toward their original biodiverse state is itself a form of creation. When this is done in small communities by landowners in partnership with a broad collaboration of individuals and organizations (Bradby, Keesing, and Wardell-Johnson 2016, 828), including visitor and tourist participation, the touristic approach is creative in both concept and outcome. That outcome is not only the observation of an external, changed, natural environment, as occurs in nature tourism, but is an internal, emotional change evoked during the restoration work or by witnessing the transformed landscape and speaking with the restorers. The creation of artworks to represent this experience is another creative outcome for the visitor.

This work is a collaborative reflection among landscape and tourism scholars on the role of tourism at the nexus of landscape and cultural restoration. As a quality-improvement initiative, we pause to carefully consider our way forward. Speaking in the context of small, relational tourism, we follow a journey of landscape and cultural reconnection that focuses on tourists' brief immersion with land restorers at the site of re-creation. This creative approach is strategic, aligning with the principles of sustainable tourism (Bradby 2016, 316), yielding mutual benefits for the restorers and their visitors.

The purpose of the chapter is to report a unique type of small creative tourism. All over the world, First Nation Peoples are embracing the opportunity to share their culture, highlighting the entwinement of people and place. We offer an example of how Indigeneity can go hand in hand with sustainable tourism development.

Restoring Landscapes and Lost Habitats

Our theme of restoration addresses the dual perspectives of restoring access for both people and wildlife to biodiverse landscapes. Our examples are located in southwestern Australia, an area designated as a global biodiversity hotspot, which is a place "where exceptional concentrations of endemic species are undergoing exceptional loss of habitat" (Myers et al. 2000, 853). Much of the habitat loss occurred through government-sponsored agricultural development from 1919 to 1930 and 1948 to 1969, now described, with hindsight, as "the post war holocaust of mass clearing . . . [that brought] so much wealth . . . and affliction" (Rijavec 2003). Thus, the habitat that remains is vital to protect.

The Noongar are the First People of southwestern Australia, having continuously occupied its landscapes (in the Noongar language, *Boodja*) for at least fifty thousand years (Turney et al. 2017, 3; Tobler et al. 2017). Noongar identity, language, and culture are universally and inextricably attached to *Boodja*, including strictly controlled rights to resources, and responsibilities for managing biodiversity and the spiritual health of its inhabitants (Meagher and Ride 1979, 67; Berndt 1979). The consensus outcome from this restoration tourism was to promote a reparative path for the relationship between people and nature in light of the hegemony of the unsustainable rate of land clearing globally (Maxton-Lee 2017, 19; Lawson et al. 2014). Entwined altruistic intent echoes loudly throughout the small and slow setting of our tourism. The altruism is focused on reparation.

Place and Touristic Place

Our place is the "Fitz-Stirling," which is a largely cleared habitat gap between the Fitzgerald River National Park, itself part of a biosphere reserve, and the Stirling Range National Park, known as *Kykeneruff* by the local Noongar. While these two national parks are recognized locally and globally for their biological richness, more recent work has identified the surrounding and connecting cleared landscapes as equally important (Gioia and Hopper 2017, 9).

Within the Fitz-Stirling, in addition to a range of efforts by the farming community to better conserve the local biodiversity, strategically located low-productivity farms are being purchased by private individuals and conservation NGOs, mostly using philanthropic funds. This cleared land is then being restored as part of a thousand-kilometre connectivity conservation area known as Gondwana Link (Bradby, Keesing, and Wardell-Johnson 2016, 828). These opportunities host the pilot small tourism ventures examined in this chapter.

Our touristic place is the *Boodja* itself, being the biodiverse land biome with its entwined Noongar spirituality in all its realms. The tourists journey into it; by interaction with it and by observation, they make their own meanings of it; they come to understand and feel its multiple functions and traditions; they create and retain their own memorable experiences. In *Boodja* there is no pre-selected "stockpile of knowledge, traditions, memories and images," as found in cities according to Scott (2010). There is the live *Boodja* and the people who live there; tourists journey, look, listen, feel, inquire, participate, and create. Their participation creates a shared social capital of mutual benefits, a reciprocal altruism between restorers and tourists (Paraskevaidis and Andriotis 2017).

Cultural Connection with "Country"

In traditional life, Noongar people lived within family groups, travelling along tracks (or in Noongar, *biddis*) and residing across specific *Boodja* to which their families had deep spiritual connections, as well as rights and responsibilities to manage. Movement patterns were seasonal, based on climate, resource availability, and social, educational, and ceremonial purpose (Nind 1831, 26; Collard and Harben 2010; Meagher 1974). Clearing of that land and fencing for agriculture, such as occurred in the Wellstead District and much of the Fitz-Stirling area, stripped the natural biodiversity from the landscape, and in doing so, not only caused harm to Noongar spiritual and educational resources and places, but also severely restricted Noongar access to both the remaining intact and the damaged *Boodja*.

Reconnecting

Initially, the Gondwana Link program had a strong ecological focus in the Fitz-Stirling, being the progressive reconnection of the two national parks so that they could eventually function again as one ecological unit. With time, a deeper understanding has formed that ecological restoration and reconnection are inextricably linked to cultural and social restoration and reconnection (Aronson, Blatt, and Aronson 2016, 42).

Noongar reconnection with *Boodja*, including the sensitive restoration of *Boodja*, will greatly enrich outcomes for southwestern Australian biodiversity and people, as well as for the tourist experience. Ecological, cultural, and social values are here entwined.

The Actors in and Design of Touristic Experiences

The restorers in our examples are also the tourism providers; they present their first-hand perspectives, offering authenticity in their ecotourism product.

Their small-group tourism was "backward-designed" (Wiggins and McTighe 2005, 36) to bring about transformative outcomes in tourists. As the consensus outcome for this community of practice was to promote a reparative path for the relationship between people and nature, this theme echoed in their tours, while still presenting distinctive experiences through the variation in landscapes the visitors toured.

To quote author M. Jane Thompson in her tour script relating to why they undertook their restoration, "to restore a bit of the planet in our own little way . . . link the country up, be part of a big scheme; one of our things is to try and inspire other people to do similar things."

The Restoration Tourists

To date, the restoration sites have received between ten and fifty visitors per month, excluding seasonal periods, when the risks of the wet (infection with dieback) or fire are prohibitive. Generally, the groups have a common interest for their visits—for example, birds, wildflowers, primary school excursions, mature age summer school, university students, project-based professionals. There is a mix of international visitors with environmental interests and local people, some being potential benefactors. They come as pairs or small groups typically of ten to twenty adults, coming for periods ranging from two hours to four days; some larger groups also visit.

Our Restoration Tourism Examples

Figure 4.1 shows the geographic location of our three examples: Chingarrup Sanctuary and Yarraweyah Falls in the Fitz-Stirling area, and Wilyun Pools Farm in the Wellstead district.

Each property was nearly 90 per cent cleared of original bush in the 1960s and '70s in preparation for agricultural use, and then farmed by conventional practices until no longer profitable, when ownership changed. Figure 4.2 shows a historical timeline of the landmark events of our three examples.

Another innovative approach to the same restoration outcome is through "balanced" farming where properties that have been worked intensively and unsustainably are subject to changed farming practices that return biodiversity to the landscape (Bawden 2018, 124; Massy 2017). Our Wilyun Pools Farm illustrates this: a long-standing family farm has transitioned to a sustainable, regenerative future. A wider adoption of sustainable regenerative farming requires the changing of a mindset that has been ingrained through generations of harsh agricultural practice. The surrounding farming community has taken a first step toward such a cultural transformation by formally recognizing Noongar natural and cultural heritage locally.

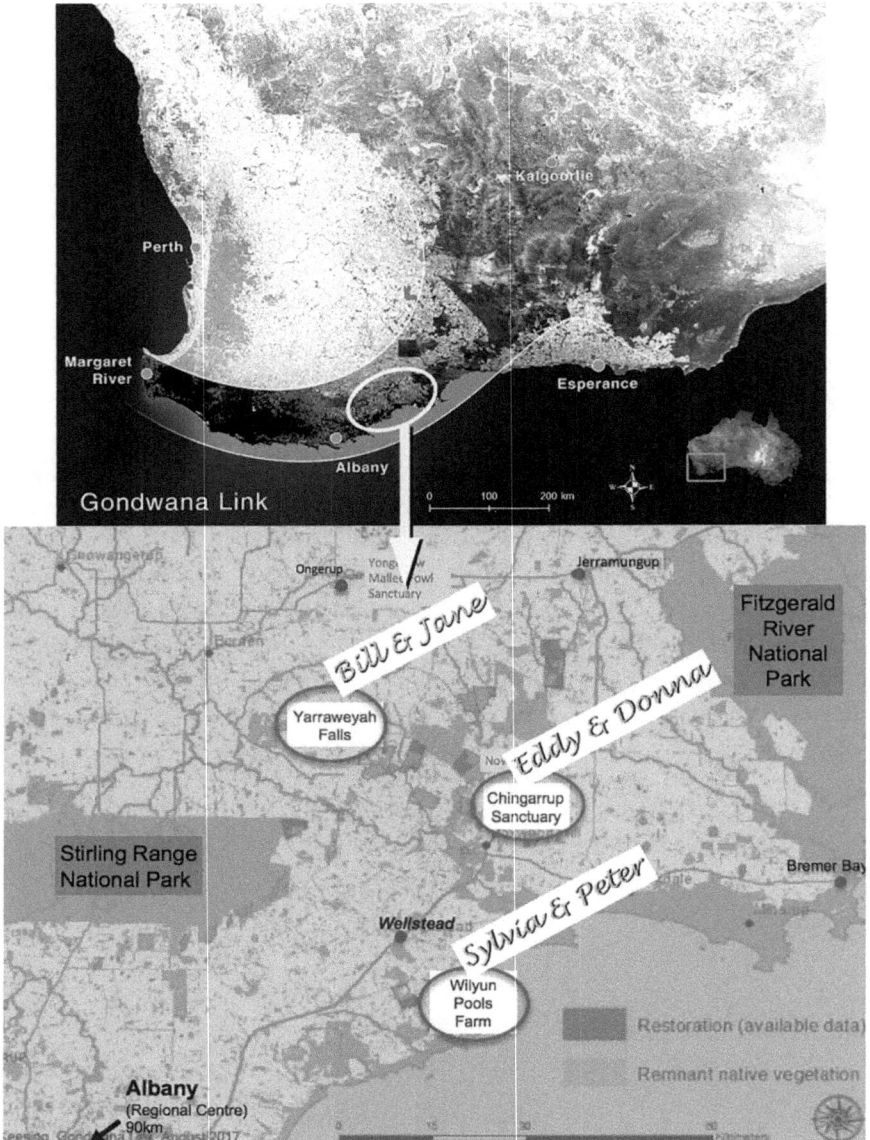

Figure 4.1: The Gondwana Link "Corridor" in southwestern Australia and the locations of three restoration tourism examples in the Fitz-Stirling.

Source: Gondwana Link Office, Keith Bradby.

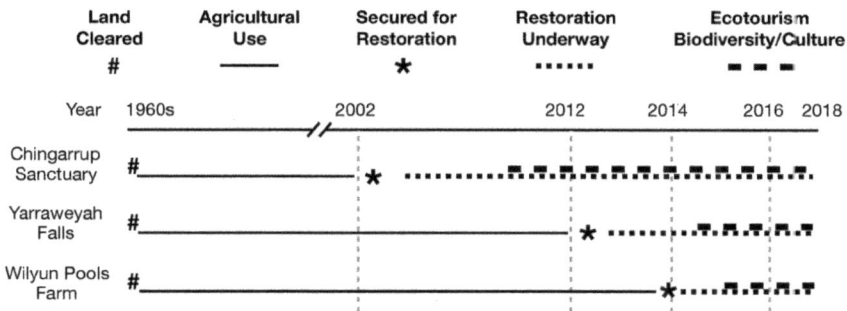

Figure 4.2: Timeline for landmark events in landscape restorations.

Source: Moira Maley and Gondwana Link.

Profiles of the Restoration Tourism Examples

Chingarrup Sanctuary

NOONGAR CULTURE

Chingarrup Sanctuary sits within the catchment of the Pallinup River, an important Noongar movement corridor between the coast and inland areas. Of particular significance on the property are the Corackerup and Chingarrup Creeks, which provided water and fertile land for people, plants, and animals, and thus were vital for hunting, plant gathering, and movement corridors. An ochre source on the Corackerup Creek was traditionally used and remains important to Noongar people. Waterways also had (and continue to have) important spiritual significance, and were traditionally the focus of ceremony and daily Noongar life, while upslope heathland and granite outcrops were important for specific plants and other resources, and again, hold spiritual significance.

PEOPLE AND PROCESS[1]

Eddy and Donna, restorers, wildflower enthusiasts, and botanists, purchased the Chingarrup property (576 hectares) in 2002 as a "bush block for conservation"; their block evolved into a biodiversity restoration project as part of Gondwana Link. Funding assistance supported the initial revegetation of 110 hectares, with ongoing restoration extended over more than twelve years, worked by the owners and many volunteers, with professional help in periodic visits, as Eddy and Donna are based in the capital city of Perth, some 450 kilometres away. Research and monitoring are carried out through citizen science (volunteer supported and grant funded) and professional groups; tourist visitations coincide with the owners' regular visits to their property.

DESIGN

In designing the tour program for visitors, Eddy and Donna traced the themes of their own emotional journey during the restoration. They aim to inspire others to recognize the importance of connected natural landscapes, and for others to learn from hands-on work in a biodiverse environment, observing and feeling personal responses to the colours, textures, sounds, and behaviours of the landscape and its wildlife inhabitants through complete immersion in it.

THE EXPERIENCE

Chingarrup Sanctuary tours are visitor-centred and range from occasional day visits with guided driving and walking tours of the property's highlights to extended project-focused camping stays. Written guides for an immersive, multiple-day program consider the goal of the period on site; a choice of the extent of personal involvement alongside more experienced participants; the range of activities; potential highlights; time-tabling of activities; skills level for participation; personal tools that would be helpful to bring; food menu and kitchen facilities; sleeping and toileting arrangements; clear directions for locating the sanctuary; and communications facilities available, as well as contact numbers. This full and frank guide projects a responsible approach to the safety of visitors and provides a clear set of behaviour expectations.

Their mature approach to visitors reflects their experience over the long term. Activities are well paced, of appropriate size for completion so as to see a result during the stay, and designed so that a participant takes away a sense of personal contribution within a continuum. Evening activities are gently creative, inclusive, and support learning around the value of connecting landscapes and people. This rich interaction embodies slow tourism where perceived value is linked to the host—tourist relationship (Clancy 2018).

A biannual illustrated newsletter containing relevant recent reports and events is distributed by the restorers to all past participants, creating strong and expansive social capital. Eddy promotes both Chingarrup Sanctuary and Gondwana Link as an invited speaker, and maintains active contact with government agencies in lobbying for environmental conservation.

These restorers were pioneers of ecotourism in the region; they showed unique courage and generosity of spirit in their venture, and their thirst for lifelong learning has led them to start other restoration sites, allowing them to progressively reinvest their wisdom.

Yarraweyah Falls

NOONGAR CULTURE

Yarraweyah Falls is also within the catchment of the Pallinup River, and thus Noongar activity and tradition reflects the situation at Chingarrup. Of particular Noongar significance are the two Yarraweyah Falls on the river, which are connected by 150 metres of rock and remain of contemporary ceremonial importance.

PEOPLE AND PROCESS[2]

Bill and Jane are experienced intensive farmers from Queensland and keen botanists, who purchased Yarraweyah Falls (1,500 hectares) in 2012 for biodiversity restoration as part of Gondwana Link, and also as a home site. The attraction was the high biodiversity of the area, the umbrella support of Gondwana Link, and the proximity to other biodiversity-driven restorations. Their previous experience had been on an organic farm located on the rim of encroaching industrial development.

Carbon sequestration funding (from the Carbon Neutral Charitable Fund), combined with Australian Government biodiversity funding supported the planting through direct seeding of a hundred hectares of local trees and shrubs that would both sequester carbon and provide biodiversity benefits; the owners undertook biodiversity infill planting with seedlings from stock they collected and propagated on the property.

DESIGN

In designing their tour programs for visitors, Bill and Jane use creative themes from their own immersion in the restoration, and they make an effort to share their joy at the outcomes of the emerging life forms that they see.

THE EXPERIENCE

Ecotourism is young in the area of Yarraweyah Falls. Visitors see a variety of features there: the re-vegetation, waterfalls, and the adjacent restoration sites Monjebup and Red Moort. Jane creates artworks with natural elements, and Bill loves walking among nature, quietly explaining special features so as to conjure the mythology of the landscape to the present moment. Visitors reflect on this later and write about it.

Creative activities form the backbone of their guided tours and stays. Their promotions offer nature-centred activities that are customized to visitors' interests and interaction with adjoining restoration properties; a family-friendly context for introducing nature and landscape connection to people of all ages; home cooking and an organic vegetable garden; and wide open skies and geological vistas.

Bill and Jane brought to their restoration tourism a combined wisdom from their own family experience, previous projects, a realist environmental commitment, and their belief in the importance of local networks. They worked on their Yarraweyah Falls property in a supported context alongside like-minded landscape restorers in the Gondwana Link community.

Wilyun Pools Farm

NOONGAR CULTURE

Wilyun Pools Farm is located in the southern part of the Fitz-Stirling corridor. For some time, local community members had recognized a need to record the local Noongar cultural history. In a spirit of cultural reconciliation, they wished to formally record local cultural heritage as an artwork for future generations. A painting depicting the local country before European settlement was commissioned from Noongar artist Nicholas Smith, who painted in the distinctive landscape tradition of the Carrolup artists of the 1940s (Wroth 2015). Nicholas began to paint in the Carrolup school when he was removed with other Aboriginal children to the Marribank Mission. His painting hangs in the Wellstead Community Resource Centre on the tourist visitor trail, and represents a strong example of cultural mapping.

Traditionally, Noongar walking *biddis* were a core human element of *Boodja* in the Fitz- Stirling. However, clearing for agriculture and cessation of Noongar management of *Boodja* has meant that the locations of *biddis* have become obscure and poorly known. To address this erasure, a recent Noongar-initiated project[3] brought together several Noongar Elder women with Wilyun Pools Farm and the local Historical and Heritage Committee to share the Elders' collective family stories and childhood memories. The project utilized early settlement maps to guide them in locating a women's cultural trail, the Gnadju Trail. Revisiting sites along the trail was an emotional experience, as they stood in a group in these places, recalling events that connected the Noongar women with their grandparents and ancestors. Documenting these stories was important for Noongar and non-Noongar participants, and has provided a valuable resource not only for their families, but for national reconciliation.

PEOPLE AND PROCESS

Sylvia and Peter, the restorers for Wilyun Pools Farm, both grew up in the South Coast region of Western Australia and were working farm children during the "million acres a year" agricultural clearing holocaust in the 1960s. As adults, Sylvia worked as an environmental conservationist and Peter in farming and plantation forestry.

Wilyun Pools Farm (1240 hectares) was a family farm developed by Sylvia's parents through clearing of the original bush, and then largely grazed with sheep from 1965 to 1991. Its use changed in 1991 when 820 hectares were planted with blue gum trees (*Eucalyptus globulus*) for paper fibre. In 2014, farm ownership was passed on to the next generation, bringing a transition to more ecologically balanced farming. Sylvia and Peter pooled their skills to restore the family farm back to a more balanced commercial agricultural business, including 120 hectares restored back to natural biodiverse landscape. Their vision is to operate more gently within the natural ecology of the landscape and incorporate wildlife as an integral part of the business.

The initial restoration of 100 hectares of biodiverse wildlife corridors across Wilyun Pools Farm has received support in the form of federal and state grant funding.[4] Peter and Sylvia collected the native plant seed used from remnant areas on the farm and built 60 kilometres of protective fencing to exclude grazing stock from the restoration corridors. They manage, monitor, and conduct ongoing participatory action research relating to biodiversity.

Inviting Noongar Elders back on *Boodja* and sitting together on land within the farm boundary was a meaningful step into a richer future of cultural respect and sharing. The culturally significant Noongar *biddis* across both the farm and the Wellstead District have now been mapped and recorded, and an ongoing dialogue is maintained with Noongar community members. Using this map, four non-Indigenous artists stayed on-site and, using a slurry of the local orange clay, created a 2-by-3-metre "Tracks of Time" canvas as a non-literal depiction of the old Noongar *biddis* that criss-crossed the landscape before the land was cleared. This artwork now moves around the region on display.

DESIGN

In designing tours for visitors to the farm, Sylvia and Peter want to demonstrate that conserving native plants and animals can be easily integrated into commercial agricultural businesses in Australia.

THE EXPERIENCE

An ever-increasing number of school children, university study groups, art groups, and agricultural interest groups visit Wilyun Pools Farm.

Although the school children are from the regional small city of Albany (only 100 kilometres away), the big open space on the farm, as well as the interactions with farm animals and machinery, has great impact. A tour for sixty children rotates them through four outdoor activities, each of which requires walking and talking with experts, building a structure, or drawing what they saw.

Discussion

The Restoration Ecotourism Experience

Regardless of the duration of the tour, the remote location of the restoration sites necessitates three tour phases: first, a journey into country; second, an orientation and intimate interaction inside country; and third, a journey back out from country. So, from the visitors' perspective, there is a big transition from their starting landscape (likely a car park or city home) to that of the restoration site in the first phase of the visit, providing an opportunity to build a relationship with the destination, and negotiate expectations. For the second phase, which commences on arrival, the visitors require an orientation to the immersion landscape before moving, participating, or creating within *Boodja*, which for them is an unfamiliar world. The third phase of the visit, leaving *Boodja*, must be undertaken with respect, acknowledging mutual contributions and also future possibilities; during the journey out, space is left for reflection but also for resolution of any issues that may have arisen. The crafting of the ecotourist's experience has to allow for changing weather, wildlife behaviour, and unforeseen natural events. All being optimal, the impact on the visitors of their engagement with nature, as well as with elements of tangible and intangible cultural heritage of *Boodja*, will be strong, lasting, and transformative. Such are the possibilities of small tourism in small places.

The restorers have deep passion, enthusiasm, respect, and understanding of the tour site's landscape. These attributes aid them in their role as interpreters and translators of cultural traditions; in landscape restoration, there is a culture of biodiversity heritage as well as the culture of the traditional people. The comfort and familiarity shown by restorers when in their landscape is a stabilizing factor for the visitors, most of whom will be out of their comfort zone to some extent, at least initially. By design, an entirely self-drive version of this restoration tourism would lack both the key relationship elements and the spaces for undistracted reflection, and would also open the possibility of disease incursion.

Meaning Making and Mentorship

In order to make sense of the restoration actions, the visitors need to re-create in their own minds a background context against which to evaluate the evidence before them. The evidence is the range of different species of plants and animals, their colours, shapes, sizes, behaviours, and the shapes of the landscapes they are in—in a word, biodiversity. The biodiversity needs to be felt through contact and actions before meaning can be made. The restorers have made their meaning from the restoration process and outcome and wish for others to do the same, so they are the best possible human interpreters and mentors (Lukianova and Fell 2015, 615). To continue on the personal journey toward understanding the value of biodiversity, visitors may repeat the tour, engage in other restoration-related activities, or other transformative travel such as guided visits in national parks (Wolf, Stricker, and Hagenloh 2015).

Wolf, Ainsworth, and Crowley (2017, 1664) derived a framework for transformative travel from their systematic review of reports on visitor-experience development in rural or urban protected areas. The experience characteristics and benefits listed in their framework also apply to the restoration ecotourism examined in this chapter. We have the additional contexts of creative and altruistic tourism in which to consider the visitor experience. These dimensions are contributed by the restorers, as well as by a focus on actively restoring the landscape.

In the spirit of lifelong learning demonstrated by the restorers to date, keeping an ongoing dialogue between Noongar traditional owners and landholders will strengthen Noongar reconnection and will enrich the tourist experience for both provider/interpreter and visitor. Sylvia and Peter's approach at Wilyun Pools includes both informal relationship building between restorers and traditional owners, as well as direct Noongar interpretation for visitors. Western scientists in Australia are just starting to recognize that over sixty thousand years of Aboriginal knowledge should inform settler ways, rather than remain as a separate historical entity (Bairnsfather-Scott 2019, 1). The restorers have the opportunity to share the dynamic journey of incorporating Aboriginal science into ecological restoration.

At Nowanup, other recent and inclusive innovations in cultural landscape restoration in the Fitz-Stirling have seen close collaboration between Noongar Elders and ecological restoration professionals that have deliberately incorporated the spiritual importance of plants and landscape in restoration design and execution (*Koori Mail* 2017, 22). This creates meaningful, comfortable human spaces on *Boodja* that can again be used as Noongar places of spiritual connection, learning, and healing. Ongoing connection between our restorers and this new, inclusive approach to restoration of Noongar *Boodja* will further enrich the biodiversity and socio-cultural outcomes of restoration, and hence the tourist experience that they host.

About People Who Restore

The restorers in our examples were committed partners, with skills related to the restoration work; they did not complete their projects alone. Their pathways to the decision to restore varied. At Chingarrup, the personal conservation decision coincided with the commencement of Gondwana Link; the restoration was paced, continuous, and evolutionary, and intermittent over fifteen years, and so was a significant part of life for the restorers. At Yarrahweyah Falls, the decision was planned and strategic, and made in collaboration with a fully formed Gondwana Link advisory group; the restoration was a full-time immersion over two years, being lived by the restorers.

The decision among the farming community to seek cultural change in Wellstead spanned a long period, giving community members time to listen, engage, and then act. On Wilyun Pools Farm, the decision for both cultural and biodiversity restoration evolved as a planned part of family succession; the restoration was paced over a term and took place alongside the farm business. It remains open to rapid change as the next generation of restorers embrace the challenges of climate change and interweave ancient knowledge with modern dynamic landscape assessment.

Although each restorer came to their place along a different journey, they shared a culture of respect for nature and connection with their landscape; this drove their actions as restorers. In executing their restorations and designing their small tourism experiences, the restorers acted akin to craftsmen, as Sennett (2009) has described in the context of achieving mastery. Craftsmen not only desire to do quality-driven work, they also have the ability required. Their high levels of skill allow them to feel fully and think deeply about what they do. Their mastery has an ethical dimension, which is slow crafting.

The restorations were arduous but were also an opportunity for personal change. As an action, restoration potentially evoked a new identity in individuals, beginning their transformation from environmental advocates to change agents who enrol others for their cause (Williams and Chawla 2016, 980). The restorers must share with others the outcomes of their work in order to create mutual benefits; by inviting ecotourists to share the experience of the process of restoration, the restorers spread the word and mature their own wisdom. Showing others is an important transaction for them. The form of collaborative, altruistic tourism is an effective strategy for aiding ecological, economic, cultural, and social sustainability, one small group at a time.

Our restorers were individuals who, through life experience and strong commitments to the value of intact landscapes and cultural respect, acted to protect and restore. Their stories are parallel journeys inside one touristic place; restorers share their own experiences with tourists, and invite them to create their own and to take with them into the future a new relationship with nature and biodiversity.

Restoration Ecotourism and Small Tourism

Our ground-driven, co-creative activities, our strategy based on need (to protect and restore habitat), and our revealing the "intangible embeddedness of the host community" defines creative tourism, according to Richards (2011, 1239). The school children's amazement at the rural open spaces, broad landscape horizons, and new sounds and smells at Wilyun Pools Farm matches urban "performative spaces" (Cloke 2007, 47), but in the rural setting. Slow tourism is another perspective in which restoration ecotourism can be considered. Hallmarks of slow tourism include quality in its social and relational aspects, environmental soundness, and economic and social benefits for destination communities (Clancy 2018).

The small context optimizes the experience potential for tourists. The restoration pathway that is core to Chingarup, Yarraweyah Falls, and Wilyun Pools Farm was the shared driving motivation, akin to environmental altruism. Our restorers' commitment to crafting a solution to their biodiversity dilemmas and their recognition of First Nation People's cultural knowledge led to personal mastery. In fact, with this interweaving of ancient knowledge and modern landscape assessment, a generational change in mindset has become evident in southwestern Australia. The wider community now embraces First Nation People's cultural knowledge, ecological science, and lore related to land management. Emerging generations increasingly recognize and demand cultural connection and its integration into future restoration projects. Looking at small things is empowering and healing; recognizing nature's strategies is humbling to humans (Bairnsfather-Scott 2019, 1; Laudine 2016, 121). Truly transformative ecotourism can only be accomplished by close observation of a small place.

Conclusion

Our collaborative reflections at the nexus of landscape and cultural restoration have shown not only a unique type of small creative tourism, but also a small, slow, and transformative restoration ecotourism. The key features that emerged were quality in the social and relational aspects of the restorer/tourist/nature interactions; environmental soundness; and the diffusion of rewards for individuals, communities, and the land.

Acknowledgements

The authors gratefully acknowledge Basil Schur (of Greenskills Inc., based in Denmark, Western Australia) for our rich discussions relating to the craft of ecotourism delivery and the presence of cultural values in landscapes.

We also acknowledge the essential roles of multiple supporting bodies in the restoration projects mentioned in this work: the Australian Government National Landcare Biodiversity Fund, the Australian Government's 20 Million Trees initiative, Landcare Australia, Bush Heritage Australia, Carbon Neutral Charitable Fund, Conservation Council of Western Australia, Greening Australia, Greenskills Inc., National Science Week (Western Australia), South Coast Natural Resource Management, Shell Reconnections, State Natural Resource Management (Western Australia).

There was no financial support for the writing of this work.

NOTES

1   Funding assistance/in-kind support was sourced from Bush Heritage Australia, Conservation Council of Western Australia, Greening Australia, Greenskills Inc., and Shell Reconnections.

2   Funding assistance/in-kind support was sourced from the Australian Government National Landcare Biodiversity Fund, Bush Heritage Australia, Carbon Neutral Charitable Fund, Conservation Council of Western Australia, Greenskills Inc., and South Coast Natural Resource Management.

3   With funding assistance from National Science Week, an initiative of the Australian Government.

4   The Australian Government's 20 Million Trees program and the Landcare Australia initiative of the State Natural Resource Management.

References

Aronson, James C., Charles M. Blatt, and Thibaud B. Aronson. 2016. "Restoring Ecosystem Health to Improve Human Health and Well-Being—Physicians and Restoration Ecologists Unite in a Common Cause." *Ecology and Society* 21, no. 4: 39.

Bairnsfather-Scott, Merindah. 2019. "The Aboriginal Way: Western Science Meets Indigenous Science." Winyama Digital Solutions, 16 October 2019. https://www.winyama.com.au/news-room/blog-post-the-aboriginal-way-western-science-meets-indigenous-science.

Bawden, Richard. 2018. "Regeneration and Its Transformational Imperative." *International Journal of Agricultural Sustainability* 16, no. 2: 124–6.

Berndt, Ronald Murray. 1979. "Traditional Aboriginal life in Western Australia: As It Was and Is." In *Aborigines of the West: Their Past and Their Present*, edited by Ronald M. Berndt and Catherine H. Berndt, 3–27. Nedlands: University of Western Australia Press for the Education Committee of the 150th Anniversary Celebrations.

Bradby, Keith. 2016. "Biodiversity Restoration and Sustainable Tourism in South-Western Australia." In *Life Cycle Approaches to Sustainable Regional Development*, edited by Stefania Massari, Guido Sonnemann, and Fritz Balkau, 312–18. New York: Taylor an Francis.

Bradby, Keith, Amanda Keesing, and Grant Wardell-Johnson. 2016. "Gondwana Link: Connecting People, Landscapes, and Livelihoods across Southwestern Australia." *Restoration Ecology* 24, no. 6: 827–35.

Clancy, Michael. 2018. "Practicing Slow: Political and Ethical Implications." In *Slow Tourism, Food and Cities: Pace and the Search for the Good Life*, edited by M. Clancy, 63–75. London: Taylor and Francis.

Cloke, Paul. 2007. "Creativity and Tourism in Rural Environments." In *Tourism, Creativity and Development*, edited by Greg Richards and Julie Wilson, 37–47. Florence: Routledge Taylor and Francis.

Collard, Len, and Sandra Harben. 2010. "Which Knowledge Path Will We Travel?" *Studies in Western Australian History* 26:75–95.

Gioia, Paul, and Stephen D. Hopper. 2017. "A New Phytogeographic Map for the Southwest Australian Floristic Region after an Exceptional Decade of Collection and Discovery." *Botanical Journal of the Linnean Society* 184, no. 1: 1–15.

Koori Mail. 2017. "Massive Animals Growing." *Koori Mail*, 6 September 2017, 22.

Laudine, Catherine. 2016. "Away from a World of Unique Truth." In *Aboriginal Environmental Knowledge: Rational Reverence*, 121–30. New York: Routledge.

Lawson, Sam, Art Blundell, Bruce Cabarle, Naomi Basik, Michael Jenkins, and Kerstin Canby. 2014. *Consumer Goods and Deforestation: An Analysis of the Extent and Nature of Illegality in Forest Conversion for Agriculture and Timber Plantations*. Washington, DC: Forest Trends Association. https://www.forest-trends.org/wp-content/uploads/imported/for168-consumer-goods-and-deforestation-letter-14-0916-hr-no-crops_web-pdf.pdf.

Lukianova, Natalia A., and Elena V. Fell. 2015. "Meaning Making in Communication Processes: The Role of a Human Agency." *Procedia—Social and Behavioral Sciences* 200:614–17.

Massy, Charles. 2017. *Call of the Reed Warbler: A New Agriculture–a New Earth*. Brisbane: University of Queensland Press.

Maxton-Lee, Bernice. 2017. "Material Realities: Why Indonesian Deforestation Persists and Conservation Fails." *Journal of Contemporary Asia* 48, no. 3: 419–44.

Meagher, Sara J. 1974. "The Food Resources of the Aborigines of the South-West of Western Australia." *Records of the Western Australian Museum* 3:14–65.

Meagher, Sara J., and William David Lindsay Ride. 1979. "Use of Natural Resources by the Aborigines of South-Western Australia." In *Aborigines of the West: Their Past and Their Present*, edited by Ronald M. Berndt and Catherine H. Berndt, 66–80. Nedlands: University of Western Australia Press for the Education Committee of the 150th Anniversary Celebrations.

Myers, Norman, Russell Mittermeier, Cristina Mittermeier, Gustavo DaFonseca, and Jennifer Kent. 2000. "Biodiversity Hotspots for Conservation Priorities." *Nature* 403, no. 6772: 853–8.

Nind, Scott. 1831. "Description of the Natives of King George's Sound (Swan River Colony) and Adjoining Country." *Journal of the Royal Geographical Society of London* 1, no. 1: 21–51.

Paraskevaidis, Pavlos, and Konstantinos Andriotis. 2017. "Altruism in Tourism: Social Exchange Theory vs Altruistic Surplus Phenomenon in Host Volunteering." *Annals of Tourism Research* 62:26–37.

Richards, Greg. 2011. "Creativity and Tourism: The State of the Art." *Annals of Tourism Research* 38, no. 4: 1225–53.

———. 2014. "Creativity and Tourism in the City." *Current Issues in Tourism* 17, no. 2: 119–44.

Rijavec, Frank, dir. 2003. *A Million Acres a Year*. Acton: Film Australia—National Film and Sound Archive.

Scott, Allen J. 2010. "Cultural Economy and the Creative Field Of The City." *Geografiska Annaler. Series B, Human Geography* 92, no. 2: 115–30.

Sennett, Richard. 2009. *The Craftsman*. London: Pearson.

Tobler, Ray, Adam Rohrlach, Julien Soubrier, Pere Bover, Bastien Llamas, Jonathan Tuke, Nigel Bean, Ali Abdullah-Highfold, Shane Agius, Amy O'Donoghue, Isabel O'Loughlin, Peter Sutton, Fran Zilio, Keryn Walshe, Alan N. Williams, Chris S. M. Turney, Matthew Williams, Stephen M. Richards, Robert J. Mitchell, Emma Kowal, John R. Stephen, Lesley Williams, Wolfgang Haak, and Alan Cooper. 2017. "Aboriginal Mitogenomes Reveal 50,000 Years of Regionalism in Australia." *Nature* 544, no. 7549: 180–4.

Turney, Chris S. M., Michael I. Bird, L. Keith Fifield, Richard G. Roberts, Mike Smith, Charles E. Dortch, Rainer Grün, Ewan Lawson, Linda K. Ayliffe, Gifford H. Miller, Joe Dortch, and Richard G. Cresswell. 2017. "Early Human Occupation at Devil's Lair, Southwestern Australia 50,000 Years Ago." *Quaternary Research* 55, no. 1: 3–13.

Wiggins, Grant, and Jay McTighe. 2005. "Backward Design." In *Understanding by Design*, 13–34. Alexandria, VA: Association for Supervision and Curriculum Development.

Williams, Corrie Colvin, and Louise Chawla. 2016. "Environmental Identity Formation in Nonformal Environmental Education Programs." *Environmental Education Research* 22, no. 7: 978–1001.

Wolf, Isabelle D., Gillian B. Ainsworth, and Jane Crowley. 2017. "Transformative Travel as a Sustainable Market Niche for Protected Areas: A New Development, Marketing and Conservation Model." *Journal of Sustainable Tourism* 25, no. 11: 1650–73.

Wolf, Isabelle D., Heidi K. Stricker, and Gerald Hagenloh. 2015. "Outcome-Focused National Park Experience Management: Transforming Participants, Promoting

Social Well-Being, and Fostering Place Attachment." *Journal of Sustainable Tourism* 23, no. 3: 358–81.

Wroth, David. 2015. "The Carrolup School and Australian Landscape Painting." Japingka Aboriginal Art, accessed 23 March 2023. https://japingkaaboriginalart.com/articles/carrolup-school/.

The Role of Cultural Associations in the Promotion of Small Tourism and Social Inclusion in the Neighbourhood of Bonfim, Oporto: The Case of Casa Bô

Andre Luis Quintino Principe

Introduction

In 2017 the city of Oporto, Portugal, was voted by tourists from 174 countries the best European destination (European Best Destinations 2017). This is the third time that Oporto has received this award, with the first two taking place in 2012 and 2014. The presence of low-cost airlines and local accommodation platforms has aided the increase in tourism; there is now a need for the city to absorb this trend.

Even amid an active pandemic, Portugal shows positive signs of the resumption of tourism, with the nomination of the city of Braga, neighboring Porto, as the best European tourist destination in 2021.

The recognition of cities and territories as ideal tourist destinations serves as an indicator for tourists hoping to choose holiday destinations. Travel destinations also attract professional, academic, and cultural events, such as themed fairs and congresses. Money is of course another factor influencing tourists, with the choice of destination being linked to "pricing issues and economic exchange rates" (Pearce 2007, 104). In this sense, the city of Oporto is attractive for visitors because it offers lower costs than, say, Lisbon. The travel website European Best Destinations mentions that travellers from countries like the United States, the United Kingdom, France, Denmark,

South Africa, South Korea, Ireland, and Canada voted Oporto as the first choice of destination in 2017.

The city of Oporto has fifteen parishes. The parish of Bonfim is the fourth most populous, with 24,265 inhabitants (or 7,956 per square kilometres). Moreover, about 65 per cent of the population is over sixty years of age. This perhaps explains another striking feature of this parish, which is the provincial character of the residents of Bonfim.

However, tourism has been changing the way cities and territories are seen; in the context of small tourism, what are otherwise endogenous traditions in a place like Bonfim can become a site of visitor engagement (Cooper and Hall 2008, 112). In this way, the perception of a place as a tourist destination is evaluated by "how relatively accessible it is and therefore its potential market for visitors" (113). Tourists who are interested in local culture arising from the traditions of a specific place gain new appreciation of the unique differences characterizing different neighbourhoods. This insight into the more subtle expressions of a particular place is an outcome of small tourism, as is the slow disengagement of local provincialism.

Tourism in Oporto has brought about economic and social change even in the city's less-visited parishes. Real estate speculation has transformed residential areas with the emergence of local hostels and lodgings, attracting tourists who seek local experiences in the city's parishes. For the local community of Bonfim, the increase in people circulating in the parish and patronizing the local markets and restaurants stimulates the local economy. Accompanying this activity is a demand for art and culture, which supports and sustains such entities as cultural associations. Small tourism can be mutually beneficial for residents, place, and visitors, combining all their experiences in a sense of social inclusion. Small tourism is the right size of tourism for parishes or other urban neighbourhoods.

Considering the significant recent increase in tourism in Oporto, the case study described in this chapter sought to examine if the Casa Bô cultural association could take the lead in establishing a new tourist option outside the central, historical, and touristic zone of the city, and, taking advantage of its small scale, offer creative tourism opportunities for tourists seeking accommodation in local lodgings, either because of the price, or because they wish to search out authentic experiences similar to the everyday life of local residents.

Case Study Setting

This case study about Casa Bô focuses on the interactions of tourists with the local community of Bonfim through the cultural association; the engagement of visitors and residents was found to produce mutual benefits, thereby promoting social cohesion and inclusion.

The Casa Bô cultural association plays a role in the Oporto parish of Bonfim that sees it embrace three social pillars: culture, environment, and social solidarity.

Casa Bô also interacts with other cultural associations in the city of Oporto, creating synergies and providing mutual help in joint cultural and social solidarity activities. Some of these institutions are Rés-da-Rua, Espaço Compasso, and Casa da Horta.

These synergies stem from the volunteering activities offered both inside and outside of these associations. In cultural associations, volunteering takes place with the help of structural reforms and improvements to associations' headquarters and human resources at events, among other activities. In external activities, volunteering takes place, for example, with such cultural activities as music classes in institutions for people with physical disabilities, or recreational activities in nursing homes. There is also participation in the cultural festivities of the city of Oporto, with typical food stalls at parties such as the Feast of St. John (or São João for the Portuguese), the biggest festivity in the city.

Other interactions between cultural associations occur with the involvement of artists travelling through the Oporto, who ask for space to perform in one of the cultural associations, and who usually end up performing in other locations due to the synergy between various groups and venues in the city. In the same way, members of the public, which often includes tourists, who attend a cultural event at a cultural association usually learn about other associative spaces.

Some of the tourists and touring artists who seek accommodation in cultural associations refer each other, so that these people have a greater opportunity to stay in these spaces, and this hospitality is often compensated by way of voluntary actions on the part of guests, which usually take the form of providing maintenance of these spaces.

The data collection revealed two striking and distinct characteristics in the parish: a cultural resistance among locals against mixing with people of

Figure 5.1: Map of Portugal.

Source: Maps Portugal, https://maps-portugal.com/maps-portugal-cities/porto-portugal-map (accessed 10 April 2023).

Figure 5.2: Location of Casa Bô in the city of Oporto.

Source: Idealista, https://www.idealista.pt/en/comprar-casas/porto/mapa (accessed 10 April 2023).

other parishes, or against attending cultural events in Bonfim that are not considered part of the local traditions or festivities, and a demographic pattern showing that about 65 per cent of the population is aged sixty or over.

Another noticeable characteristic in Bonfim is the number of vacant houses. Portugal has the second-highest number of vacant houses in Europe, just behind Spain, at around 730,000, which corresponds to around 14 per cent of the total number of houses in the country. Of the 25,000 empty houses in Oporto, approximately 2,000 are in Bonfim. This reality negatively influences social cohesion and inclusion in the neighbourhood, transforming parts of the parish into deserted places and leading to isolation, social exclusion, and an absence of adequate local small business and social infrastructure.

Figure 5.3: Aerial view of Casa Bô and neighborhood.

Source: Google Maps (fair use policy).

About Casa Bô

The Casa Bô cultural association resides in a century-old three-storey build-ing that was once one of the parish's large stock of abandoned buildings. Based on an agreement with the owner of the property, a symbolic ten-year lease was concluded for the use of the space; in exchange, the cultural associ-ation committed to working toward the rehabilitation of the building over the same period. Since Casa Bô was founded in 2015, an internal revitalization of the building has been completed, and more recently, structural work has begun on the rear facade, carried out by members and volunteers.

The association's activities can be divided into three pillars (Principe 2016, 45). The first pillar is culture, and the association schedules concerts, literary events such as weekly poetry nights, dances, and creative workshops, among others.

The second pillar is environment, with the association supporting en-vironmental awareness through initiatives involving permaculture and vegetarian food. Casa Bô has a vertical vegetable garden in the backyard of the building containing crops that are used in the vegetarian social dinners offered before nighttime cultural events.

The third pillar, social solidarity, is expressed through voluntary activities and initiatives both inside and outside of the association. Some of these regular initiatives include volunteer visits to nursing homes and music education projects at institutions such as the ACAPO, or theAssociação dos Cegos e Amblíopes de Portugal (Association of the Blind and the Amblyopia of Portugal).[1]

Economic Sustainability and Management

As a non-profit organization, Casa Bô follows a management model focused on its sustainability; it also employs a horizontal organizational structure with no decision-making hierarchy in its volunteer governing body.

Non-profits or third-sector organizations are entities focused on generating the social economy. That they do not have profit as their primary objective presupposes the use of an economic surplus for the purpose of sustainability. Instead of seeking profit, the social economy reuses economic surpluses mainly by reinvesting in growth for scale or making investments in new social projects, with a view to fostering greater social intervention (Azevedo, Franco, and Meneses 2010, 19). The mission of cultural associations, as well as foundations, mutual societies, and co-operatives, is to meet demands that are otherwise not satisfactorily met by the public sector (Ramos 2005). In this sense, cultural associations can often compensate for creative and cultural shortfalls in peripheral and non-touristic residential areas.

Casa Bô has low fixed expenses (leasing, water, and electricity) and has a high number of members and volunteers. Having begun in 2015 with 6 volunteers, it currently has more than 200 (15 of whom participate in the direction of the association); these volunteers contribute and take turns in the activities of the organization, including in such areas as event management, social dinners, cleaning, and maintenance (Principe 2016, 71). This economic model allows the association to adopt the practice of conscious donation in order to meet its financial needs and thereby sustain its activities. The conscious donation consists in suggesting a value for both social dinners and cultural events, so as not to influence public participation through advance or door ticket sales, thereby removing any financial barriers. Those wishing to attend are asked to provide the event's suggested fee to the best of their financial ability. However, this model can only function well in a small context. The association retains 30 per cent of the revenue, with 70 per cent going to the event's artists. The social dinners feature a small variation, with the association retaining 40 per cent and the volunteer who has provided the meal receiving 60 per cent (Principe 2016, 119–32).

With the onset of the COVID-19 pandemic, experiments have been conducted in relation to financial contributions for participation in events. One of these was the creation of three price ranges, with each person attending being free to choose the price that they deem best suited to their financial reality. The idea is to maintain ease of access while also maximizing financial return.

Records of cultural events in our observation diary show that the average attendance was eighteen people at cultural events and nine at social dinners (Principe 2016, 128). In addition, about 75 per cent of the participants contributed the suggested donation. The fact that 25 per cent of participants can engage with the association's activities for free without jeopardizing the economic sustainability of Casa Bô attests to its ability to make good on its commitment to social inclusion and solidarity.

Of the 174 cultural events held during the period of analysis—October of 2015 to August of 2016 (Principe 2016, 36)—it is estimated that 3,155 people attended the evening events, and that at least half of this audience (1,566 people) also participated in the social dinners. Given that 25 per cent of the attendees did not pay, we can see that about 788 people benefited from the practice of conscious donation, with about half of this number also enjoying social dinners without barriers to entry.

The Casa Bô community comprises members and volunteers of the association, residents of the local community of Bonfim parish, residents of other parishes of Oporto, students, and a solid representation of national and international tourists. In addition to the cultural events it offers the community of Bonfim, Casa Bô promotes events directed especially to certain tourist niches. One of these initiatives consists of weekly meetings for participants in the digital hosting platform Couchsurfing, which attracts travellers who are looking for local experiences and free accommodation.

The research methodology was primarily qualitative, supported by some quantitative research, providing material for an empirical analysis of both the organization and its users in their different social roles. The quantitative research collected events from nine cultural facilities all over Oporto in order to classify cultural events by type, especially those in the so-called creative industries. Casa Bô does, in fact, represent an emerging cultural focus for creative tourism in Oporto: the study shows that more than 65 per cent of its events are linked to activities considered to be within the creative industries. It is a place where residents and artists have developed activities with the effective participation of tourists attending cultural events. Creative tourism offers visitors an immersive and authentic experience on a small scale, with the possibility of a participative cultural learning experience. This is seen to be an effective strategy for expressing the special character of a place, connecting visitors and locals in a living cultural heritage experience (UNESCO 2006, 3).

The study concludes with some suggestions as to the potential of the cultural association to operate as a pole of attraction and a method of diffusion for creative tourism initiatives; it could also contribute to the growth of tourism in Oporto through such initiatives, as well as assist in building social inclusion and cohesion in the parish.

The pandemic has clearly underlined numerous uncertainties as regards the activities of cultural associations. The abrupt drop in tourism beginning in the spring of 2020, the stricter and more restrictive rules for the use of closed spaces, and the economic loss already accumulated in the period since the beginning COVID-19 can render the sustainability of these spaces unfeasible, even forcing their closure in extreme cases. In this sense, an even more creative strategy is needed to readjust the business model employed by these associations, so that they can continue to have a positive impact on their communities and fulfill their potential as creative and sustainable small tourism options.

Methodology

The purpose of this study is to identify creative small tourism initiatives in cultural associations, and to explore how these initiatives could possibly contribute to social inclusion and cohesion within the local community, with the added benefit of developing sustainable tourism options.

This chapter is based on a master's thesis in innovation economics management, successfully defended before the University of Oporto's Faculty of Economics under the title "Cultural Associativism and Creativity: Innovation, Social Cohesion and Sustainable Change—a Case Study on Casa Bô" (Principe 2016). A case study was chosen for the research, once it was established that the particular example was significant and representative, in order to justify a generalization for similar situations (Severino 2007, 121). The approach was qualitative, as the research addresses various subject areas at the intersection of sociology, management, and economics. Indeed, qualitative research is particularly suitable for cross-disciplinary studies (Denzin and Lincoln 2006, 16). Data collection took place in the period from June to September 2016. The qualitative research techniques included document analysis, interviews, and an observation log, providing a sound strategy for the cross-checking and interpretation of data (Denzin and Lincoln 2006, 17).

Seven documents were collected and analyzed, among them Casa Bô's social statute, as well as other documents requested or mentioned in the interviews and in the field during the observation phase. Nineteen semi-structured interviews (Bauer and Gaskell 2015) were conducted, producing approximately seven hours of recorded and transcribed interviews. These interviews were conducted with agents representing different social roles involved in all areas, within and without the cultural association. The interviewees represent eight nationalities and were members of Casa Bô, temporary guests of the cultural association, public, local, and foreign artists, volunteers at the association's cultural events, and employees of the local Council of Bonfim. Five of the nineteen interviews were conducted by email. In order to document and analyze data collection in the field, an observation log was created. Each event observed was assigned an entry consisting of three fields: a header that categorized basic facts such as the classification of the event or its funding; a lengthy description of the observations; and the observer's contextual reflections. For the initial classification of events, a thesaurus was used to create a standardized and controlled vocabulary. Harpring describes a thesaurus as "a controlled vocabulary arranged in a specific order . . . to promote consistency in the indexing of content and to facilitate searching and browsing" (2013, 236).

There was a total of 21 records in the observation journal (Principe 2016, 182–289), of which 10 were related to internal events at Casa Bô, such as cultural events and social dinners, and 11 to external ones, which were activities directly involving the participation of Casa Bô at, for example, a cultural festival in the city of Amarante, located approximately sixty kilometers away from Oporto, and a volunteer mission in the rural areas of Aboadela, Sanche, and Várzea, in the district of Amarante.

Two more external events involved one artist who had performed at Casa Bô; these events were observed outside the context of activities directly related to the association. One of them was a concert put on by another cultural association called Rés-da-Rua, in Oporto, and another held at Rua das Flores, a tourist destination also in Oporto known for its outdoor cultural and artistic activities.

The quantitative research comprised an analysis of the number of cultural events in Oporto so as to understand how many of these events could be linked to creative industries. Data was collected using event schedules from nine cultural facilities in the city, five of them established cultural venues (Casa da Música, Fundação Serralves Foundation, Maus Hábitos, Hard Club, and Coliseu do Porto) and four cultural associations (Rés-da-Rua, Espaço Compasso, Casa da Horta, and Casa Bô) (Principe 2016, 35).

Analysis of the cultural events agenda took place from October 2015 to August 2016. The data collection process consisted in the use of a computer script to export event calendars from the website Viral Agenda Cultural[2] to Microsoft Excel. This website aggregates information on cultural events and distributes it through Facebook. It captures the information and organizes it graphically in its platform through the use of APIs (application programming interfaces). A total of 5,155 entries were collected, providing the total number of events offered by the nine cultural organizations. Of this total, 1,128 events (21.88 per cent) were offered by the cultural associations, and 4,027 (78.12 per cent) by the established venues (Principe 2016, 35).

For the classification of events, the table of creative industries included in the creative economy report of the United Nations Conference on Trade and Development (UNCTAD 2012, 8) was used as a reference. This classification divides the creative industries into four groups and nine categories, as follows:

- Heritage groups: (1) cultural sites and (2) traditional cultural expressions
- Arts groups: (3) performing arts and (4) visual arts
- Media groups: (5) audiovisuals and (6) publishing and printed media
- Functional creations groups: (7) new media, (8) creative services, and (9) design

The cultural events included in this analysis found correspondences in the first six creative industry categories. The classification of the samples was carried out manually, with interpretation and use of keywords, whenever it was possible to make the proper correlation (Principe 2016, 159).

Comparative and percentage analyses of the total number of events were performed from this quantitative data, forming the basis of three comparative tables. The first table encompasses the nine cultural facilities together; the second considers only the four selected cultural associations; the third compares the events in the five traditional cultural facilities to those put on by Casa Bô. The tables identified fourteen categories of events as related to the creative industries. From this starting point, information in the tables was analyzed (Principe 2016, 80–9), facilitating an understanding of the relevance and role of the cultural associations in terms of cultural production and diffusion in Oporto, and particularly in Bonfim. Together, these mixed research methods provide the basis for the following discussion.

Results

The research revealed six opportunities for and initiatives in small-scale tourism carried out by Casa Bô, which in turn promoted greater social inclusion in the local community of Bonfim. In each case, a note is added on how each of the items has been affected by the fundamental paradigm shift COVID-19 has caused.

1. Attracting Creative People

Casa Bô welcomes many visitors and artists who promote cultural events from different creative industries. It is a heterogeneous audience, formed by consumers and practitioners in the performing arts (musicians, actors, dancers), traditional cultural expressions (artisans, artists of local and regional cultural traditions), visual arts (painters, sculptors, photographers), media and literature (journalists, writers, poets, storytellers), and audiovisual arts (film and documentary producers), among others. Many of these people are active members in the leading categories of the creative industries. Casa Bô, then, acts as a meeting point where these practitioners can develop and disseminate their ideas and activities in a small venue.

According to Florida (2002), the ability of a territory to attract members of the creative class is a *sine qua non* for the development of the so-called creative economy; Florida plots this ability along three axes, named for the three *t*s of the creative economy: talent, technology, and tolerance. Tolerance is a factor that is predominantly linked to the capacity of individuals to feel social inclusion in a community. One of the pillars of the Casa Bô is social solidarity, and within its social values, the association promotes the integration and participation of all people through voluntary initiatives and social solidarity actions. Art and cultural functions attract people, and the conscious donation strategy supports their integration without financial barriers. With these initiatives, the association both promotes social inclusion and operates as a tourist venue accessible to all types of visitors interested in the small cultural events offered by Casa Bô.

IMPACT OF COVID-19

Since the pandemic, there has been an abrupt drop in creatives seeking space for presentations, resulting in part from the lack of audiences, the crippling impact on tourism, and also the fact that creatives themselves cannot be as mobile as they were pre-pandemic. Currently, they are simply not passing through the city in high numbers. To address this situation, Casa Bô transformed the use of its usual space for cultural events into artistic residencies, necessitating much less mobility. During the peak of the pandemic, there were about fifteen residents, all of whom were paid a small monthly stipend, likely not enough to cover all their expenses while living in Oporto, but enough to contribute to their stay at Casa Bô and to help keep the association sustainable.

Since late 2021 and early 2022, the cultural and tourist sector has resumed its activities with greater intensity thanks to the reduction of pandemic-related health restrictions. Casa Bô followed the trend toward normality with the increase in audience-oriented cultural activities.

2. Producing Cultural and Creative Events

Cultural events play an important role in social inclusion, as they allow integration and collective participation in a community. Creativity is an inherent element of art and culture, and as such plays a strategic role in the cultural landscape of a community or city. Greffe (2011, 200) argues that a landscape comprises the visible features of an area; when it is shaped by human activity, a landscape becomes a cultural landscape. In this sense, cultural events are a collective and participative manifestation of this landscape in a certain place. Greffe advocates for the importance of listing and displaying the elements

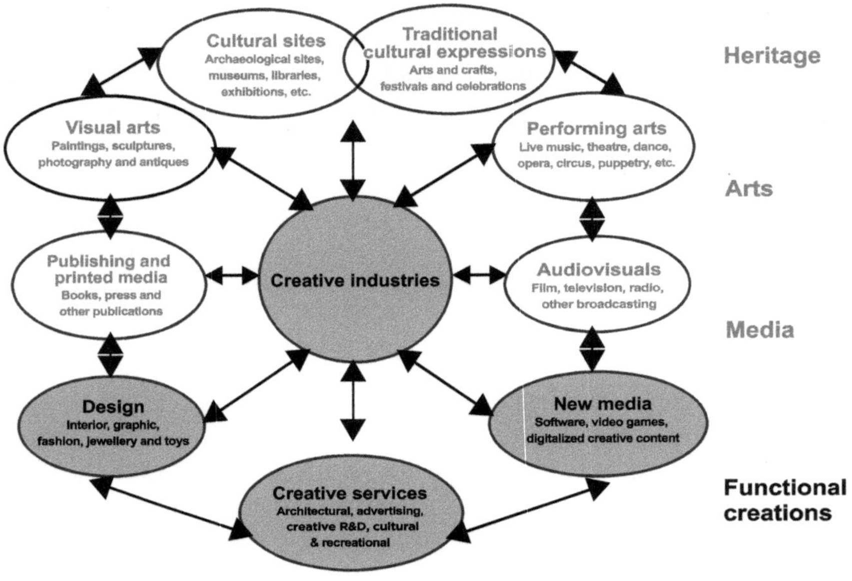

Figure 5.4: Classification of creative industries. In grey text are the areas attracted by Casa Bô (highlighted by the author).

Source: UNCTAD.

that can make the cultural landscape more amenable to the implementation of creative cities. Cultural associations can contribute can make a significant contribution to such work.

The cultural events put on by Casa Bô were classified within the creative industries in three of the four existing groups (heritage, arts, and media), and in six of the nine categories (audiovisual, performing arts, traditional cultural expressions, visual arts, and publishing and printed media) within UNCTAD's creative industries classification cited earlier. In percentage terms, the 178 cultural events held by Casa Bô fell into 14 of the 21 types of cultural events, and about 67 per cent were classified in at least one of the categories of the creative industries. This shows the same level of creative engagement as Casa da Música in Oporto, which recorded 1,516 events in the same period, of which 71 per cent were categorized as creative. Small still works.

A good example of an intimate creative event at Casa Bô is its poetry night. This weekly event is part of the association's cultural agenda. The event consists of readings of poetry, whether or not it is authored by the particular participant performing the reading. Usually there is always at least one guest musician, and whenever possible, other musicians are invited to participate in an improvised way. In other cases, dramatizations or dance performances are also held. This integration of various art forms, as well as the spirit of improvisation, stimulates the creative character of the event.

Music concerts provide another example. At Casa Bô, concerts are often scheduled on short notice, depending on the availability of the association, of the resident artist, or of musicians passing through Oporto looking for a space to present their work. It is common to see artists adjusting their set lists a few hours before the start of the concert, after checking the physical conditions of the venue, the audience present on a given day, and the time available for presentation. There have already been cases where there was only one scheduled concert, and since there was additional time available, and an audience present, two other groups eventually performed on the same night—a plus for all stakeholders, since each event is a unique and exclusive experience. Smallness allows for such flexibility.

IMPACT OF COVID-19

From 2020 to 2021, artistic interactions continued in the association, mainly between residents and active members of Casa Bô, but with limitations on capacity. There were naturally a reduced number of cultural and public events.

Since the beginning of 2022, with the improvement of the events agenda and the resumption of tourism, the schedule of performances has resumed as usual.

3. Connecting Social Agents

Casa Bô is an open space for the whole community. The interactions between social agents (members of the association, artists, and the public) are dynamic and easy as most of the spaces are intended for common and collective use. Greater social interaction takes place most prominently at the vegetarian dinners that occur before evening cultural events. Event artists, members of Casa Bô, and the audience share a long table with seating for about sixteen people, or other tables around the kitchen and library room. During dinner, everyone sits at a table with no marked places, and usually the members of Casa Bô sit and interact with visitors so that there is more interaction and contact between all. This initiative allows for the beginning of new friendships between residents, tourists, artists, and volunteers of the cultural association.

In these gathering, an exchange of synergies happens spontaneously, and this is what sets the Casa Bô experience apart from the experience that a tourist might have at a conventional cultural event, such as a concert at Casa da Música in Oporto. In this case, the tourist will have a very different perception and experience in terms of social interactions, since traditional cultural venues are larger, formatted spaces, with a more rigid agenda, and a less intimate space (Principe 2016, 108). The focus is less alternative and more commercial or touristic; there is very little interaction among people in this more formalized space. Cultural associations can break this paradigm with their events, using their small size, ability to accommodate changes, and intimate character to their advantage.

Another initiative that favours social interactions in the Casa Bô cultural association is the practice of workshops, usually focusing on craft making or other types of endogenous knowledge. The workshops normally take place in small groups. Both members of the cultural association and people passing through Oporto hold these events; similarly, the attendees are both residents and tourists. At one of the workshops observed (Principe 2016, 210), a volunteer member of Casa Bô instructed those present in sewing techniques for cushion covers. Among the attendees, there was a Hungarian tourist who had never run a sewing machine. The interaction of this Hungarian tourist with members of the cultural association resulted in that person staying a few nights in the space in return for help with the daily activities of Casa Bô. As the Hungarian tourist was travelling with little money, they took the opportunity to strengthen ties with the members of the association and to interact in a more direct way with the local culture of Oporto.

IMPACT OF COVID-19

During the peak of the pandemic, even amid a tentative resumption of cultural activities, the decrease in the regular public and the limitation of the association's cultural events schedule reduced social interactions, and this was aggravated by the need for social distance, use of masks, and limitations on things like opening hours.

The workshop activities, as well as the musical concerts, etc., started again in 2022 with the resumption of tourism and other cultural events.

4. Promotion of Tourist-Themed Events

The cultural association has already promoted thematic events aimed at a portion of tourists in the city of Oporto. This event is the weekly Couchsurfing meeting. The Couchsurfing organization forbids payments for stays—the concept is to bring together people of different cultures within homes, thus providing an experience of everyday life in the destination community. One of the hosts of Couchsurfing in Oporto chose Casa Bô as a weekly meeting place, with the result of bringing together local residents of Oporto and tourists of different nationalities. The Couchsurfing meetings occur before the evening cultural events, so part of the Couchsurfing audience takes the opportunity to stay for the social dinners and subsequent events.

IMPACT OF COVID-19

Thematic events linked to tourism have basically halted since the pandemic began.

This specific type of event has not yet returned to normality due to the consequences of the pandemic and out of public health concerns related to social proximity.

5. Positioning Casa Bô as a Local, Alternative, and Authentic Tourist Spot in Oporto

With the ascendancy of mass tourism in Portugal, and the increase in tourists in Oporto, there has been a significant increase in local accommodation offerings in the city. Digital platforms like Booking.com and Airbnb have empowered private citizens by giving them the opportunity to transform apartments and townhouses into alternative forms of tourist accommodation. According to data from RNAL (Registo Nacional de Alojamento Local), the number of households offering accommodation in the parish of Bonfim grew from only 1 in 2010 to 210 in 2016. While in Oporto there are 3,761 rooms with a capacity of 9,630 tourists, the parish of Bonfim supplies 436 rooms with a capacity of 1,094 tourists, or about 11 per cent of Oporto's capacity.

This migration of a portion of tourists from the traditional hotel chains to local guest houses in the parishes has created an opportunity and a demand for cultural and leisure options in parishes that can absorb this new flow of tourists staying farther from urban centres. The empirical analysis demonstrated that Casa Bô engaged with tourists hosted in the parish of Bonfim, and that the tourists had chosen to connect with the local association not only because of proximity, but also for the opportunity the association gave them to experience a cultural event like a local resident. Small tourism activities that take place in small places will almost always provide a more personal, authentic experience for all stakeholders.

IMPACT OF COVID-19

Casa Bô and other cultural associations lost their status as local references and tourist alternatives, as they suffered more intensely from the lack of effervescence in the city as a result of the pandemic. On the other hand, people of artistic and creative natures travelling in Portugal started to think of Casa Bô as a medium- or long-term refuge since the transformation of the space into an artistic residence.

With the effects of the pandemic diminishing and tourism resuming, Casa Bô intends to once again assume its role as a tourist alternative in the city of Porto.

6. Linking Casa Bô Outside the Parish

In addition to cultural events within the Casa Bô association, volunteer members hold external cultural and volunteer events. One of these events is the association's participation in the Feast of St. John celebrations on the night of 23 June. St. John is the most revered saint of Oporto, of pagan origin and associated with the celebration of the summer solstice. Celebrations include dancing, eating, and fireworks. Casa Bô set up a bannered food tent where it sold delicacies made by its members to festival goers, including a significant number of tourists, who participated in the celebrations in the streets of Oporto. In addition to the typical food stall, volunteer members also played traditional songs to celebrate the date (Principe 2016, 67).

Another external initiative observed during the data collection was the Bô Festival (Principe 2016, 70), a multicultural event that took place in the city of Amarante in August 2016, with the participation of 11 organizations, including other cultural associations in Oporto, with about 170 volunteers, more than 60 cultural activities such as concerts, workshops, seminars, lectures, etc., and the offer of about 16 services such as massage and therapy sessions, food trucks, traditional crafts, etc. The festival raised funds for the urban rehabilitation of Casa Bô and was attended by an estimated 700 people, including residents of Amarante and Oporto, domestic tourists, and tourists from different countries such as Germany, Australia, Spain, and France, among others.

IMPACT OF COVID-19

With the sudden reduction in the movement of visitors, combined with capacity restrictions and stricter rules for holding cultural events, no external events were held from the beginning of the pandemic until the end of 2021.

The festivities of São João and other external events were celebrated again starting in 2022.

Discussion

Cultural Associations and Small Tourism

Cultural associations can be locations of emergent creativity; in larger cities, they are small clusters and creative spots that provide unique conditions endogenous to their own place. They can attract highly creative people who are in search of space to present their art and vocation, or who wish to join or create networks. Because they do not aim for profit, cultural associations enjoy autonomy and openness, engendering a more propitious space for creative expression, individual engagement, and resident-visitor collaboration. Generally operating with a very flexible agenda, few rules and formalities, a no-blame culture, and few entry restrictions, cultural associations become cultural laboratories, functioning as talent incubators and spaces for experimentation on the part of both creatives and visitors, spaces where synergies and knowledge sharing occur in workshops, in cultural events featuring the active participation of visitors, and in the social activities like the social dinners that take place before nocturnal events. In this way, cultural associations like Casa Bô contribute particularly to social and cultural sustainability and social inclusion, while offering a consummate local small tourism adventure in a small place.

Casa Bô and COVID-19: Challenges and Initiatives

Since the beginning of the pandemic, Casa Bô has struggled to survive. Without events, no revenue flowed into the association, even though fixed expenses such as rent, water, and electricity continued. New solutions, such as the artistic residency once the lockdown was lifted, allowed Casa Bô sufficient income to cover its expenses. During the lockdown period, community building continued on its social networks. Crowdfunding was also used to raise funds for a structural renovation of the house's skylight, with incentives to offer members' crafts for donations of certain amounts. However, the in-person cultural events agenda has been almost completely paralyzed since the beginning of the pandemic.

Until there is a normalization of tourist and cultural activities in Portugal, the challenges facing Casa Bô are directly linked to its own economic sustainability.

The cultural and tourist sectors were among the most affected by the pandemic. In response to COVID-19, in order to compensate for losses, many countries have implemented public investment initiatives to support actors in these sectors. In Portugal, the government adopted grants and subsidies for cultural sectors, offered compensation for losses, and initiated investment initiatives (OECD 2020).

Conclusions

Cultural associations have an important role to play in the preservation and development of small local cultures, as well as in the ability of these cultures to attract visitors and multicultural creatives to the local communities that exist in larger cities.

They are a meeting point for artists and artisans, and a venue for the diffusion of art and culture. Local associations meet a need for accessible cultural dissemination in communities that are not in the major tourist zones of larger cities. They also create collaborative social networks involving other associations and other organizations, offering new inclusive initiatives and social cohesion. According to Bridge, Murtagh, and O'Neill (2009, 186), social networks facilitate innovation and the development of skills and knowledge, as well as providing for their dissemination.

Before the pandemic, with the increasing tourist demand in Oporto, a change of behaviour regarding the migration of tourists to more residential parishes of the city was perceived as a beneficial alternative to the standard offer of hotels located in more central and touristic areas. This behaviour is motivated by tourism trends such as short-term holidays, low-cost flights, empowerment of a new wave of low-income tourists in search of low-cost local accommodation options, and a growing demand for small tourism, in which visitors seek not only to gaze on official tourist attractions, but also to immerse themselves in local experiences, to feel like they are temporary residents. Local associations can play a prominent role in this quest. Within the tourism value chain proposed by the Confederação do Turismo Português (2005, 850), accommodation, transportation, catering, events, local cultural events, and public services are vital components in the tourism industry. Casa Bô contributes to this value chain mainly by both supporting and providing local events as its core business. Catering can also be considered in the form of the vegetarian social dinners, as a complementary service within this value chain.

The attraction of tourists to more residential neighbourhoods contributes to the social inclusion of the local community in that it generates economic opportunity for local commerce, favouring local producers, residents with small family businesses such as cafés, taverns, grocery stores, small shops, and day-to-day services such as hairdressers, shoemakers, seamstresses, and other local businesses present in the more residential parishes. If Casa Bô can help to bring in the right number of tourists to support—and who are interested in—small tourism, it can establish social interactions and integration of these tourists with the local community. According to Zanoni and Janssens (2009), increasing cultural diversity in cities can be an important way to stimulate creativity and innovation as an alternative form of economic sustainability.

For the social integration between tourists and the local community, cultural associations such as Casa Bô, because of their intimacy, openness, and flexible agenda, can offer a unique and local tourist option, facilitating synergies and exchanges of experiences between the local community and the emerging trend of a tourism that is increasingly interested in not only checking items off a list of touristic sites and taking the requisite selfies, but also in engaging in the routine and habits of residents.

Right now, it is difficult to predict whether Casa Bô and other cultural associations like it will maintain the role they played pre-pandemic. Will we ever return to life as we knew it before 2020? What can be said is that even in the face of this adverse scenario, Casa Bô found a way to reinvent, transform, and sustain itself—even if in reduced circumstances—and it continues to add social capacity for its small community. Hopefully, it will return to its small tourism initiatives.

NOTES

1   https://www.acapo.pt/.

2   https://www.viralagenda.com/.

References

Azevedo, Carlos, Raquel Campos Franco, and João Wengorovius Meneses. 2010. *Gestão de Organizações Sem Fins Lucrativos—o Desafio Da Inovação Social*. Porto: Imoedições—Edições Perriódicoas e Multimédia, Lda. (Grupo Editorial Vida Económica).

Bauer, Martin W., and George Gaskell. 2015. *Pesquisa Qualitativa Com Texto, Imagem e Som: Um Manual Prático*. 13th ed. Rio de Janeiro: Editora Vozes Limitada.

Bridge, Simon, Brendan Murtagh, and Ken O'Neill. 2009. *Understanding the Social Economy and the Third Sector*. London: Palgrave Macmillan.

Confederação do Turismo Português. 2005. *Reinventando o Turismo Em Portugal. Estratégia de Desenvolvimento Turístico No 1º Quartel Do SéculoXXI.*

Cooper, Chris and Colin Michael Hall. 2008. *Contemporary Tourism: An International Approach*. Oxford: Routledge.

Denzin, Norman K., and Yvonna S. Lincoln. 2006. "A Disciplina e a Prática Da Pesquisa Qualitativa." In *O Planejamento Da Pesquisa Qualitativa: Teorias e Abordagens*, 2nd. ed., 15–41. Porto Alegre: Artmed.

European Best Destinations. 2017. "Best Places to Travel in 2017—Europe's Best Destinations." European Best Destinations, accessed 23 March 2023. https://www.europeanbestdestinations.com/best-of-europe/european-best-destinations-2017/.

Florida, Richard. 2002. *The Rise of the Creative Class. And How It's Transforming Work, Leisure and Everyday Life*. New York: Basic Books.

Greffe, Xavier. 2011. "Creativity: The Strategic Role of Cultural Landscapes." In *Sustainable City and Creativity: Promoting Creative Urban Initiatives*, edited by Luigi Fusco Girard, Tüzin Baycan Levent, and Peter Nijkamp, 199–223. Farnham, UK: Ashgate Publishing.

Harpring, Patricia. 2013. *Introduction to Controlled Vocabularies: Terminology for Art, Architecture, and Other Cultural Works*. Los Angeles: Getty Research Institute.

OECD (Organisation for Economic Co-operation and Development). 2020. "Culture Shock: COVID-19 and the Cultural and Creative Sectors." OECD, 7 September 2020. https://www.oecd.org/coronavirus/policy-responses/culture-shock-covid-19-and-the-cultural-and-creative-sectors-08da9e0e/.

Pearce, Philip L. 2007. *Tourist Behaviour: Themes and Conceptual Schemes*. Reprint, Clevedon, UK: Channel View Publications.

Principe, André Luis Quintino. 2016. "Associativismo e Criatividade: Inovação, Coesão Social e Mudança Sustentável: Estudo de Caso—a Casa Bô." Master's thesis, Universidade do Porto. http://hdl.handle.net/10216/87160.

———. 2018. "Associativismo Cultural, Criatividade e Sustentabilidade." *Análise Associativa—Revista Da Confederação Portuguesa Das Colectividade de Cultura, Recreio e Desporto*, no. 5:86–104.

Ramos, Maria Conceição. 2005. "Economia Social, Inclusão e Responsabilidade Social Empresarial." *Investigação e Debate Em Serviço Social*. Associação de Investigação e Debate em Serviço Social (Portugal).

Severino, Antônio Joaquim 2007. *Metodologia Do Trabalho Acadêmico Científico*. 23rd ed. São Paulo: Cortez.

UNCTAD (Conferência das Nações Unidas sobre Comércio e Desenvolvimento). 2012. *Relatório Da Economia Criativa 2010: Economia Criativa Uma Opção de Desenvolvimento. Nações Unidas*. Brasília; São Paulo: Secretaria de Economia Criativa/Ministério da Cultura; Itaú Cultural. http://unctad.org/pt/docs/ditctab20103_pt.pdf.

UNESCO (United Nations Educational, Scientific and Cultural Organization). 2006. "Towards Sustainable Strategies for Creative Tourism." *Creative Cities Network*, no. 1/11/2006:1–7. https://unesdoc.unesco.org/ark:/48223/pf0000159811.

Zanoni, Patrizia. and Maddy Janssens. 2009. "Sustainable DiverCities." In *Sustainables Cities: Diversity, Economic Growth an Social Cohesion*, edited by Maddy Janssens, Dino Pinelli, Dafne C. Reynen, and Sandra Wallman, 3–25. Cheltenham, UK: Edward Elgar Publishing.

Small Tourism in a Big City: The Story of 5Bogota

Diana Guerra Amaya and Diana Marcela Zuluaga Guerra

Introduction

Before COVID-19, the tourism industry in Colombia was beginning to gain traction, even if it was an exclusive industry that has always favoured the same actors, hotels, and travel agency chains, most of them internationals. Its relatively slow growth traces its origins to the mid-twentieth century, when the first international organized trip to the country was documented. The growing political and social insecurity caused by drug trafficking and internal guerrillas, however, hindered the evolution of the industry.

In the new millennium, the creation of the Ministry of Foreign Trade and Tourism signified the government's commitment to a resurgence of tourism. Branding sought to minimize the safety concerns of potential visitors with the slogan "the only risk is wanting to stay." This helped to restore Colombia's status as a tourism destination on the world stage. However, given the country's permanent economic crisis and high unemployment rates, it has been difficult for any actors other than traditional providers to offer tourism services, thereby limiting the industry's impact on the general population. The official campaigns did achieve their desired end, which was increasing the number of visitors coming into the country. These travellers of the new millennium, though, have come in search of experiences different from those offered by traditional tourism suppliers. These visitors are aware of how their choices relate to recent domestic peace initiatives, and to the cultural consequences caused by Colombian years of isolation as a peripheral tourism destination.

Because of a limited number of airlines and routes, Colombia was traditionally accessible to international travellers only via the capital of Bogotá. From there, travellers could go on to Cartagena and Medellín. Recently, more tourism campaigns have opened up both of those cities to visitors, but it is still typical for them to connect through Bogotá. The capital is socially and culturally complex, with over seven million inhabitants spread over a vast land extension. Most of its population lives in financially vulnerable conditions, where they are viewed as a mass, closer to being numbers than persons. All this hardly made Bogotá a tourism destination. Still, it is under these conditions that small tourism can flourish as a tool for social inclusion, as well as an attraction for socially conscious travellers.

The secret formula to do this is more conspicuous than one might imagine: it is to be found in everyday life, in local people, in their routine and cultural practices, in the flavours, the colours, the crafts, the architecture, and the passersby. Intangible heritage is synonymous with the ordinary. That is why we at 5Bogota decided to create a project that opens the possibility for real and everyday people to break into the tourism industry through the concept of small, creative tourism, such as that offered through our company, 5Bogota, a private small tourism start-up located in Bogota, Colombia, co-founded in 2013 by Diana Guerra and Diana Zuluaga, who, in addition to being partners, are also mother and daughter.

Diana Guerra is a business administrator. For over thirty years, she worked as a financial and administrative consultant for entrepreneurs through entities such as Women's World Banking. She was also a university professor at the Colombian School of Hospitality and Tourism.

Diana Zuluaga is a publicist; she studied and lived outside the country for more than eight years, and when she returned to Bogotá, as a result of an experience working in the historical district of the city, she had the opportunity to meet local artisans, cooks, and artists in states of economic vulnerability, who were trying to improve their income but who did not know how; although they were located in the most touristic area of the city, they could not find work within the traditional tourism sector.

The experience of Diana Guerra as an entrepreneurial consultant and tourism teacher, along with Diana Zuluaga's expertise in the creative field, gave rise to 5Bogota: they could see the gap between travellers looking for different and authentic experiences in the country and the locals who possessed this authenticity, and who needed work. They subsequently compiled a business model that envisioned a marketplace that could shorten the chain and more directly connect travelers with local hosts. Due to the difficulties involved in operating a company in Colombia, the structure is quite simple: instead of direct employees, the organization has collaborators, specifically the same local hosts who are hired for each service that the traveller requires. At the national level, there are around twenty collaborators.

5Bogota is a small tourism start-up that connects travellers with local hosts who showcase the country realistically and uniquely. At 5Bogota, we design tours and experiences that are completely authentic, through which travellers learn about our culture and our people while supporting local development. This has the potential to transform the Colombian travel industry, making it more inclusive and participative. Gastronomy is a powerful bond between cultures, and of course, a well-known aspect of tourism. When they do anything related to food and beverage, travellers discover much more than a destination's cuisine. Through food, travellers can discover and understand social practices, local dynamics, and some of a location's values. For this reason, 5Bogota has focused on gastronomic experiences. Especially in Bogotá, gastronomy is marked by multiculturalism. As Bogotá is the country's capital, many Colombians regard it as a place of opportunity and make it their home, and these people bring their traditions with them. This makes it possible to sample the entirety of Colombian cuisine along the city's streets.

This chapter aims to share the methods we at 5Bogota have designed to reimagine tangible and intangible cultural assets and to build creative experiences around them, engaging travellers with endogenous aspects of small sections of a large city. Our strategy will allow anyone interested in gastronomy and creative tourism to craft experiences focused on the five senses, authentically representing neighbourhood culture and turning such experiences into a significant source of income for locals. We will share the process we use to highlight a neighbourhood and its inhabitants, and to design routes and tours with the everyday life of the host as a starting point. Bogotá offers enough space and variety for residents to represent their own spaces and to set their geographical limits as they wish. Each *Bogotano*'s perception of the city and the relationship they have with it is unique, intimate, and personal. We share three of our local hosts' gastronomic small tourism adventures.

How to Deploy the Five Senses to Represent a Neighbourhood

For over seven years, we have designed tours for visitors based on the five senses and people's daily lives; we hope this establishes our credibility in offering 5Bogota as a case study.

Our objective here is to craft small tourism experiences in which every individual matters, even in a city as large and complex as the Colombian capital. It is vital to convince the locals that their daily lives are important and worth sharing with others. One could say that each inhabitant creates their version of a place based on their relation to it and their experiences of it. Elements such as their area of residence, the cafés, pubs, and restaurants they visit, their usual meeting places with relatives and friends, their homes, and their particular urban landscape create the uniqueness of the destination, making it different for each individual. This is our first and most important principle.

Our senses are the means through which we explore our surroundings. Before you attempt to design a tourism initiative for small groups in a designated area—in our case, within a large city—you must immerse yourself in that micro-culture. We think of this as the road map of our community. How will you do that?

Walking

This involves getting to know the environment such that a mental map might emerge. Walking allows you to commit to memory every corner, every place and building, enabling you to understand the time and distances involved in each route. It is essential to know every street in order to identify new paths and urban sights. These walks should occur daily to ensure that the locals recognize you and allow you to become part of the community; only then will you be part of its daily life, able to share it with future guests.

Observing

This is about sharpening the senses. It is not just about watching but also about listening, smelling, tasting, and touching the cultural heritage of the local community. It is necessary to find the gems hidden in daily life, those recurrent traditions that distinguish a given destination from all others. The goal is to get to know the iconic locations in a route, as well as the locals, finding out who they are and whether there are possibilities for visitor interaction with them.

Exploring the Community's History

While texts, news reports, and written histories are helpful, oral traditions—the stories that inhabitants offer when asked and that only a few can tell and remember—are equally valid, perhaps even more so. The process that starts with walking and that includes observation must involve conversations with the locals. It is impossible to represent a community without knowing how the locals perceive it, especially not without understanding the features of the environment that locals wish to share and emphasize. The importance of the material heritage of the neighbourhood cannot be understated. To that end, any museums, churches, parks, monuments, and libraries in your chosen zone should be included in the route. However, as these locations are part of the traditional tourism circuit, it is vital to include voices that will describe them from a different perspective.

Establishing Relationships with the Locals

The mapping of iconic locations and must-see stops to represent a location must also include establishing relationships with principal and secondary parties. Do engage with local leaders, but also with those who work in trades that can be shared: the carpenter, the vegetable vendor, the baker, the architect, the cook, the writer, the butcher. They and all their spaces will be essential in the crafting of sensory experiences. Leaving your comfort zone and seeing beyond the obvious is key to discovering the wonders of a neighbourhood.

Interviewing Local Parties in Search of Allies

You will need to develop these relationships with locals in order to provide engaging experiences. These locals are the main way your visitors will engage with the everyday life of the community. Conduct interviews with possible partners and develop a specific questionnaire designed to discover their personal histories and their relationships with the location to help you understand their desires and intentions. What are they willing to share with visitors? This will also allow you to customize a proposal for them that encourages these potential allies to participate. Their needs and financial expectations, available time, and relevant personality traits should be identified in order to establish their trust and create long-term commitments. You may well find some people are not interested in sharing their knowledge or tastes with visitors. They are still locals, and you will still see them. For this reason, it is essential to maintain good relationships and propose other options to them, not necessarily involving direct contact with foreigners. For example, a route may include a stop where these people work, and a short interaction without any responsibility beyond carrying on with their jobs as they usually do. At 5Bogota, the different stops at a farmers' market had precisely this objective: the individual preparing coffee or fruit juice was a fundamental aspect of the route but did not have any additional responsibilities with the visitors, unlike those whom we call local hosts.

Crafting Sensory Experiences

We build experiences that rely on the five senses through a series of creative lab sessions and conversations with our local hosts. Each host has the opportunity to select a sense they consider to be a prevalent aspect of their local experience, and then to create their offer with the input of the other hosts in the lab session. The key is to create stories instead of tourism products. With that in mind, each experience must include a series of moments that contribute to our ultimate goal: fostering memorable small-group adventures that deeply impact travellers' lives.

Mapping in the Lab Sessions

A map is the graphic piece summarizing the locally led planning we have described. Once the locations, the local parties, and the type of relationship the locals will have with your routes have been established, it is advisable to record the tour in a map; this will then be used to guide the visitor experience. The map thereby becomes a local guide, created by locals, about their community. It might be good to have a local illustrator design the map as this can function as both a promotional piece and a souvenir—and engage a local creative to make it.

Our Strategy for 5Bogota Experiences

Using the experience gained at 5Bogota, we have developed a methodology to create our offerings. They key here is that we work in, and design for, small groups.

First, it is essential to identify the aspects each local would be willing to share with travellers who match their interests. To this end, it is crucial to listen to and witness their routines so that ideas may freely flow. Remember that the goal is authenticity.

Once the elements with the most excellent chance to become sensory experiences have been identified, the future host is invited to an experience lab, which features techniques that drive the creative process such that the result will stem from the work contributed by the potential host, ensuring their motivation and ongoing commitment. The lab is a collaborative and multidisciplinary session with the objective of reimagining local hosts' every-day activities and turning these into experiences that convey a sense of their community to a small group of visitors. Stimulating creative thinking is key if hosts are to understand what is worth sharing out of everything they do. During this phase, it is indispensable for hosts to look at their community and their skills through the eyes of a tourist. Every idea produced by this exercise is understood to be equally valid. Every word may become the trigger that gives birth to an experience. The expected result is a list of concepts that all the hosts can use, and which continually renews the basis for our routes. In this way, the lab not only produces the foundation of our visitor experiences, but also develops social capital, creates social inclusion, and sustains local culture.

Part of our strategy is to create stories, not products. This calls for a practical exercise during the lab, during which hosts write a narrative de-scribing the experience they will offer as if told by a traveller. The narrative includes their own name, age, place of origin, and general aspects of their personality—anything they are likely to share with visitors. Hosts will have to determine what they expect the tourist will find noteworthy during their visit. By having the host take the traveller's place, we seek to alter how the host perceives their community, and to revitalize its tangible and intangible cultural assets.

While the relationship between each host and traveller is unique, having clarity about how the experience is to be delivered minimizes the risk of un-pleasantness or outright disappointment. It will ensure that the experience is always memorable. The final part of our methodology is to have the local hosts understand what we see as the three significant moments in the visitor experience. Every traveller will require variations on the plan laid out for each moment, which means we must be ready for any and every kind of re-sponse a traveller may offer, and always be ready to execute alternate plans. Still, a fairly uniform format makes the experience more fluid and easy.

It is worth remembering that this is not about following a script. Hosts must always act naturally while at the same time executing each activity with confidence and trusting the people involved in the route, being respectful of timings, and upholding the value proposition at play.

At 5Bogota, we have identified the following as critical moments.

Breaking the Ice

The meeting place, the greeting, and the first activity, and especially the first conversation, must be planned. The impressions created during the first few minutes will provide a better understanding of the traveller's expectations. In some cases, it will be necessary to explain the route and how it will be travelled. In other cases, the element of surprise may be your best resource. The host must read the travellers and quickly understand which aspects of the route need to be emphasized. This is why the first conversation may use specific questions.

The "Wow" Factor

This is the turning point, when you surprise and offer travellers an unexpected sensation. To achieve this point, it is crucial to select a predominant sense, one that will take centre stage owing to a specific activity. It may be an emotion, a flavour, a scent, an unexpected sight, or a turn of phrase. Whatever is selected, it must be sure to elicit a profound reaction from the traveller. This moment will become richer with every traveller you welcome. It is they who will inform your approach through their expressions and reactions as to what made an impression on them during the experience. Here again, the role of the local host is paramount as they must sharpen their senses to read travellers' emotions.

Brand Awareness

It is unlikely, although not impossible, for travellers to return repeatedly to your offering. The goal should therefore be to encourage them to recommend your experience to their relatives, friends, and social networks. How will you convert your visitors to become your leading promoters? One of our strategies is to ensure that they have a keepsake to remember us when they return home. In this sense, a souvenir is your best friend. However, just as your experience is different from traditional touristic products, your souvenir cannot be something that is available to anyone passing through the airport.

Each experience should produce a result, whether tangible or intangible. Small creative tourism enterprises frequently provide items such as a piece of handiwork that the traveller makes themselves. But not every experience will produce such a souvenir. The perfect example is cooking lessons, where the souvenir will be the recipes and techniques learned by the travellers.

Gastronomy as a Guiding Principle: Flavour Itineraries

Gastronomy is always present in any community as an element representing the local culture. Visitors are of course inclined to sample the cuisine of the places to which they travel. Even when breakfast, for example, includes the same basic ingredients from location to location, its presentation will vary. In some cases, it will include ingredients unusual for that time of day from another international perspective. Such is the case with all local customs surrounding food. Gastronomy represents the first, closest, most natural and vivid approach to local culture for travellers looking to immerse themselves in a particular enclave. Food and all its associated activities generate stories that become part of an oral tradition, and as such, are one way that culture is sustained. The ingredients used, where they are found, how they are combined, the traditional flavours and scents of the different kitchens, and the secrets each recipe has held through generations, are the culinary treasures that help provide a sense of place.

As such, gastronomy is one of the crucial elements to research if you want to share with your visitors the customs of local culture; meals can foster moments of profound connection with locals and their customs. These moments happen organically as visitors and residents enjoy the flavours and scents of a meal, snack, or beverage. During these activities, language barriers are also reduced for both foreigners and locals, increasing social inclusion for all.

Owing to the many domestic in-migrations in the late twentieth and the early twenty-first centuries, caused mainly by insecurity in intermediate cities and rural areas, Bogotá is now home to many internal migrants, which has caused the city to almost double since the end of the previous century. These circumstances have turned Bogotá into a gastronomic centre where people from all Colombian regions offer their traditional dishes using equally traditional ingredients and recipes. The city's gastronomic mix is so rich that it is no stretch to say that here it is possible to taste the cuisine from every Colombian region without visiting those places. Small tourism experiences based around gastronomy can flourish where individuals from different places and customs meet. There are neighbourhoods in the city where restaurants from different regions converge, providing a strong level of purchasing power for restauranteurs. The historical neighbourhoods usually play host to these food communities. This is where 5Bogota has laid its food routes.

Indigenous Cuisine

The Colombian Indigenous and Black communities have been working for centuries to preserve their cultures, often using gastronomy as a fundamental component to do so. For the country, these communities' ingredients and recipes are a valuable and respected heritage. Additionally, domestic and international travellers have contributed to the appreciation of this heritage in recent years, finding in gastronomy an element of cultural immersion. Corn, for instance, is native to Mexico and was transported south, becoming one of the main ingredients of Central and South American Indigenous cookery. Corn is used in a variety of ways and is present in many dishes and meals. Endemic herbs, with medicinal, magical, and/or culinary properties, contribute flavour, scent, and magic to meals, as Indigenous communities attribute otherworldly powers to their plants.

Farmers' Markets as Cultural Spaces

During the era of colonialism and the transition to independence, and even into the twentieth century, farmers' markets were urban spaces where rural food producers met with local city dwellers. Farmers' markets were the meeting point to exchange products brought in from the countryside, and to share customs.

For many years these marketplaces were located outdoors in town squares, until local governments stepped in, building spaces to contain the markets in hopes of improving their cleanliness. As marketplaces grew more popular, smaller satellite markets appeared in various city neighbourhoods, making it easier for buyers to access them. This led to many more of these spaces in urban areas. Bogotá was no exception. Many farmers' markets were established in neighbourhoods, where they became a relevant part of the traditions of the city. They assumed the status of iconic places where different kinds of products were offered, not only foodstuffs, but also artisanal utensils for the home and kitchen made by locals. As time progressed, a few small businesses offering prepared meals appeared in the marketplaces. Now, these historical farmers' markets host real food courts. What is more, the areas surrounding the markets saw many small businesses spring up, offering a wide range of products and services. This phenomenon took place around all the marketplaces, turning their neighbourhoods into iconic sectors of the city.

Unfortunately, since the late twentieth and the early twenty-fist centuries, farmers' markets have deteriorated as a result of abandonment by local governments, as well as by the emergence of new, modern grocery stores that have taken centre stage, rendering traditional farmers' markets less competitive, and even causing them to disappear in some cases. The few remaining are attractive sites for small-group tourism experiences, not only because they represent local culture, but also because surrounding businesses are eager to counter their degradation, leading to multiple route allies. This scenario provides marketplace labourers who tell their own stories or those of their products, as well as their origins or uses; local hosts who share thematic anecdotes; locals who demonstrate how the farmers' markets function nowadays; and store owners or service staff available in spaces that are open to the public, both within and outside the marketplace.

5Bogota Experiences

Colombian gastronomy is the product of the cultural mixture resulting from the Spanish conquest, the arrival of the African slaves, and the ingredients endemic to our lands. The richness of the meals produced by this mixture is now influenced by new migrations from Colombian regions currently taking place. This has turned the country into a gastronomic centre, with autochthonous and diverse cuisines that rely on their origins, the climatic conditions of each region, and its ingredients.

Bogotá could very well be considered the gastronomic capital of Colombia, a qualifier with an unprecedented and regrettable origin. Forced displacements, brought about by the violence caused by guerrillas and drug trafficking, have precipitated the migration of people from all over the country to the capital. As a result, Bogotá has become a showcase for national gastronomy. As is the case in most cultures, one of the main ways Colombians connect with foreigners is to share their rich cuisines. Sharing a meal is considered one of the most effective methods of bonding, whether at home or at a restaurant. 5Bogota broke into the tourism-provision market with little competition, as most tourism services providers focus on typical products like beaches, festivals, and adventure tourism. Our approach, based on local culture and customs, focused on the strong bonds gastronomy creates between strangers, and so we chose it as our guiding principle, with the possibility of adding other themes and topics as appropriate.

Our tenets were as follows:

- To transform places common for traditional tourism into creative spaces. To this end, we introduced the use of the five senses as a fundamental tool.

- To implement the concept of small tourism in a city as large and complex as Bogotá. We sought to have offers available in different neighbourhoods, thus turning them into creative hubs outside the traditional tourism circuit.

- To create thematic links between the outskirts and the inner city through an urban tourism offer with hints of countryside tourism in nearby zones.

- To foster social inclusion by bringing wealth created by tourism to communities usually overlooked by the industry.

These tenets are most evident in the experiences detailed below. We have crafted these small experiences in collaboration with local hosts. We have selected examples where innovation is the leading factor.

El Regateo, La Ñapa y La Vaca

Location

This route is in the 7 de Agosto neighbourhood. This is an emblematic location for two reasons: first, it is one of the most traditional commercial sites in the city, where it is possible to find just about anything, though it is especially famous for its numerous automotive shops; and second for its farmers' market. While farmers' markets are usually frequented by tourists visiting Colombia, the one in the 7 de Agosto serves primarily local customers due to its status as a place customarily considered dangerous, and thus outside the traditional tourism circuit. At first glance, the location did not seem to have great potential because of its visual and noise pollution and its primary commercial function. However, the route has flourished.

Local Hosts

The hosts are the Amapola Cartonera, a collective of visual artists and writers who create artistic books using recycled materials such as discarded cardboard. It operates a bookshop located in the 7 de Agosto neighbourhood. This social enterprise promotes reading through fair and accessible prices for the most vulnerable communities. Since cardboard is their primary material, the farmers' market is their supplier.

The Experience

The hosts take visitors to the historic 7 de Agosto farmers' market. The name of the experience is taken from local expressions used in the farmers' markets, which the members of Amapola Cartonera encourage visitors to use during the route.

Register (haggling): Asking for a lower price is a long-standing practice at farmers' markets that distinguishes the social dynamics of this cultural space.

Ñapa (freebies): Asking for an extra unit as a present after completing a large purchase at one of the marketplace's stands is typical.

Vaca (whip-rounds): This is the name given to the money collected by a group of friends or relatives to purchase something, usually an alcoholic drink. For the experience, the purpose of the whip-round was the purchase of a fruit salad for everyone.

The Gastronomic Element

Participants taste local fruits, fresh coffee, and typical neighbourhood dishes. They also stop at stands selling fresh herbs and listen to descriptions of their different uses. The world of medicinal and cooking plants—and those with mystical properties—is a central aspect in Colombian farmers' markets.

Itinerary

The travellers visit the marketplace accompanied by a member of Amapola Cartonera, stopping at coffee shops, at fruit and local specialty stands, and at artisan shops to experience various textures. It is an opportunity to perceive tastes, scents, colours, and sounds. The last stop includes purchasing the cardboard that the traveller will use to create their keepsake.

The travellers walk through the neighbourhood for a few blocks until they arrive at the bookshop, disproving the neighbourhood's reputation as a dangerous place. Once at the bookshop, travellers are guided by the artists at the collective to construct a handmade cardboard book from scratch—a book the visitors will take with them. The book's content records their experience at the farmers' market, including drawings of the fruits and their names, and records their feelings and their most significant experiences. At the end, the traveller leaves a space blank to record their later reflections.

Becoming a Salt Artisan in Zipaquirá

For years, one of the most popular and traditional tours offered to international and domestic travellers has been visiting the Salt Cathedral at Zipaquirá, located forty-two kilometres from the capital. In the mid-twentieth century, this church was built inside a salt mine, which constitutes its main appeal. The surroundings of the cathedral boast a solid tourism infrastructure, an excellent artisanal offer, and many traditional restaurants, hotels, and parks, among other amenities.

Local Hosts

Our partners here are La Maloka Moderna, a cultural project located in Zipaquirá. Their objective is the creation of artifacts using salt as raw material. Employing ancient techniques, the artists at La Maloka Moderna pay homage to the Muiscas, one of the Indigenous tribes that inhabited the high plateau of Bogotá. These artists design interior decor objects with salt at the core, producing artifacts for the home, which feature the added value of the well-being and prosperity thought to be induced by the chemical properties of this mineral, as well as the historical property of the value salt held for bartering among our ancestors. Their products range from lighting and decoration artifacts to medicinal and relaxing bath salts.

The Experience

A La Maloka Moderna member accompanies a small group to the famous Salt Cathedral in Zipaquirá. In addition to completing the established tour, the traveller also spends time with a salt expert who shares the role salt played in the Indigenous economy. This is an inspiring space as there are many structures and sculptures made of salt along the way.

The Gastronomic Element

This experience presents a gastronomic challenge as the location is often the object of over-tourism, which affects the authenticity of the gastronomic offer and the quality of the restaurants, which are often quite crowded. The answer to this challenge is a picnic using regional, endemic ingredients with the company of the hosts, which is ideal as the cathedral is surrounded by nature. With that, travellers are removed from the tourism mainstream and have the opportunity to try food prepared in an artisanal manner—with a little salt!

Itinerary

A guided tour of the cathedral is led by the location staff and the local host. Once travellers leave the church, they go to the picnic area to enjoy their locally based meal. At the end of this activity, visitors follow the artisan to the workshop, where they are shown the different tasks necessary to create salt sculptures. They are then given face masks and gloves and, with the guidance of one of the La Maloka Moderna members, create a salt sculpture to take back home with them.

Bar Experience: Ethnic Rituals

Location

The Quinta Camacho neighbourhood is a symbol of the mid-twentieth-century capital city, and was declared a heritage site in 2000. It is considered to be an open-air architectural museum integrated within the modern city. Over the last fifteen years, the location has earned a reputation as a gastronomic and cultural hub, boasting a wide array of restaurants, art galleries, antiquaries, theatres, unique cafés, and themed hostels. These businesses were initially conceived for the local population as the neighbourhood was not included in traditional tourism circuits, being located away from the historical centre. The traffic in Bogotá is known to be slow and difficult. Quinta Camacho was therefore not recognized in the tourism world as a possible destination for travellers, and little effort was made to promote it.

Local Host

Enter Mauricio Pardo, a young bartender born in Ubaté, a township just outside Bogotá. For Mauricio, who goes by Mao, it was not easy finding his way into the bar scene, as the profession had at this point barely gained traction. Looking for new opportunities, Mao decided to share his knowledge by crafting a 5Bogota route, where the traveller moves undetected through the neighbourhood's nightlife.

The Experience

Our host hinges this experience on sacred rituals as the protagonists in this route are the liquors of our ancestors. These liquors are often credited with magical powers and were used in group ceremonies to pay homage to deities or to heal the body and the soul.

The Gastronomic Element

Visitors taste artisan-produced ancient liquors using recipes from the Indigenous peoples of different regions: Chirrinchi from the Caribbean, Viche from the Pacific, and RC (*rompe calzón*, or "knicker breaker") from the Amazon.

Itinerary

The meeting point is the first bar. There, the traveller must provide the bartender with a clue they received previously. The bartender will then recognize them and will initiate the ritual by preparing the cocktail. At the same time, and as the traveller drinks, the bartender tells them the myths surrounding the liquor in question. The traveller then receives a new clue they must provide at the next bar, where the next bartender will present them with a new ritual and tell them the story of the liquor being used. This route includes three or four stations.

How Is 5Bogota Doing?

Since the creation of 5Bogota, revenues have been showing a growth trend. To illustrate, in December 2019, before the pandemic, 385 travellers engaged in different experiences with our local hosts. This number of travellers generated income that positively impacted the value chain, and we succeeded in our objective of allowing tourism income to reach people outside the traditional circuit, who achieved a positive economic impact by sharing their daily lives. During this period, the income generated corresponded to a value greater than fifty minimum monthly wages in force in Colombia for that year, which, according to the Ministry of Labour, was US$285 per month. The sales behaviour had achieved stability and continued its upward trend; in other words, it was expected that 2020 would exceed our expectations. 5Bogota was on the top list for local experiences. It was in the first position in gastronomic experience on Tripadvisor in Bogotá for more than three years and listed in printed guides such as *Lonely Planet* and *Bradt*. Reservations as of March 2020 exceeded twenty minimum wages in value, in addition to pre-paid advances that helped our cash flow and made it possible to project sales for double the value of 2019.

That said, the impact of the pandemic on the industry, and in particular, on tourism ventures, is undeniable.

The post-pandemic financial situation is critical. The business was suspended for more than a year. And just in the first quarter of 2022, 5Bogota slowly started resuming its activities, with just seven to ten travellers per month, a volume that does not allow the required operational stability.

It is worth mentioning that tourism ventures did not receive government support during the pandemic, which is why many of them, including 5Bogota, had to suspend their economic activities until the arrival of international travellers becomes normalized.

The future continues to be uncertain for 5Bogota. Although the network of hosts has remained active, the number of international travellers arriving in the country is still insufficient to make any economic forecasts.

Conclusion

We built 5Bogota from scratch in a large, complex, majestic city full of striking social phenomena. In that context, it was no easy task to implement a small creative tourism concept. It posed a significant challenge, because at first glance, it did not seem possible to offer small, bespoke tourism in a destination with over seven million inhabitants. However, we found that the city functions differently in each neighbourhood, and even within micro-cultures in each location. A farmers' market can feature specific dynamics that distinguish it as a self-contained community. Building micro-tourism experiences based in the belief of the importance and attractiveness of local culture—such as those practised at local farmers' markets—allowed us to rescue the life stories of the inhabitants of these locations and provide visitors with the opportunity to experience them.

From a sustainability perspective, tourism must be seen as a social phenomenon, a bonding space for people. Benefits for locals should transcend financial profit, and in the same way, the ultimate goal for the traveller must exceed mere leisure. In our experience, the implementation of creative, slow, and small tourism reclaims the dignity of the daily life of locals while at the same time impacting the lives of visitors in profound and moving ways. We believe in community-led tourism planning that creates social capital by integrating local communities as hosts, and including under-recognized locations as tourism territories. We hope our concept can help spur a social phenomenon: locals reasserting a sense of ownership of their own community, creating cultural sustainability. Crafting visitor experiences based on the traditional and everyday occurrences of the hosts and their cultural heritage revitalizes and stimulates the recognition of their own cultural wealth, playing a central role in preserving intangible urban heritage assets. As well, our small tourism business model allows for the social redistribution of wealth, with earnings from these services going back into communities that would not receive them otherwise. Offering these activities in a domestic in-migration capital like Bogotá allows travellers to interact with cultures far from their chosen destination. Small tourism can integrate small zones, small products, and small areas that exist within a large territory. Perhaps the chaos COVID-19 has caused in the traditional and largely unsustainable tourism industry offers us a positive way forward: travellers have the opportunity, through small tourism in small places, to engage with local lives and practices that, in the long run, can help redefine the image of a country. We hope we have provided a potential way forward for locally focused, small tourism providers in the model of 5Bogota.

Cultural Festivals in Small Villages: Creativity and the Case of the Devil's Nest Festival in Hungary

Emese Panyik and Attila Komlós

Introduction

When visitor-resident interaction is seen as paramount in a tourism experience, it is often best facilitated in small groups in a place of manageable size. Creative tourists not only visit places, they also make them by actively engaging their skills and knowledge to enrich the local experience of a particular destination (Richards 2011). One of the main issues within creative tourism is the authenticity of the experience (Chhabra, Healy, and Sills 2003; Prentice 2001; Steiner and Reisinger 2006), which is strongly linked to the place it stems from. To put it simply, "one can learn to dance salsa from world-class dancers in many countries but only Cuba provides the atmosphere that attaches the symbol of authenticity to the salsa classes experience" (Ohridska-Olson and Ivanov 2010, 3). While cultural tourism is based on tangible cultural resources, creative tourism relies equally on tangible and intangible resources. Thus creative tourism is less place-bound than cultural tourism, because the creative experience is not staged but being produced "on the go" in collaboration with the visitors using intangible cultural resources, such as dances, singing, crafts, festivals, and painting (Prentice and Andersen 2003).

The main challenge of creative tourism is, therefore, not only to attract visitors to a place but also to involve them in the co-creation of the authentic experience based on tangible and intangible resources. Furthermore, authentic experiences are often segregated, hidden in isolated places far from urban areas or popular tourist attractions or destinations. Larger tourism enterprises are typically ill-suited for small, creative tourism experiences.

This chapter presents a case study that aims to explore the challenges of small creative tourism. While festivals have been identified as a form of creative destination (Prentice and Andersen 2003), attention is focused principally on big cities such as Edinburgh (Prentice and Andersen 2003) or St. Petersburg (Gordin and Matetskaya 2012). Little is known about the potential of festivals to draw attention to underdeveloped, small, and isolated regions. We aim to address that research gap in this chapter.

The context for this case study is an iconic cultural festival in Hungary, Ördögkatlan Fesztivál (Devil's Nest Festival), organized since 2008 in a group of villages in one of the most underdeveloped regions of the country, South Baranya. The study offers a retrospective exploration of the long-term impacts of the event on local development. While large-scale music festivals are usually organized in remote, natural areas in order to isolate the visitors from the residents—that is, to maximize the visitor experience and minimize the impacts on the local population (e.g., Tomorrowland in Boom, Belgium; Ozora Festival in Dádpuszta, Hungary; Boom Festival in Idanha-a-Nova, Portugal, etc.)—Ördögkatlan was born in a remote limestone quarry located about twenty kilometres from the closest city, Pécs, as a small-scale arts festival, through the collaboration of four neighbouring villages and two wineries. The quarry functions as an open-air contemporary arts exhibition and statue park, and each of the villages became a festival location linked by a free festival bus. The growth of the festival has been exponential. From 5,000 visitors during three days in the first year, it has reached 85,000 visitors during five days in 2017. The objective of the organizers was to create a grassroots multicultural festival drawing on local values and resources, which grows spontaneously in accordance with the interests, ideas, and feedback of the visitors, residents, and organizers alike.

Within this context the chapter reflects the residents' perspective on the indirect impacts of the festival during and beyond the event. To this end, key-informant resident interviews were conducted in the low season, January through March 2018, in the principal festival location, the small village of Nagyharsány. The interviews highlight the level of resident-visitor interactions, and the involvement of residents and visitors in co-creating their experiences during the festival.

Festivals as Creative Destination

Today, festivals and special events are one of the fastest-growing types of tourism attraction worldwide (Crompton and McKay 1997; van Heerden 2003; Getz 1997; Thrane 2002 cited in Saayman and Saayman 2005). Festival tourism creates place attachment, and provides new paths of rejuvenation for destinations.

Previous research on festival consumption identified the sharing of company and socialization as the most frequent motivations for festival consumption (Prentice and Andersen 2003). Such factors may be independent from the place, and their recurrent importance may imply that the festival itself becomes the destination, rather than being merely one among (many) other attractions of a destination (Prentice and Andersen 2003). But this depends on whether the festival is defined by the place in which it occurs and therefore relies more on its tangible and intangible cultural resources, or is more global in its thematic orientation (Ling and Lew 2012). Furthermore, festival tourists may not all be mainstream festival goers. This is especially true for festival destinations that attract tourists year-round (Prentice and Andersen 2003).

The location of a festival is a significant factor in its economic impact. Previous studies on arts festivals highlighted that a particular festival attracts most of its visitors from its own and neighbouring regions (Saayman and Saayman 2005). Visitor expenditure is generally higher by visitors from higher-income regions, while locals spend less than visitors because they do not spend on accommodation. It is therefore suggested that regional governments foster the establishment of new events in small towns, since these contribute significantly to income generation in these towns. Preferably these towns should be easily accessible from high-income areas to attract high-spending individuals (Saayman and Saayman 2005).

South Baranya, Hungary

The festival is located in southern Hungary, in the southernmost segment of Baranya County, approximately 13 kilometres from the Croatian border. The festival villages and wineries, as well as the Statue Park, are all accessible by public roads, both from Hungary and neighbouring Croatia, and from the Pécs-Pogány International Airport, which is about 20 kilometres away (see figure 7.1). The closest cities are Pécs, the regional capital, located 36 kilometres from the festival, and Villány, which is on the route linking the festival

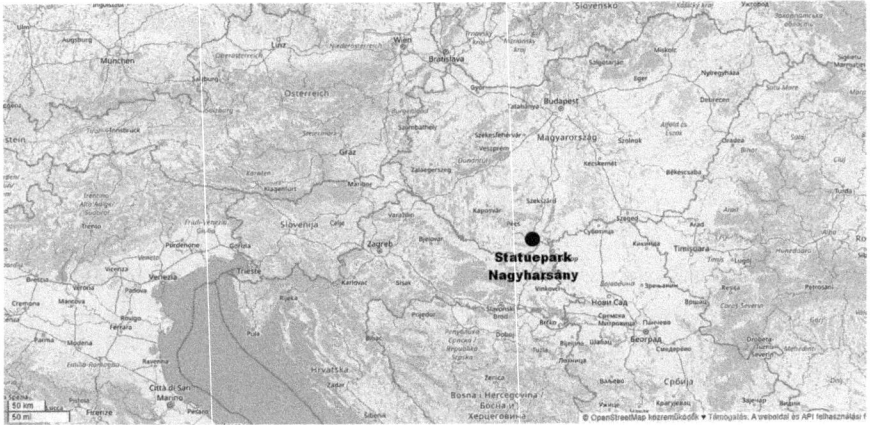

Figure 7.1: The festival location.

Source: Google Maps (fair use policy).

locations. The four villages of the festival are Kisharsány (population 351), Nagyharsány (1,500), Beremend (2,500), and Villánykövesd (227), and two wineries (Mokos Pincészet and Vylyan) also participate; these are linked by a 40-kilometres route by car or by bus (see figure 7.2). Beremend, where the limestone was processed in a factory drawn from the Sársomlyó hill, is located right at the Croatian-Hungarian border.

The economy of the region is based on three pillars. Wine production and related tourism and hospitality services are undoubtedly of decisive importance. The Villány Wine Region is one of Hungary's most famous wine regions, producing the highest-quality wines, acknowledged by various prizes won in national and international wine competitions. Hungary's first wine road was established in this area in 1994 (https://villanyiborvidek.hu).[1] Based on the local wine culture, many events are held in the region, with an ever-increasing service infrastructure. In addition to the cellars, there are also hotels, guest houses and local accommodation that provide high quality services for guests arriving individually or in groups. In addition to wine production and tourism, the Beremend Cement Factory and its associated limestone quarry of Nagyharsány are important employers of the region.

The most significant landscape in the area is the Szársomlyó hill, the highest elevation of the Villány Mountains (442 metres). The region has been

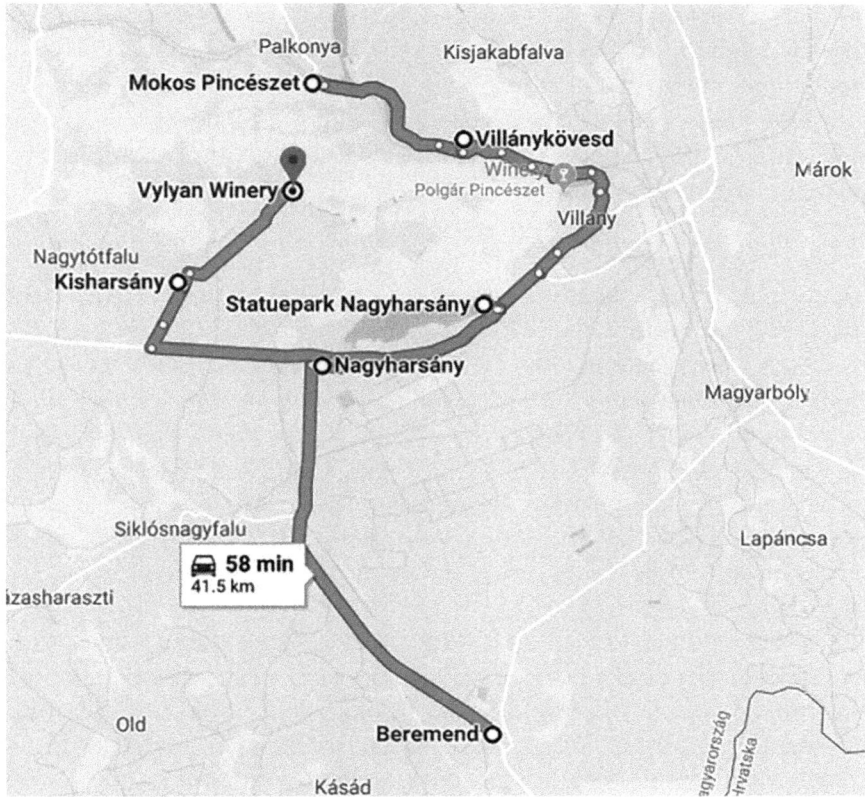

Figure 7.2: Map of the festival villages.

Source: Google Maps (fair use policy).

inhabited for more than two thousand years, and was part of the Pannonia Province of the Roman Empire. The history of the area's peoples during the last two millennia has resulted in a rich archaeological and cultural heritage (wine cellars, Siklós medieval castle, Gothic church in Nagyharsány, Roman ruins at the top of, and next to, Szársomlyó, etc.). The shape of the mountain has for centuries moved the imagination of people living here, creating myths expressed in folk tales, folk songs, and poems. Among them, the legend of the "devil's thorns" stands out, which served as a source for inspiration for the festival's name. The hill has been a national nature reserve since 1944, and as such is one of the oldest in Hungary. Since 1967, a creative arts camp has been functioning on the eastern side of the hill, where Hungarian and foreign sculptors from Japan and France have worked in the open sky for decades. The sculptures can be seen in the open-air sculpture park, which is called by the artists "the Devil's Nest," referring to the legend of the mountain and the extreme heat of the summer in the area.

The Devil's Nest Festival

The origins of the festival can be traced back to 2001, when a small arts festival was born far from the current location (close to Lake Balaton), where it had been organized until 2007 with the collaboration of three villages. The festival ran under the name Bárka Harbor. In 2008, the ten-day festival, the schedule of which had already been finalized, was cancelled at the last minute due to financial problems. In order to provide an immediate solution for the problem, the main organizers had to find a new venue for the festival and the planned program. The new location was selected based on its natural beauty, remoteness, and the willingness of the small villages to collaborate and participate in the event.

The central location of the festival became the Statue Park in Nagyharsány, on the mountainside of Szársomlyó. This former limestone quarry now hosts the festival's annual closing concert. The mountain is called the "Devil's Mountain" by locals. According to the myth, the devil wanted to marry Nagyharsány's most beautiful daughter, Harka. In order to get her, he had to remove the mountain by dawn. He failed to do so, and all that was left behind of his attempts is the quarry. The organizers also call the festival the "Barefoot Festival." The experience that the organizers aim to create is based on what Prentice and Andersen (2003) calls gregariousness, or a carefree and spontaneous but immersive social-cultural interaction between visitors, artists, educators, locals, and organizers—very informal, and as such suitable for bare feet.

The concept and aims of the festival have remained essentially unchanged since the first edition in 2008:

- to expose the region's cultural-artistic richness;
- to create an international, cross-cultural community in the small villages of Baranya during the festival, by inviting artists and hosting visitors;

- to provide economic, intellectual, and cultural assistance to the participating villages in one of the most underdeveloped areas of the country;

- to contribute to tourism development in the region; and

- to enhance the magnitude of the festival with the involvement of more settlements over the medium term, including Croatian Baranya, and to celebrate the multicultural values and common history through a Baranya Joint Arts Festival in the tourism market of Europe.

Methodology

Between January and March 2018, six key-informant resident interviews were conducted, three of them during a field trip to the main festival village, Nagyharsány. While the festival is currently organized in four neighbouring villages and two wineries, the central location with the highest number of programs, administrative tasks, and infrastructural contribution is Nagyharsány. Thus, the interview series started with the mayor of Nagyharsány. Then, a snowball method was used to identify key-informant residents in the small settlements who were actively involved in the festival. The mayor, two winery owners, one winery marketing director, and two main festival organizers were interviewed. The interviews were semi-structured and followed an interview guide in which nine topics were identified (see below). They lasted on average one hour, and were recorded and transcribed. We performed a standard qualitative data analysis procedure, in which we organized segments of the six interviews under the nine interview topics. We used coding to identify patterns in each column. We then proceeded with the interpretation of data, in which we presented the issues that unfolded during the analysis and used citations from participants to illustrate/highlight those issues.

Key-Informant Interview Topics

1. The geographic, economic, and social position of the villages in the region.

2. The impact of the festival on the region's image during the past ten years.

3. The direct and indirect impacts of the festival on the development of the region.

4. The potential of the festival to highlight the region's social and economic problems.

5. The potential of the festival to improve the networking capacity of the villages.

6. Practices to involve residents and visitors in the creation of the festival experience using local tangible and intangible cultural resources.

7. Local participants (associations, wineries, service providers, businesses, voluntary groups, etc.) in the festival.

8. The challenges of resident involvement.

9. Logistical, infrastructural, or other problems during the festival.

Socio-economic Impacts of the Festival

Discussion of the topics revealed three key issues regarding the socio-economic impacts of the festival: growth in visitor numbers; direct tourism-related infrastructural developments in the villages and their benefits for the local population; and the festival's contribution to the preservation and promotion of local heritage and culture. The interview responses raised a series of questions, such as: How can the festival transform local attractions into a tourism product? How can it change the image of the region? How does it influence the strategic position of the settlements?

Growth in Visitor Numbers

Considering the visitor numbers, the festival has demonstrated a stable and remarkable growth since 2008. As can be seen in table 7.1, from 5,000 visitors at the beginning, it crested at 90,000 attendees in 2019. This is in line with the growth in festival locations, which started at twelve and has reached twenty-seven locations in the five festival villages (table 7.1). The growth in visitor numbers have been accompanied by a growth in festival locations, and of course by the diversification of the festival program. In economic terms, new local accommodation options have been established. However, there is a need to further advance service provision in the villages. The number of supermarkets, ATMs, and scheduled transport between the larger cities and the festival is still lower than necessary. (There is, for example, only one ATM available among the festival locations.)

During the past years, all local accommodation facilities have been re-served months before the event, bringing the occupancy rate to 100 per cent. This is not surprising because there are no hotels in the festival villages, only a couple of guest houses, local accommodations that include wine cellars, private home rentals, and a large-scale, temporary festival camp at the local sports field in Nagyharsány. The local tax defined by the municipality is 200 HUF per person per night (about EUR 0.6), paid by the guest to the accommodation provider, who remits it to the municipality. According to the mayor of Nagyharsány, there are about 450 houses registered in Nagyharsány, 200 of which provide local accommodation during the festival. This is equal to 44.4 per cent of all houses in the village. One interviewee commented that there were 170 tents set up in one private backyard during the 2017 festival. This accommodation income for a local host is about 100,000–200,000 HUF (EUR 330–660), which corresponds to the average monthly income in Hungary, allowing local homeowners to buy firewood for the following winter, as well as consumer goods such as new furniture for their houses.

Table 7.1: Growth in visitor numbers (2008–21)

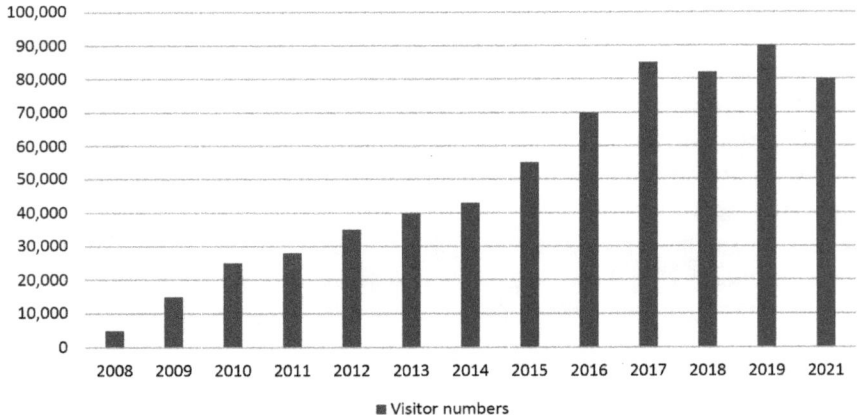

Source, authors, based on www.ordogkatlan.hu

Table 7.2: Changes in the number of festival locations

	2008	2009	2010	2011	2012	2013	2014	2015	2016	2017
Nagyharsány	4	6	7	7	8	7	8	8	12	12
Kisharsány	4	6	5	5	6	6	10	8	6	7
Palkonya	4	6	5	6	7	8	9	9	1	1
Kisjakabfalva	0	0	0	0	0	0	0	1	0	0
Beremend	0	0	0	0	1	2	2	2	2	3
Villánykövesd	0	0	0	0	0	0	0	0	3	4
ALL	**12**	**18**	**17**	**18**	**22**	**23**	**29**	**28**	**24**	**27**

Source: Authors

Direct Tourism-Related Infrastructure Developments

In order to meet the enormous demand during the festival, accommodation provision requires continuous improvement and expansion from both quantitative and qualitative perspectives. Service providers are often in a dilemma, wondering whether it is worth investing in infrastructure development for five days only when there are no festivals of such volume in the region for the other 360 days of the year. However, the nearby Villány-Siklós Wine Route organizes a number of weekly programs from April to October (HúSvét!, Rozé Maraton, Ha péntek akkor Villány, Palkonya Open Cellars, Red Wine Festival, etc.), so the increasing number of participants in these events will also use the accommodation of the surrounding settlements. Wine cellars therefore have begun to expand, such as Kovács Cellar in Nagyharsány, which in recent years has evolved from a winery to a local accommodation provider, operating three guest houses in the region.

Food services have also been impacted. Most overnight festival visitors are young, with lower discretionary income, and so choose simple, cheaper food options from the local grocery stores, rather than from restaurants. Day visitors typically choose the festival market and street food. Because there are no supermarkets in the villages, the stocks and income of the few local grocery stores multiply during the festival. This is not, regrettably, a year-round situation.

The Festival's Contribution to Local Heritage Sustainability and Promotion

The visitor numbers in local exhibitions and museums in the villages increase during the festival period; instead of a few visitors per day, these venues see hundreds on a daily basis. Most wineries sell local, handmade products such as jams, syrups, wine by-products, as well as pesto and honey, which are of great interest to tourists, thereby providing an additional income for local entrepreneurs. One interviewee, who is a wine producer and cellar owner, owns two buildings in the village. One is the family home and includes a small souvenir shop for local products and an ethnographic collection of woven fabrics in the back. Some of the antique fabrics preserved in this collection are the last ones of their kind and are unique pieces.

The other building is currently an empty house in poor condition. The interviewee plans to reconstruct it in the near future in order to create a permanent space for the collection, with the intention of providing a workshop for small creative tourism activities such as local weaving practices.

Co-creation Practices

One of the festival's main values is interactivity, and various new creative forms of artistic expression have been developed during the past ten years in which local entrepreneurs, visitors, and residents participate. In addition to clothes painting, an analogue photography workshop—where visitors take pictures on glass or film negative, develop their photos, and show them in an exhibition room—and painting of old, unused wine barrels by artists that become part of the Vylyan wine cellar's decor, the following innovative activities are noteworthy. In all cases, these creative activities are carried out either by individuals or by small groups of visitors.

Land Art Workshops

Visitors have the opportunity to create their own art works at the Statue Park Land Art sessions in which objects found in nature, such as dried trees and stones, are painted and/or assembled. The pieces created by the visitors remain on the scene until the closing day of the festival, so an open-air artwork museum is created in real time, and subsequently expands daily. The different stages of work are captured in photographs and animated short films to show the creative process.

Living Ethnography

Living ethnography is a contemporary project that aims at preserving folk art on the edge of extinction. Today, there are fewer and fewer places in the world where folk traditions are not just brought out on holidays but are actually still an integral part of everyday life. At the turn of the twentieth century, various ethnographers became internationally recognized for researching such living folk art, such as Hungarians Béla Bartók (folk music) and Zoltán Kodály (folk music), Finn Elias Lönnrot (Kalevala), the Grimm brothers from Germany (folk tales), or the Pole Hugo Kołłątaj (folk culture). Nowadays, Hungarian Miklós Both is carrying out similar research in Ukraine, and he has brought small groups of singers from three small Csernyihiv villages in Ukraine, where this musical folk culture is an aspect of daily life, to perform at the festival. Their visit was supported by the Hungarian cultural organization Pro Progressione, the French Di Mini Teatro—Commedia Dell'Arte contemporaine (contemporary art theatre), and the Ivan Honchar Museum in Russia as part of the Creative Europe Programme (2014–20).

Village Tourists: A Partly Improvised Open-Air Comedy

Village Tourists is one of the hallmark performances of the festival, offered numerous times a day as a result of the exceptionally high interest shown by audiences. Participation is limited for each session because this live experience and engagement by visitors requires small groups. Well-known artists from the National Theatre of Pécs organize a satirical tour in the villages for the participants, which they partly improvise to present village life, show the main attractions, and embody rural characters.

Local Legends Theatre

Similar to the living ethnography project, this initiative focuses on the preservation of local legends, myths, and oral traditions in the small, peripheral festival villages. In addition to Pécs, nearby Kaposvár is also famous for its arts culture, particularly theatre art. Kaposvár's experimental theatre company, K2, comprised of young artists, has been a permanent performer since 2014. That year, members of the company arrived weeks before the festival and carried out extensive research in the villages, engaging in conversations with the local people. They were especially interested in the elderly population and talked to various older residents about interesting stories that have been preserved throughout the generations by way of oral tradition. These stories and legends became the inspiration for new theatre pieces that were performed at the festival. The first piece, in 2014, was *The Bride of Nagyharsány*, followed by *The Groom of Kisharsány* in 2015, *The Bridesman of Villánykövesd* in 2016, and *The Beremend Wedding* in 2017, each of which was based on stories from one particular village. The pieces were performed at open-air locations using minimal design and accessories, usually in the gardens of private homes opened for the festival.

Analogue Facebook

Analogue Facebook is an offline, retro version of Facebook in which the organizers used a large wall in the central village for festival "residents" to message one another, draw, or just write anything they liked. The wall also called attention to the fact that Internet access is usually limited at the festival locations, which is considered to be part of the experience.

Besence Open

In 2016 the festival organizers launched a fundraising call in order to support the participation of children from the poorest villages in the region. From the donations of festival visitors, 14 children from Besence, a small village of 126 mainly Roma residents, could spend their holidays at the festival. Besence has no school, kindergarten, community spaces, or job opportunities, but the village has become well-known in Hungary through its resilient mayor, who won a tennis court for the village on a national tender. The mayor then contracted an instructor to give tennis classes for the entire village. A documentary entitled *Besence Open* has been made based on the story, and the mayor was invited to a forum during the festival to talk about the challenges of fighting poverty in the village. Such is the emphasis on smallness that it becomes a topic at the festival. Here we can see true resident-visitor interaction.

Resident Participation

Reciprocally positive resident-visitor interaction is a defining feature of both small and creative tourism, and the Devil's Nest Festival is no exception. Nagyharsány, being the central festival village, has more tasks and responsibilities than the smaller villages, which host fewer activities. The municipality is responsible for street cleaning, waste removal, repairs, electricity supplies, portable toilets, and toilet paper stocks. Between 100 and 120 sacks of garbage are collected daily at the festival. According to the mayor, while the tourism tax growth during the festival provides a small municipal income, there is no positive financial benefit for the municipality's participation in the festival, but then neither is that the objective. As he says, "It has to ripen like an apple so that it can be harvested when the time comes." In addition to the municipality, the local Association for Nagyharsány is responsible for organizing the campground at the sports field in the village. The income the association derives from festival-related tasks is spent on community development, such as on toys for the local kindergarten in 2017.

Participation of the local population in the festival is very high, thanks to the favourable conditions provided for local residents. The regular 12,000 HUF full pass (EUR 40) costs residents only 2,000 HUF (EUR 7). In addition, the streets, roads, and squares, which are usually empty during the off-season, become crowded with people from all over the country and abroad, and there are activities on almost every corner. Concerts and theatre pieces are included in festival passes, and resident attendance—with or without a pass—at these events is free of charge, again enhancing social inclusion. The mayor estimates that about 800 of the 1,500 residents visited at least one festival location during the 2017 event.

Most of the festival program includes national and international artists, but the local culture is also represented in various ways. Nagyharsány's local folk dance group has performed for three consecutive years; the Seniors Club organizes barbecues and group singing, and the local rock band was also included in the program for the first time in 2017. The minority associations of the Roma population organize concerts, forums, and games to draw attention to social problems such as segregation and discrimination.

The Festival and COVID-19

COVID-19 caused the cancellation of the thirteenth edition of the Devil's Nest Festival, scheduled for 2020. With the mitigation of the first wave of the pandemic in the summer of 2020, but still without permission to organize festivals, the organizers planned to replace Devil's Nest with a long weekend mini-festival called "Devil's Day," to run 20–22 October 2020. However, this practice could only occur when the vaccination rate reached at least 50 per cent. Similarly, large-scale festivals such as OZORA, for example, also organized "back-up events" resembling the original but with a considerably lower number of participants. The aim was, on the one hand, to provide an opportunity for artists who had lost their jobs and income during the pandemic, and, on the other, to reduce, at least partly, the loss of tourism income for the local communities. Although the preparations had begun, the second wave of the virus in the autumn eventually thwarted the organization of these initiatives.

In 2021, large-scale festivals were all still cancelled in Hungary, but the Devil's Nest Festival, being small, could be held on the usual dates in the first week of August. The motto of the 2021 edition was "Exceeding Ourselves," clearly referring the festival's resilience in the face of all the difficulties created by the pandemic. While the event was very similar to previous years, it was considerably less crowded, because most events could only be attended with the presentation of a COVID-19 immunity card. Children had to be accompanied by vaccinated adults even at the free children programs.

Conclusion

The Devil's Nest Festival (Ördögkatlan Fesztivál) is a cultural and music festival that has operated since 2008 in one of the most underdeveloped, rural areas of Hungary. It takes place over four small villages and with the participation of two wine cellars, with twenty-seven locations at the festival's height in 2017. The economy of the small villages traditionally relies on primary stone mining and cement production, grape production and winemaking, and wine tourism (based on the Villány-Siklós Wine Route). The festival has fundamentally changed this situation by creating new tourism products and thereby complementing the region's traditional wine tourism with cultural festival tourism. The festival has also elevated the profile of the small participating villages. It has shown an outstanding growth in visitor numbers, having started at 5,000 in 2008 and reaching 85,000 national and international visitors in 2018, proving that local cultural assets, both tangible and intangible, in small places can attract tourists. Unlike traditional summer music festival culture, Devil's Nest promotes a meaningful local experience based on authentic cultural values. Ördögkatlan events are held in central places in the villages to promote interaction with the local communities. The local wine cellars and municipalities are part of the organization as they do not only provide venues but accommodation as well. Tasks are allocated to non-governmental organizations to redistribute the profit generated during the festival for local development. For the only grocery shop and second-hand clothes shop in the main festival village, Nagyharsány, as well as for the private homes that register as local accommodation providers, the festival has become an important complementary source of income during the month of August.

The festival's name refers to a myth related to the symbol of the surrounding natural reserve, Szársomlyó hill, which highlights the organizers' view that in order to create an authentic experience, tourist events should reflect the origins of the place. As interactivity and community-led planning and participation are among the chief festival objectives, various new creative forms of artistic expression have been developed in which local entrepreneurs, visitors, and residents actively co-create, mostly by means of open-air performances, with minimal design and accessories, drawing on local resources. Furthermore, one exemplary festival fundraising initiative has successfully engaged both visitors and residents in a cultural sustainability initiative.

While the 2020 edition was cancelled due to the pandemic, a smaller 2021 edition was successfully held, despite all the organizational challenges related to health and safety measures. Tourism experiences in which the small local community is deeply engaged, and which are based on that community's own tangible and intangible cultural assets, can become sustainable such that, as in the case of the Devil's Nest Festival, not even COVID-19 can erode them.

NOTE

1   https://villanyiborvidek.hu.

References

Chhabra, Deepak, Robert Healy, and Erin Sills. 2003. "Staged Authenticity and Heritage Tourism." *Annals of Tourism Research* 30, no. 3: 702–19.

Crompton, John L., and Stacey L. Mckay. 1997. "Motives of Visitors Attending Festival Events." *Annals of Tourism Research* 24, no. 2: 425–39.

Getz, Donald. 1997. *Event Management and Event Tourism*. New York: Cognizant Communication.

Gordin, Valery, and Marina Matetskaya. 2012. "Creative Tourism in Saint Petersburg: The State of the Art." *Journal of Tourism Consumption and Practice* 4, no. 2: 55–77.

Ling, Ma, and Alan A. Lew. 2012. "Historical and Geographical Context in Festival Tourism Development." *Journal of Heritage Tourism* 7, no. 1: 13–31.

Ohridska-Olson, Rossitza, and Stanislav Ivanov. 2010. "Creative Tourism Business Model and Its Application in Bulgaria." *Proceedings of the Black Sea Tourism Forum "Cultural Tourism—The Future of Bulgaria,"* 12 October 2010. https://ssrn.com/abstract=1690425.

Prentice, Richard. 2001. "Experiential Cultural Tourism: Museums and the Marketing of the New Romanticism of Evoked Authenticity." *Museum Management and Curatorship* 19:5–26.

Prentice, Richard, and Vivien Andersen. 2003. "Festival as Creative Destination." *Annals of Tourism Research* 30, no. 1: 7–30.

Richards, Greg. 2011. "Creativity and Tourism: The State of the Art." *Annals of Tourism Research* 38, no. 4: 1225–53.

———. 2020. "Designing Creative Places: The Role of Creative Tourism." *Annals of Tourism Research* 85, no. 1. https://doi.org/10.1016/j.annals.2020.102922.

Richards, Greg, and Julie Wilson. 2006. "Developing Creativity in Tourist Experiences: A Solution to the Serial Reproduction of Culture." *Tourism Management* 27, no. 6: 1209–23.

Saayman, Melville, and Andrea Saayman. 2006. "Does the Location of Arts Festivals Matter for the Economic Impact?" *Regional Science* 85, no. 4: 569–84.

Steiner, Carol, and Yvette Reisinger. 2006. "Understanding Existential Authenticity." *Annals of Tourism Research* 33, no. 2: 299–318.

Thrane, Christer. 2002. "Jazz Festival Visitors and Their Expenditures: Linking Spending Patterns to Musical Interest." *Journal of Travel Research* 40, no. 3: 281–6.

Van Heerden, Adriette. 2003. "Economic Impact of the Aardklop National Arts Festival." Master's thesis, Potchefstroom University for CHE, Potchefstroom.

Artistic Micro-Adventures in Small Places

Donald Lawrence

Introduction

In 2014 I was invited to contribute a project to Art Marathon, an annual festival of artists' projects and events organized by Eastern Edge Gallery in St. John's, Newfoundland. Since renamed "Holdfast," the festival presented a dynamic mix of activities in and around the gallery, including the ground level of an adjacent parkade, and at off-site locations around the older part of town. Being a participating artist during Art Marathon parallels my experience of participating in two other similar events: in 2008 as a participating artist in Ice Follies, a biennale organized by the W. K. P. Kennedy Gallery in North Bay, Ontario, and as the lead artist/researcher of the Midnight Sun Camera Obscura Festival, realized in Dawson City, Yukon, in 2015, in partnership with the Klondike Institute of Art and Culture. A consideration of what these three events may offer for small tourism in small places—for the opportunity presented by such art-activated activities—is what I take up here. I do not undertake anything like a sociological study of tourists' responses to these projects. Rather, I am drawing upon what I have created as my own contributions to these events, what I have observed of visitors' interactions with these projects, and a sampling of other projects and visitors' responses to them from these same events.

These three events have much in common, including a basic interest in bringing a performative dimension to the viewer's experience; each of the events takes a chance on foregrounding projects that are being realized for the first time, effectively collapsing the idea of experimentation and dissemination into a single moment. Often, there is no rehearsal. For both the artist and the viewer there is something adventurous in this and the condensed duration of events like these suggests a parallel to the "micro-adventure," a term and a pursuit made popular in 2014 by the British adventurer Alastair Humphreys. A micro-adventure is characterized as having "the spirit (and therefore the benefits) of a big adventure; it's just all condensed into a weekend away, or even a midweek escape from the office" (2014, 14). The way that viewers, including tourists, are invited to take a chance on entering into something unexpected, sometimes becoming participants themselves, is in the spirit of Humphreys' idea, to push people to take the chance to experience something outside their comfort zones.

By way of these events, tourists and other "normal people with real lives" are given, or sometimes stumble upon, the opportunity to learn something of contemporary art, a realm that they may consider to be for other people, but that they might welcome and perhaps engage in when encountering it unexpectedly.

For the purposes of this contribution I am taking "tourists" to be those who have come from somewhere other than the host communities of these arts events. Typically this may mean a small number of such visitors, perhaps at times not many more than the collective number of event organizers and participating artists themselves. In this case, several opportunities and challenges may be kept in mind. First, the context of this volume may simply be a good opportunity to call attention to such arts events as these for practitioners and scholars of tourism, in the hopes of interesting tourism promoters in small arts festivals. Second, in some respects, these sorts of events work best because they are organized by a small collaborative network in a local community, including artists, and perhaps some artists from other places. The tourists, maybe small in number, who purposefully or otherwise find themselves in the middle of such events, will experience something special, something genuinely experimental and/or local in conception—often a one-time-only experience. Third, though the artists and curators who come from away to participate in such events may not be tourists in the typical sense, they are often highly engaged visitors to such communities, contributing to local economies and intent on building important linkages between small places, networks comprising members of an extended cultural community, which may be an important ingredient for the sustainability of small tourism in small places.

My own artistic practice in recent years includes two primary interests. First, it is an exploration of simple, pre-photographic optical principles and apparatuses, including the creation of projects that invite participants to gain an embodied, multi-sensory experience of early image formation. Second, in some of these projects, I look at the meeting place of urban culture—of art, early forms of popular entertainment, etc.—and the culture of outdoor recreation, for which Humphreys' concept of the micro-adventure is particularly analogous in some instances. The specific, historical form of the public camera obscura informs some of the projects that I consider in this contribution, so an explanation of these structures is a good place to start.

Cameras Obscura

Latin for "dark room," a camera obscura is in essence a darkened space into which light is admitted by way of a lens or open aperture, with an image of whatever surrounds the structure cast inside by this simple means, much like the formation of an image inside one's own eye. The projected image will be upside down and inverted, cast on a wall or cast downwards onto a circular table via a mirror, and perhaps with a rotating optical apparatus to provide a moving, panoramic image. In its simple form as a darkened room, the camera obscura's image represents an early form of optical projection, the forerunner of all such optical technology developed over the past five hundred years or so, and smaller, portable cameras obscura are the forerunner of the modern camera. Knowledge of this history is of course not essential to know in relation to most contemporary artistic practices that a visitor will encounter, but it does inform some of the artworks considered in this essay, and there is a connection to the development of modern tourism that may be mentioned here. Having emerged in Chinese, Islamic, and ancient Greek cultures, and while being an advanced imaging technology in early modern Europe, the camera obscura was eclipsed by emerging technologies—including photography—by the mid-nineteenth century. However, at just the time when the camera obscura's usefulness to science declined, modern tourism emerged in the nineteenth century with an expanding middle class, enhanced options for travel, etc. In this climate, walk-in public cameras obscura began to populate seaside and other popular locations for tourists to take in the surrounding view. If no longer "advanced technology" during the latter nineteenth century, the walk-in camera obscura was a popular means of seeing a live, moving image and doing so in advance of the invention and popularity of film over the next decade or two. Sometimes aligned with the interests of another phenomenon, that of amateur astronomers, and sometimes identified as "observatories," these early multimedia sites inhabited the tops of converted towers or took the form of small, pavilion-like buildings. Many such cameras obscura continued to be built or existed well into the twentieth century, and there are a few extant examples from around that time.

Occasionally I combine art making and related research interests with purposeful travel, with particular historical sites as a destination. In the pre-COVID summer of 2019 I made such a trip, visiting and studying cameras obscura in Greenwich and Bristol and on the Isle of Man, creating studies and detailed measurements of these places along the way. The Clifton Observatory in Bristol is a good and extant example of a nineteenth-century camera obscura in which visitors wind their way to the top of a repurposed tower, entering into a darkened space at the top. A circular, and slightly dish-shaped table fills the middle of the space, with an image of the surrounding landscape projected across its surface. The image is cast by way of a simple optical housing at the top of the tower, comprising a mirror and one or more lenses, with the optical housing being rotated 360 degrees. Captivating today for the very lucid, somewhat dream-like quality of the projected image that results when an image is pure light, unmediated by anything more than the lens and mirror, the effect would likely have been even more alluring for the burgeoning number of tourists in the nineteenth century, with these early spectacles of media culture emerging alongside the still new medium of photography, the photographic album, and the yet-to-emerge medium of film. The postcards seen here of the Clifton Observatory and the interior of a similar camera obscura in Dumfries, Scotland (in which an attendant continues the long-standing practice of offering a guided tour of the town by way the projected image), also evidences the role that the production and circulation of printed images has played in the network of tourist sites that includes these cameras obscura.

Playing off the tradition of such structures I realized the Nanton Camera Obscura in partnership with the University of Lethbridge Art Gallery between 2016 and 2019, at the university's Coutt's Centre for Western Canadian Heritage, on a farm a few miles east of Nanton, Alberta. Nanton is a centre for the surrounding farming communities and a popular tourist destination for its many antique stores, historical buildings and museums, and for its general smalltown appeal. I've had the opportunity to show the camera obscura to

Figure 8.1: Great Union Camera Obscura (1892), Douglas Head, Isle of Man.

Source: On-site journal study by author, 2019.

Figure 8.2: Clifton Observatory and Camera Obscura (1828), Bristol, England, postcard, ca. 1900.

Source: Author.

many visitors, whether they have come from such close-by centres as Calgary and Lethbridge or from anywhere else.

What is experienced inside is a surprise for most visitors, particularly as the outward appearance of the structure is generally utilitarian, a corrugated steel grain bin similar in design to ones seen across the farmlands, but small in comparison to most for being one of the earliest on the western Prairies, dating to 1927. Some visitors first wonder about the system of rough gearing on the roof, and perhaps see the optical structure at the top rotating if others are inside already operating the gearing. The rotating lens seems to be as much a magnet to bring people inside as the nearby, somewhat jovial roadside making the claim that this is the "World's Most Corrugated Camera Obscura" (punning off the language and visual culture of tourism learned

Figure 8.3: Dumfries Camera Obscura (1836), Dumfries, Scotland, postcard, ca. 1970s.

Source: Author.

early, during family road trips). Once inside, visitors experience something else, as Louise Barrett has described:

> Once the door is closed . . . and the room darkens, the space is utterly transformed: an image suddenly appears before you on the table—an image that seems to glow from within, with a brilliant, painterly quality. There is a moment of genuine wonder as you realize that the prairie grasses in this "painting" are actually blowing gently in the wind, and you recognize that what you're seeing is not a still life, but the moving image of the landscape outside. (2021, 289)

Figure 8.4: Donald Lawrence, "Nanton Camera Obscura," Coutts Centre for Western Canadian Heritage, Nanton, Alberta, 2019.

Source: Author.

Entering the camera obscura is for some visitors an easy decision, while for others it is taking a chance. Many, perhaps most, first-time visitors do not know what is inside but come away with a new experience. Interior signage, information handouts, and, for some, guided tours offer visitors the opportunity to learn something of the basic principles of image formation, including in the human eye, the historical roots of the imaging devices and technology that are so ubiquitous today, and how such structures relate to the origins of modern tourism. Thus "entertainment"—the default assumption of traditional tourism's objective—and the more contemporary tourism interests of education and transformation are brought together as one experience, something that visitors may not anticipate upon first seeing the old grain bin.

I have seen this working best at the Coutts Centre during events programmed by Josephine Mills, curator of the University of Lethbridge Art Gallery. Mills has worked carefully to create events that will not only bring artists and scholars together but that will do so in a way that is welcoming to broad audiences, including visitors to the centre. An example is the 2016 Prairie Sun Festival, which saw the first opening of the then in-process camera obscura. Such curatorial impulses extend the realms of artistic creation outside the confines of the art gallery in a way that is paralleled and contextualized by looking to arts festivals organized by art galleries, particularly those staged in small places.

Ice Follies: Celebrating the Peripheral

Ice Follies was imagined by Dermot Wilson, curator of the W. K. P. Kennedy Art Gallery, and first realized in 2004. Ice Follies is rooted in the landscape and culture of North Bay, two hundred miles north of Toronto. As Wilson relates, the Follies "began simply about the place, a white-on-white canvas," and he observes that "small places have space" (Wilson, interview with author, 7 July 2021). With the vast expanse of frozen Lake Nipissing in mind, Dermot's observation is an interesting one, something of an inversion of the principles embedded in the source of his metaphor, Kazimir Malevich's 1918 *Suprematist Composition: White on White*. Whereas Malevich's small canvas, arguably a key instance in the development of abstract painting, invokes a purity and distance from the concerns of daily life, Wilson turned exactly to daily life, looking to what he characterizes as "the architecture of ice fishing huts" (Wilson, interview), at the daily pursuits and subcultures of North Bay. He understood that such an approach to community-based arts events goes against the grain of mainstream art practices:

> At the time, the Canada Council[11] saw Ice Follies as anomalous. There weren't so many projects going out into nature; setting up projects in nature made sense—in the place and in the culture of the place. So, the Council considered that Ice Follies would match the culture and that the W. K. P. Kennedy Art Gallery could actually do this. (Wilson, interview)

There are three dimensions to what Wilson recounts of the Canada Council's support of Ice Follies that are important to the success of such arts events and to their contribution to small-place tourism. First, the cultural activity must be true to the place: smaller communities will have a closer-knit identity and local traditions. Second, the Canada Council seeks to fund projects that, even if unusual, are likely to succeed; it recognized that the W. K. P.

Figure 8.5: Donald Lawrence, "One Eye Folly" (in tow on Lake Nipissing), camera obscura, Ice Follies, North Bay, Ontario, 2008. Source: Peter Nickle.

Figure 8.6: Christine Charette and Jeremy Bean, "Rewind in Fast Forward," installation (on Lake Nipissing), Ice Follies, North Bay, Ontario, 2008. Source: Author.

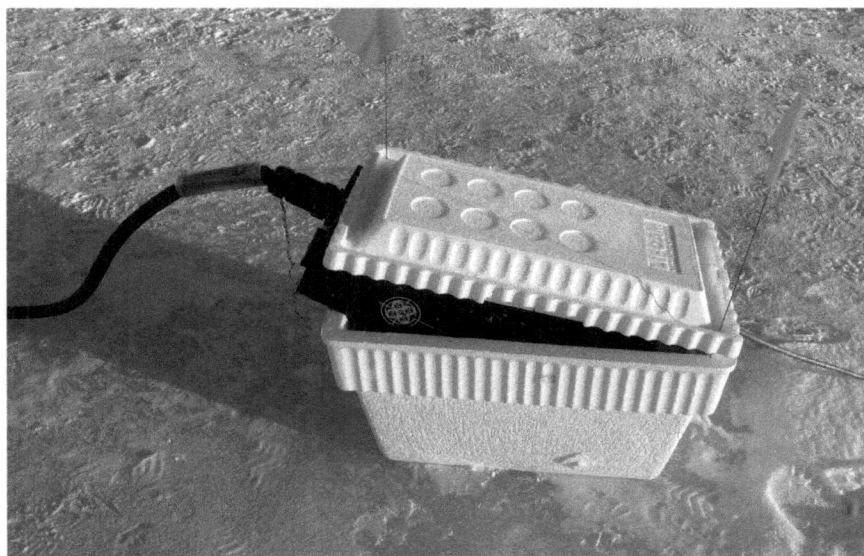

Figures 8.7a and 8.7b: Peter Nickle, "Ice Cracks," installation (on Lake Nipissing), Ice Follies, North Bay, Ontario, 2008. Source: Author.

Kennedy Gallery, its community members and partners, are woven throughout the broader landscape and subcultures of North Bay, where everyone knows everyone (or at least someone), which creates a network that can enable projects to happen. Third, if there is an expectation of appealing to and engaging a broader audience, things must not stay too insular, and Wilson understood that, even if hosted in a small place, there was a "need to be able to show that this was a national exhibition" (Wilson, interview). How can such an annual event unfold in North Bay, and yet become tangible for the artists, the community, and to visitors? While the proportion of participating artists from the North Bay region versus those from elsewhere across the country varies from year to year, there is always a balance of the two. This serves to keep the Follies rooted in the community, while at the same time enjoying a national profile and significance. As an artist coming from British Columbia, the following is what I experienced and observed.

In the immediate lead-up to the opening day, I worked in a temporary warehouse studio setting alongside a few of the other artists, variously creating their projects or, as in my case, assembling the pieces of the sculptural follies that we had created, partially disassembled, and shipped to North Bay. A few of the other artists were out on the ice constructing their projects on-site, two of them involving the casting/freezing of ice or, like the activity of ice fishing, drilling through the ice to the lake below. The last thing I did in the studio was to construct a simple sled to get my "One Eye Folly" onto the ice. Through the day before the opening, local resident and outfitter Baden Brownlee employed his 1950s Bombardier snow bus to pull several of the structures onto the ice—an informal parade of sorts and itself a community event that signals the lead-up to the Follies each year. After spending the day on the ice finishing up the installation of my project and visiting the other artists as they did the same, I camped out, sleeping on the ice and listening to the booming sound as it cracked through the night. From that experience I came to understand something of the sounds and characteristics of that landscape, sounds that Peter Nickle planned to capture, recompose, and broadcast from "Ice Cracks," the mobile sound lab that he had created, with its customized microphones embedded in the ice. Then in the morning, the visitors to the festival arrived, walking out onto the ice and speaking with the artists or taking in the fun of the snow bus as Baden toured visitors around the projects all day long. In the evening there was a large gathering and dinner attended by the artists, a mix of community members, and particularly

Figure 8.8: Donald Lawrence, "One Eye Folly," camera obscura (on Lake Nipissing), Ice Follies, North Bay, Ontario, 2008.

Source: Author.

engaged festival visitors. The evening was semi-structured, an opportunity for Wilson and the artists to speak to their projects, but also an opportunity for informal gathering and celebration. It was an eclectic group that gathered that evening in North Bay, reminding me at the time of what I had seen a few years previously, in 2004, in another relatively small place, Dawson City, and that I kept in mind a few years later when planning the 2015 Midnight Sun Camera Obscura Festival.

I am used to art gallery openings in which a couple of hundred people gather, as well as ones where just a small number of people gather. I was not expecting what I saw at Ice Follies. At the end of the day I expressed to Dermot Wilson how surprised I was that perhaps 150 to 200 people showed up at the "One Eye Folly," a half-mile off shore. In reply, Wilson said that the day's overall turnout had reached 750, and from the discussions that I had throughout the day, I knew that at least a modest number of visitors travelled to North Bay for the event.

This speaks to both the opportunity and the challenge of small-place art festivals such as this. It is clearly evident from my experience at Ice Follies, Art Marathon, and the Midnight Sun Camera Obscura Festival that those from away—tourists—can become highly engaged by such off-site projects, including some visitors who come upon the events unexpectedly. These visitors became fully engaged in dimensions of the local landscape and community in a manner that is different from what is offered by mainstream tourism. On the other hand, despite finding visitors who come upon such projects unexpectedly, it is true that the most potentially responsive and engaged of those who take in such events are themselves already dedicated members of the arts community. This is not a bad thing. Every cultural activity has its core followers, and it is important to note that they themselves effectively become "tourists" as they travel from place to place to participate in exhibitions, music events, or theatre festivals, etc., with small places often the location of some of the favoured venues. Observing that there is an insular dimension to the audience for such events is, especially in the context of the present volume, a call to those working in and studying tourism to look more closely, and more regularly, at these sorts of events and to consider the increased role that they may play in (small) place promotion.

Art Marathon: Micro-Adventure, Micro-Festival

One of Canada's longer-running artist-run centres, Eastern Edge Gallery sits near the harbour, the kind of place that a small number of tourists will seek out and that others may come upon as they wander around the older part of St. John's, Newfoundland. In 1999 the staff and community of artists supporting Eastern Edge opened the gallery's first twenty-four-hour Art Marathon event, effectively enacting an art-world version and precursor to Alastair Humphreys's micro-adventures, with artists gathering to create and exhibit artworks through the day and night. I was invited to participate in the by then long-running event in 2014, which had by this time been reinvented as a "Spectacular 5 day Extravaganza of Art Music and Performance" (Eastern Edge Gallery 2014).

Those attending Art Marathon in 2014 could take in, and in many respects could participate in, several kinds of activities. The gallery hosted an opening reception at which each of the invited artists gave mini-talks about their projects, and from there visitors could follow a printed map to find their way to artists' off-site and pop-up projects. Some of the projects ran through the night, including illuminated Morse code signals coming from the windows of Signal Hill's Cabot Tower as part of Halifax-based artist Michael McCormack's "Beacon," and Baltimore-based artist Rachael Shannon's inflatable "Breastival Vestibule," which became a welcoming and communal space for discussion and relaxation through the duration of the festival. Eastern Edge was a hub of activity, with artists creating components of off-site projects inside, while outside festival goers could take in Sara Tilley's "Wiener Temple," in which performances were enacted throughout the festival inside the playful, circus-like temple constructed of cardboard and fabrics by Tilley, Kyle Bustin, and Elling Lien. The ground floor of an adjacent parkade was used by local artists for the Art Marathon proper that represents the origins of this event: a twenty-four-hour period in which participating artists created artworks that were then put up for auction. Charmaine Wheatley's artists' parade wound its way through the streets, culminating in a performance composed of local artists, volunteers, and—memorably—at least one enthusiastic visitor.

For me, Art Marathon provided the opportunity to create the floating "Quidi Vidi Camera Obscura" that participants would enter into and paddle through in sea kayaks to take in a projected image of Quidi Vidi Gut, the small harbour and village a mile or so from downtown, a popular spot for tourists in St. John's. The opportunity to imagine and realize this project combined the heightened sensory experience of entering a camera obscura[22] with the basic ingredients of a micro-adventure for participants. Through the one-day event, a crew of volunteers assisted a steady stream of people suiting up and getting into kayaks while I and a local kayaker ensured their safe return from their camera obscura adventure. Locating the experience of a sea kayak mini-adventure to the floating artwork of the Quidi Vidi Harbour was a means of enacting a small-tourism experience for viewers in a way that drew upon and extended my experience of participating in Ice Follies, and it coincided with my planning toward Dawson City's Midnight Sun Camera Obscura Festival for the next year, as discussed below.

An added dimension to such projects as these is the opportunity to be welcomed into the small cultural communities that congregate around places like Eastern Edge. My experience in the projects I document here is that visitors from outside the host communities—tourists—have the unique opportunity to become fully immersed in the experience and fully engaged in small tourism in a small place. One example stands out. Bradley Peters,

Figures 8.9a and 8.9b: Sara Tilley, Kyle Bustin, Elling Lien, "Wiener Sugar Dance Magic," construction by Kyle Bustin, performance by Sara Tilley and Kira Sheppard, Art Marathon, St. John's, Newfoundland, 2014. Source: Author.

Figures 8.10a and 8.10b: Charmaine Wheatley, "What Is the Role of Women?," performance, sculpture, dance, painting, writing, printed matter, Art Marathon, St. John's, Newfoundland, 2014.

Source: Author.

Figure 8.11: Rachael Shannon, "Breastival Vestibule," inflatable installation, Art Marathon, St. John's, Newfoundland, 2014.

Source: Author.

from British Columbia's Lower Mainland, arrived in St. John's the day before I did. As a tourist, he found himself staying in one of the homes along the harbour in the historic Battery area, the same home in which I was billeted. Asking casually about the nature of my project, Peters soon became my most dedicated volunteer helper over the next few days. As a construction worker, Peters gravitated to the pile of two-by-fours that were to be assembled into the camera obscura's framework, all of them to be lashed together with rope, much of which was donated by the fishermen living and working in the stages adjacent to the launch site. Adapting to the method of using rope for my structure rather than the usual methods of his trade, Peters offered the observation that "there don't seem to be any rules." He was referring to my structure but also, I think, to the arts festival as a whole. This of course is not quite true; Peters likely recognized the extent of organizing, planning, and dedication that made Art Marathon a success. Perhaps he really meant

Figure 8.12: Curator Mary MacDonald entering Donald Lawrence's "Quidi Vidi Camera Obscura," Art Marathon, St. John's, Newfoundland, 2014. Source: Author.

Figure 8.13: Traveller Bradley Peters lashing together the framework of the "Quidi Vidi Camera Obscura," Art Marathon, St. John's, Newfoundland, 2014. Source: Author

that his full immersion in the festival community was free from the tropes of traditional tourism. In varying ways and in varying degrees, such events as these welcome and encourage visitors to engage in the experience at hand in different ways, to not stand back as passive observers.

Kai Bryan, one of the festival's key volunteers in 2014, and more recently the executive director of St. John's Storytelling Festival, considers St. John's to be a "medium-small place," the determining factor being scale. Large by comparison to Bryan's outport hometown of Ferryland, St. John's is small in comparison to places such as Toronto. Bringing knowledge of large-city cultural experiences and infrastructure after moving back to Newfoundland from Toronto in 2012, Bryan joins others in recognizing the efforts and successes that Eastern Edge's director/curator at the time, the late Mary McDonald (1985–2017), made toward creating connections to art practices from across the country. Bryan recalls that McDonald succeeded not only in connecting Eastern Edge Gallery to the national community but, at the same time, sought to make the gallery "almost as much like a community living room as an art space" (interview with author, 20 August 2021). There is both significant opportunity and challenge for arts organizations around such ambitions, including where they intersect the interests of tourism. As Bryan relates, McDonald came from a small community herself—Pictou, Nova Scotia—and studied art making in small communities. While such organizations as Eastern Edge Gallery are explicit in seeking to engage a tourist audience—such objectives were built into funding proposals for Art Marathon—the challenge "of running arts festivals in small places" that Bryan identifies is to not misrepresent a region and its cultural traditions, that "there is a knife edge" (Bryan, interview) dividing what may be a meaningful encounter between outside engagement with smaller communities and a too superficial, or even too exploitive, approach to welcoming visitors. Even in Quidi Vidi itself, and though I felt welcomed into the community, it is not difficult to see where such concern can lie, with gentrification increasingly transforming this small enclave, as well as other places in the bays more distant from St. John's.

Midnight Sun Camera Obscura Festival: Big Culture, Small Place

Where I grew up in Victoria, British Columbia, a neighbour's van featured a bumper sticker that boasted, as I recall, "We drove the Alaska Highway.

Yes dammit, the whole way!" The great North American adventure of this particular road trip has been a goal of many tourists since the mid-twenti-eth century. Though made easier by way of upgrades to the original "Alcan" highway over the decades, the appeal is still there, with Yukon's Dawson City (population 1,400) as a primary destination for tourists. For many, perhaps for most, but with varying degrees of comfort, luxury, or travel time, the ap-peal of the journey to Dawson City that has lingered since the Klondike gold rush, and its unique culture of place promotion even as early as the 1890s, is still present.

Much of the architecture of Dawson City remains from the gold rush per-iod, with many buildings carefully preserved by Parks Canada. Some build-ings, including West's Boiler Shop, are maintained in a way that preserves evidence of their weathering over the years, a sort of perpetual time capsule of the image of the boomtown present at the time that tourists began venturing there on the gravel highway in the 1950s.

The highway crosses the Yukon River at Dawson City by way of the *George Black* ferry. Beside the ferry landing at West Dawson and around the time of the 2015 summer solstice, Lea Bucknell's "False Front" existed as one of nine off-site projects that were part of the Midnight Sun Camera Obscura Festival. Considered by Bucknell to be a laterally compressed version of West's Boiler Shop, "False Front" referenced the facades of commercial buildings en-trenched in frontier town architecture by the 1890s, at the same time as allud-ing to the jovial gesture of the entire facade of "False Front" swinging open on oversized hinges to let visitors into the shed-like structure. Once inside, the glittering gold-clad exterior gave way to an inverted optical projection filling the back wall of the structure, facilitated by an eyeglass lens set into the oversized front door. This provided viewers not only with a multi-sensory ex-perience akin to simple walk-in cameras obscura of pre-photographic times, but also an image of the real town of Dawson City across the river, effectively unadorned by the imagery of the town's gold rush past that is otherwise an ever-present tourism strategy in Dawson City.

Working with the Klondike Institute of Art and Culture (KIAC), and with funding from the Social Sciences and Research Council of Canada, as well as the Canada Council for the Arts, the festival was realized in 2015. Its origins, however, were in 2004, when a few of us imagined the idea following the success of a "48hr Pinhole Photography Workshop" led by Whitehorse-based photographer Mario Villeneuve, that saw KIAC and its darkrooms as

Figures 8.14a and 8.14b: Lea Bucknell, "False Front," (exterior view and interior projection), camera obscura, Midnight Sun Camera Obscura Festival, Dawson City, Yukon, 2015.

Source: Lea Bucknell.

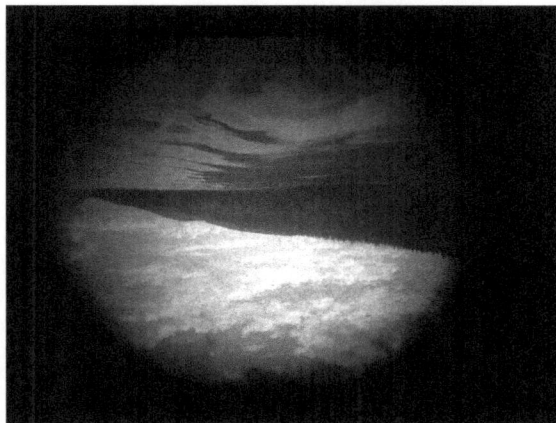

Figures 8.15a, 8.15b, and 8.15c: Donald Lawrence, "George Black Camera Obscura" (overall view, interior projection, canoeists viewing interior projection), camera obscura on *George Black* ferry, Midnight Sun Camera Obscura Festival, Dawson City, Yukon, 2015.

Source: Author.

Figure 8.16: Bo Yeung. "Hold Tight, Keep It Adrift," off-site project for the . . . *strange things done* . . . exhibition, Midnight Sun Camera Obscura Festival, Dawson City, Yukon, 2015. Source: Author.

a base for participants to create and use simple DIY cameras. In a manner that has obvious affinities with Ice Follies and Art Marathon, this 2004 event included such adventures as a couple of participants driving their van north along the (still gravel) Dempster Highway to the Tombstone Mountains, turning the van into a giant darkened pinhole camera, and then returning to KIAC to process their large-scale exposed photographic paper, however having to repeat that process a time or two in order to achieve a successful image.

Learning from these and the other collective experiences, an international team met in Dawson City in 2014 to plan the next year's events. The team included artists, scholars of optics and science in early modern Europe, researchers on the entertainment culture that emerged through the nineteenth century, an education theorist and wilderness canoeist, curators, several undergraduate research assistants, and recent visual arts alumni. Alongside the off-site projects the festival included a gallery-based exhibition of related

Figure 8.17: S. S. *Klondike* Workshop (participants with drawings and drawing inside temporary camera obscura), with the Yukon Arts Centre, Whitehorse, Yukon, 2015.

Source: Author.

works by the team's artists and . . . *strange things done* . . . , an exhibition in the Yukon School of Visual Arts (SOVA) of projects created by the festival research assistants; a series of artists' talks, lectures, and panel discussions in KIAC's former ballroom; and a series of public workshops. One such workshop, "Pretty Noisy," was initiated by research assistant Eliza Houg with the specific and successful intent of engaging the youth community, which is a key part of the vibrancy of Dawson City in the summer. A student of the Nova Scotia College of Art and Design University at the time, Houg was herself an alumna of SOVA; working with such locally engaged individuals is crucial to the success of such events in small places, and the scale of Dawson City is right for projects such as this.

Conclusion: Participating in the Community

The social networks that Eliza Houg and her peer group activated through their hosting of the Pretty Noisy workshop in Dawson City is indicative of the level of community networking and engagement that lies behind the success of the activities in Dawson City and the other arts festivals examined here. In their 2021 analysis of the importance of small-scale arts festivals in Portugal, Fiona Eva Bakas and colleagues recognize similar patterns, foregrounding the way in which "local residents (and often the visiting participants themselves) also engage in activities such as volunteering to help in the running of the festival as well as practices of mutual aid in the form of cooperating with artists to create artistic performances" (12). As a participating artist in Ice Follies and during the early planning stages of the Midnight Sun Camera Obscura Festival, the first part of Bakas's observation was familiar to me—the importance of the local community and social networks in the success of small-place arts festivals. What is particularly resonant for me is Bakas's allusion to the potential of "visiting participants," for the way that it recalls the experience during the Art Marathon on Canada's East Coast of seeing Bradley Peters, a hitchhiker arriving by chance that week from the West Coast, becoming a key enabler and participant of my own and other artists' projects through the duration of the festival. Bakas makes the case that

> small-scale local festivals also act as development frameworks for creative tourism activities. The integration of creative tourism activities, which are defined as experiences that include elements of active participation, creative self-expression, connection to place, and community engagement. (12)

The intent of the present contribution is to argue that these attributes are already built into the lived experience of many small-scale arts festivals in small places, that if the value of such an approach is recognized, then the broader context in which such artworks exist, a context that includes such surprising small arts festivals as North Bay's Ice Follies and St. John's Art Marathon (now Holdfast), may also be considered as successful examples of small tourism in small places. This is an opportunity to encourage tourists to engage in current, often experimental, dimensions of contemporary art, to take a chance on participating in an art micro-adventure. The challenge is to move past or through assumptions that such practices are the preserve of small sub-communities, to not wait until the energy of such events is domesticated through processes of normalization and gentrification. It is perhaps in small but culturally savvy settings that this can happen best, where a visitor may step into a new place one day and potentially be an active part of it the next.

NOTES

1   The Canada Council for the Arts is the primary funding agency for artistic practices in Canada.

2   For further reading on the experiential nature of walk-in cameras obscura, see for example Sven Dupré, "The Camera Obscura on the Move: Body, Animation, Imagination, in *Art, Research, Play: The Midnight Sun Camera Obscura Project*, ed. Donald Lawrence, Josephine Mills, and Emily Dundas-Oke (Lethbridge, AB: University of Lethbridge Art Gallery, 2021), 183–95.

References

Bakas, Fiona Eva, Nancy Duxbury, Paula Remoaldo and Olga Matos. 2019. "Social Utility of Small-Scale Art Festivals with Creative Tourism in Portugal." *International Journal of Event and Festival Management* 10, no. 3: 248–66. https://doi. org/10.1108/IJEFM-02-2019-0009.

Barrett, Louise. 2021. "Poking and Prying with a Purpose: The Working Art of Donald Lawrence." In *Art, Research, Play: The Midnight Sun Camera Obscura Project*, ed. Donald Lawrence, Josephine Mills, and Emily Dundas Oke, 285–99. Lethbridge: University of Lethbridge Art Gallery.

Eastern Edge Gallery. 2014. Art Marathon Poster. St. John's, NL: Eastern Edge Gallery.

Humphreys, Alistair. 2014. *Microadventures: Local Discoveries for Great Escapes*. London: Harper Collins.

The Power of Small: Creative In-Migrant Micro-Entrepreneurs in Peripheral Japanese Islands during COVID-19

Meng Qu and Simona Zollet

Introduction

Population decline, out-migration, and ageing in peripheral rural areas are issues of concern in many countries. Japanese rural communities disproportionately suffer from these issues, given Japan's status as the first "hyper-ageing" society (Manzenreiter, Lützeler, and Polak-Rottmann 2020). As a response to the depopulation issue, in recent years the Japanese government has been attempting to promote domestic urban-to-rural migration and new economic activities in rural areas. Many rural in-migrants are engaged in tourism, creative professions, and local revitalization projects that creatively engage with and enhance local communities' cultural, social, and environmental resources (Cunha, Kastenholz, and Carneiro 2020; Qu, Coulton, and Funck 2020). There is, however, a persisting tendency to focus mainly on the economic outcomes of in-migration, tourism, and rural entrepreneurship (Kalantaridis 2010; Stockdale 2006), both in policy and research. This contrasts with the growing literature on the contribution of small businesses to rural communities' quality of life (Olmedo, Twuijver, and O'Shaughnessy 2021). Furthermore, it has been suggested that in smaller communities tourism can be developed more sustainably, including through creative approaches (Baixinho et al. 2020; Richards 2021). Research on rural resilience and revitalization processes driven by creative in-migrant entrepreneurs is therefore becoming more valuable.

In addition to the common problems with socio-economic decline faced by many rural regions, the COVID-19 pandemic has brought further negative impacts to peripheral areas that depend on tourism. COVID-19, however, offers an unprecedented opportunity to examine how small-scale, creative tourism initiatives are responding to the disruptions caused by the pandemic. The double challenge micro-businesses are facing is how to maintain vital tourism flows in peripheral and resource-constrained communities while at the same time ensuring the safety of their elderly residents.

This chapter aims to qualitatively explore the creative strategies employed by in-migrant tourism micro-entrepreneurs to increase the resilience of small tourism destinations, focusing on their dual role as both tourism businesses and community-engaged enterprises. Fieldwork was conducted at a Japanese heritage site, the town of Mitarai, located in one of the peripheral islands of Japan's Seto Inland Sea. We employed participant observation and interviews with small-scale tourism businesses both before and during the COVID-19 pandemic to describe the creative activities performed through newcomer-resident-tourist co-creation, and we highlight some representative cases to demonstrate the role of in-migrant micro-entrepreneurs in enhancing community resilience. The fieldwork carried out after the COVID pandemic began is especially useful in illustrating how "the power of small" entails a diversified and organic approach to co-creating new cultural assets while preserving community resources and social resilience. The results suggest that small-scale tourism plays a key role in community resilience in peripheral rural contexts, as well as in ensuring that revitalization goals can be pursued even in the face of unpredictable events such as COVID-19. The chapter concludes by highlighting that the power of small hinges upon creating flexible, low-cost, multi-functional tourism businesses, and upon advancing strategies for balancing both community and tourism needs. These considerations can also provide valuable lessons for the revitalization of other small rural communities around the world. Small and peripheral destinations also emerge as potential attractive destinations for entrepreneurial in-migrants in the post-pandemic world.

Why Do Creative In-Migrant Micro-Entrepreneurs Matter on Small Islands?

Approaches that focus on creative enhancement (Mitchell 2013) are more likely to occur in tourism destinations with insufficient visitation and limited resources, often in "small or isolated settings" (Mitchell 2013) characterized by small-scale events and businesses (Qu and Cheer 2021). In small-scale peripheral rural communities, especially in the Global North, research has been increasingly engaging with the role of small or micro-businesses and creative entrepreneurs (Korsgaard, Ferguson, and Gaddefors 2015; Stone and Stubbs 2007; Yachin and Ioannides 2020), with growing attention paid to their embeddedness through social innovation and network-building abilities. In the tourism sector, creative artistic entrepreneurs help to revalue the local landscape and cultural capital through tourism (Crawshaw and Gkartzios 2016; Prince 2018).

Entrepreneurs, particularly those who are in-migrants to a community, further enhance their socially embedded roles through the creation of local to extra-local networks (Bosworth and Atterton 2012). In-migrant entrepreneurs and their networks can help to establish effective linkages between visitors and new migrants, and they facilitate business integration into the local destination and regional cultural context (Stone and Stubbs 2007). In-migrant entrepreneurs' capacity to be a bridge between the local community and the outside has been described as "mixed embeddedness" (Kloosterman and Rath 2001) and "placial embeddedness" (Korsgaard, Ferguson, and Gaddefors 2015) because of their role in integrating local and extra-local resources as well as structuring social networks and capital flows. Entrepreneurs establish a relational resource exchange mode through processes of "market-exchange, redistribution and reciprocity" (Olmedo, Twuijver, and O'Shaughnessy 2021). While research has mostly focused on international in-migrant entrepreneurs, domestic urban-to-rural in-migrants also play the relational function of connecting intra-community networks with extra-local networks (Bosworth and Atterton 2012). The presence of networks of in-migrant entrepreneurs within rural communities helps to create an environment that facilitates new opportunities for sustaining rural communities (Dinis 2021).

In some cases, creative tourism entrepreneurs also play a socially and community-engaged role (Duxbury and Campbell 2011; Qu, McCormick, and Funck 2022), reflecting the broader literature on the social role of small businesses in fulfilling community needs (Barraket et al. 2019; Michaelis et al. 2020; Olmedo, Twuijver, and O'Shaughnessy 2021), thus also contributing to sustainable community development. Tourism micro-businesses founded by lifestyle in-migrants, in particular, are often both business-oriented and community-engaged, due to the fact that they focus more on lifestyle rather than economic outcomes (Cederholm 2018). As such, they play multi-faceted roles in structuring diversified innovation networks for resilience building (Michaelis et al. 2020; Qu and Cheer 2020), sustainable development (Qu, McCormick, and Funck 2022; Yachin and Ioannides 2020), and regional revitalization (Qu, Coulton, and Funck 2020; Qu and Cheer 2020).

Rural creative entrepreneurs, however, also suffer from obstacles such as geographical isolation, inefficient policy and network supports, inadequate markets, and conservative neighbourhood relationships (Woods 2012). And yet entrepreneurs in resource-constrained communities faced with an uncertain future are also more likely to display a higher resilience and to succeed in weathering sudden shocks (Michaelis et al. 2020). In resource-constrained contexts, small businesses tend to adopt a multi-faceted nature and functions to sustain themselves (Michaelis et al. 2020). Literature engaging with small or micro-businesses describes their behaviour variously as entrepreneurial bricolage, resourcefulness (Barraket et al. 2019; Michaelis et al. 2020; Yachin and Ioannides 2020), and frugality within a resource-constrained environment (Michaelis et al. 2020).

Small islands can be seen as resource-constrained environments (Arias and Cruz 2019; Burnett and Danson 2017), often characterized by a fragile ecological, economic, and social structure (Karampela 2017). As a result, they also face more challenges when it comes to the potential for tourism development, especially in relation to issues of long-term sustainability and resilience (Karampela 2017; Qu and Cheer 2020). Tourism on a small island can be developed by way of a creative or artisanal entrepreneurial bricolage, and especially through the use of locally embodied narratives and cultural resources (Arias and Cruz 2019). Although the role of creative entrepreneurs for the economic revitalization of declining peripheral areas is often emphasized, especially in tourism, the direct economic benefits of creative industries are hard to evaluate (Woods 2012). On the other hand, their social role is often overlooked. In this research, we seek to explore how the individual attributes and network characteristics of creative in-migrant micro-entrepreneurs contribute to make them more resilient in the face of unexpected external impacts such as COVID-19. Furthermore, we investigate the role of in-migrant networks in providing a bridge between individual and community-level resilience. We argue that places like small peripheral islands provide an especially suitable context in which to explore the power of small.

Small Tourism, Creative Entrepreneurs, and Community Resilience in Mitarai

Mitarai village, located on Osakishimojima island, in the Seto Inland Sea (see figure 9.1), is a typical small island destination with a population of about two hundred people. Mitarai is a Japanese heritage site due to its preserved Edo-period townscape, with high historical and cultural appeal. Despite its potential for tourism development, there is a lack of young and innovative people engaging in tourism-related activities. More than two-thirds of the island population consists of elderly people over sixty-five; of these, almost half are over eighty (Qu, Coulton, and Funck 2020). In the past decade, however, Mitarai has attracted ten in-migrant micro-entrepreneurs; these people have subsequently established restaurants, accommodation facilities, as well as an art festival, and their efforts have started to provide a model for rural revitalization (Qu, Coulton, and Funck 2020).

The Japanese government has been trying to attract young domestic in-migrants and their families to rural areas in the expectation that such migrants would play an important role in decreasing the speed of depopulation (Schrade 2019). Previous research conducted in Mitarai, however, found that among the micro-entrepreneurs who move to the community, there are both long-term settlers as well as transmigrants who live in the community only for certain periods, such as on weekends (Qu, Coulton, and Funck 2020; Qu and Cheer 2020). Some of the businesses in the town are run by commuters. Compared to settled entrepreneurs, commuters are less welcome by the community, which perpetuates their social distance from locals. However, these "unsettled" transmigrants can also play an important role in bringing social innovation to local tourism-development efforts (Qu, Coulton, and Funck 2020), enhancing creative community-engagement (Qu, Coulton, and Funck 2020; Qu, McCormick, and Funck 2022), and building social resilience (Qu and Cheer 2021). Mitarai can be considered representative of small peripheral island communities struggling with decline and who treat tourism development and in-migrant entrepreneurs as their last ray of hope. This case study

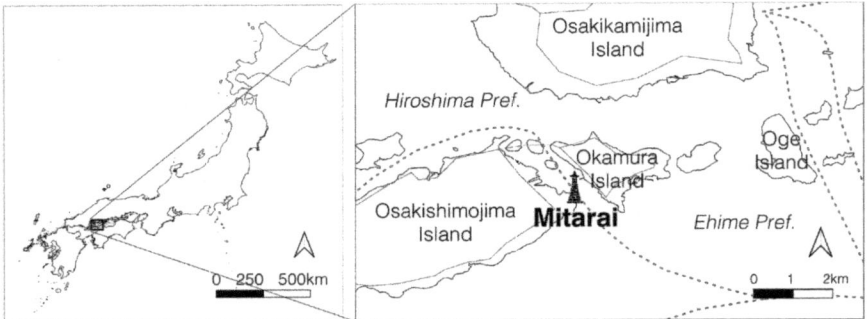

Figure 9.1: Location of Mitarai (authors' illustration).

Source: Geospatial Information Authority of Japan, https://www.gsi.go.jp/kankyochiri/gm_japan_e.html (accessed 10 April 2023).

can therefore contribute useful insights applicable to the transformation of other small islands or rural communities facing similar conditions both nationally and globally.

Methods

Much of the work on the role of small-scale in-migrant entrepreneurs in rural contexts is located at the intersection of the rural entrepreneurship, lifestyle migration, and creative tourism literatures, where social innovation (Olmedo, Twuijver, and O'Shaughnessy 2021), tourism innovation (Richards 2020), rural creativity (Borch et al. 2008; Woods 2012), resourcefulness (Barraket et al. 2019; Qu, McCormick, and Funck 2022), as well as frugality within a resource-constrained environment (Michaelis et al. 2020), allow a cross-regional exchange of social capital, restructuring, and reciprocity in small rural communities (Lysgård 2016). According to the literature on networks, social innovation can play a relational role that facilitates local to extra-local social capital exchange, as well as aiding in the transformation of resources tailored to local conditions after the establishment of a networked community by in-migrants. This creative and relational-based framework suggests that rural in-migrant entrepreneurs' ability for creative transformation and networking should play a central role in producing innovative strategies for the resilience of their businesses as well as their communities under the double strain of depopulation and the COVID-19 pandemic.

The fieldwork was conducted over four years, both before the pandemic (October 2017 to December 2019) and during (March 2020 to August 2021). The exploratory research used qualitative methods (Creswell 2017), including formal and informal interviews and naturalistic and participatory observation. Interviews were conducted with micro-entrepreneurs, elderly residents, and government officials before and during the pandemic. The events and activities documented include tourism and research visits, community event volunteering, local board meetings, university on-site projects, international education workshops, as well as online promotion events organized by tourism entrepreneurs. Additionally, archival documents and online information, including internal reports and documents from the local government and small-scale tourism enterprises, were collected during the entire fieldwork. The type and quantity of data is extensively documented in table 9.1.

Adopting a longitudinal research method allows us to observe how in-migrant entrepreneurs' activities and attitudes change over time, and to compare their efforts before and during the COVID pandemic both at the individual and community level. Qualitative research is also very suitable for small numbers of participants, such as the ten entrepreneurs in the village. Interview questions before the pandemic included interviewees' understanding of depopulation and decline issues in their community, the current tourism-development issues, and the connection between their business visions and community-revitalization goals. Follow-up interviews during COVID-19, most of which were conducted online, focused on understanding the impact of the pandemic, the change in business patterns, and entrepreneurs' creative strategies and adaptation. Participant observation during the pandemic also provided on-site confirmation of interviewees' statements. All interviews lasted an average of thirty minutes and were recorded and transcribed in Japanese before being translated into English. The content was analyzed through a grounded theory approach (Strauss and Corbin 2011), following open, axial, and selective coding methods (Creswell 2017). The results and discussion are presented together and organized by themes.

Table 9.1: Research methods and data

SCALE	DATA		SOURCES	QUANTITY
Mitarai village	Observation	Naturalistic	Field observations from before (2017-2019) and after the COVID-19 pandemic (2020-2021), documentary videos, field notes and photographs	Approx. 50 days of observation (30 days before and 20 days after COVID impact) with 120 pages of fields notes, 50 minutes documentary videos, 300 photos
		Participatory	Participation in 4 community events (2019-2021) as volunteer or co-organizer; informal interviews	Approx. 10 days of observation with 20 pages of fields notes
	Interview	Local entrepreneurs	Semi-structured interviews before the COVID-19 and online follow up interviews during the COVID-19	10 semi-structured interviews with 30 pages of transcript
				5 online follow-up interviews with 10 pages of transcript
		Elderly residents	Un-structured interview during COVID-19	8 un-structured interviews with 5 pages of transcript
Regional		Government	Semi-structured interviews and public lecture before COVID-19 Online promotion event during COVID-19	3 unstructured interviews with local tourism association and government officials, 5 government-organized public lectures, and 1 online promotion event with 15 pages of transcript
	Archival documents, online information		Official tourism information, SNS, online articles, municipal reports	20 sources
	Secondary data analysis		Number of visitors (2019-2020), regional COVID-19 cases (2020)	2 years of data provided by the Mitarai Tourism Association.
				2020 COVID infection number by (Chugoku News Digital, 2021)

Source: Authors

Results and Discussion: Small Community, Stronger Engagement

A Taxonomy of In-Migrant Entrepreneurs

In the decades before the COVID pandemic, Mitarai was one of the many shrinking island communities unable to revive its economy, with its original industrial structure declining while new tourism development lagged behind. Besides the scarcity of tourists, underlying causes such as the lack of residents and in-migrants and insufficient promotion efforts to attract tourists (Qu, Coulton, and Funck 2020) suggested that this small declining community did not have the necessary internal energy to thrive. In the last decade, however, the growing importance of micro-entrepreneurship for community revitalization and resilience building has become more and more apparent.

It is possible to identify three broad categories of in-migrant micro-entrepreneurs based on their migration pathways: (1) Regional Revitalization Corps program (*Chiiki Okoshi Kyōryokutai* in Japanese) members, who moved to a rural community through a government-funded community development scheme (Zollet and Qu 2019, 2023); (2) young and/or middle-aged in-migrants moving to rural destinations independently and with no previous connections to the community; (3) in-migrants with previous family ties to the community (e.g., their family was originally from the island, but they were not born there), including return migrants. Within these three categories, the motivations for moving to the community and opening businesses vary, with some being more lifestyle-oriented and others more economy-oriented. In-migrants can be further categorized by two types: the first includes those who settle down as new residents, despite remaining connected to the urban areas where they lived and worked before; the second contains cases of "non-settled" in-migrants, such as commuters who only run their business in Mitarai, or transmigrants who move between two locations (e.g., Mitarai on the weekends and a larger urban area during weekdays). Although previous research shows that the latter group receives less of a welcome from the local population, non-settled in-migrants also contribute to community-level revitalization efforts, sometimes significantly (Qu, Coulton, and Funck 2020). One such example is the founder of Mitarai's Shiosai art festival, who resides in Mitarai mainly on weekends.

This case also shows the increasingly important role of creative tourism in the revitalization of Mitarai. Creative tourism here includes the transformation of vacant semi-abandoned historical buildings into new tourism facilities and cultural attractions, as well as the establishment of new artistic events that bring additional visitors to Mitarai, such as the Shiosai art festival (Qu and Cheer 2021). In a broader sense, however, creativity also contributes to the building of new social assets that locals can also benefit from (Qu, McCormick, and Funck 2022; Schrade 2019). Since most micro-businesses open mainly during the holidays and weekends, this frees up time for in-migrant entrepreneurs to play other roles, including those of artists, writers, non-profit organization leaders, designers, and community supporters. Several in-migrants, for example, were involved in the organization of social events or in community groups such as the local volunteer firefighter group. From a tourism perspective, however, despite the developments brought by in-migrant entrepreneurs, pre-COVID tourist flows remained lower than entrepreneurs' expectations due to Mitarai's peripherality.

Small Equals Safer: Tourism Recovery during COVID

During the three COVID waves of 2020 (see figure 9.2), tourism all over Japan came to a near halt, particularly at the beginning of the virus's emergence. Similarly, in Mitarai there were almost no visitors in April and May 2020. Due to the continued interruption of international tourist flows, government efforts turned to domestic tourism, with the implementation of the "Go to Travel" campaign in July 2020. The campaign, however, was suspended only a few months later due to the beginning of the third wave of the pandemic.

Over the course of 2020, 26.9 per cent of tourism businesses nationwide reportedly went bankrupt as a result of the pandemic (Kankokeizai News 2021). Mitarai, however, was not as severely impacted, and none of the town's tourism businesses closed because of COVID, even though Mitarai received no visitors for nearly two months. In the following months, with domestic tourists starting to privilege smaller, more rural, and safer travel destinations, the number of tourists started climbing back up, and was subsequently unaffected by the second and third outbreak waves. By November 2020, the number of tourists had nearly bounced back to that of the pre-pandemic period. As noted by one of Mitarai's in-migrant entrepreneurs,

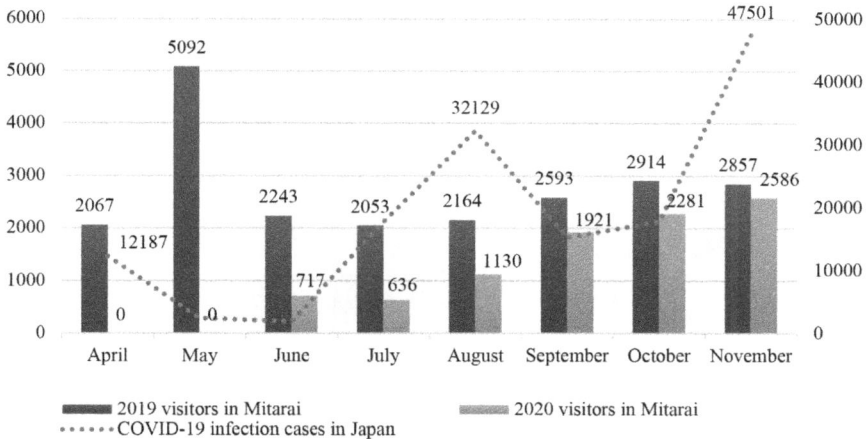

Figure 9.2: Number of tourists in Mitarai compared to 2019–20, and nationwide COVID infection cases in 2020.

Source: Authors

> During the partial-lockdown time, in the beginning, tourism has been increasing... more people are 'escaping' to the islands because they probably feel it's safer here, or they want to escape the cities and the stress of COVID. (In-migrant entrepreneur A)

From tourists' perspective, Mitarai is a history-rich travel destination that, despite being small and relatively remote, is still close enough for a day trip for Hiroshima Prefecture's residents, and its relative isolation makes it feel safer compared to larger mainland destinations. As more and more tourists chose to make day trips from the nearby cities, Mitarai's micro-tourism businesses faced both opportunities and challenges. The key challenge was how to continue tourism services while at the same time ensuring the safety of local—mostly elderly and thus vulnerable—residents. This caused concern among locals, as evidenced by the following statements:

> Local people themselves believe that [Mitarai] is a place where it's unlikely to get COVID, unlike cities, so they rarely wear masks while walking on the street. (Resident A)

> If a local resident gets infected with COVID, it takes more than an hour to reach the closest hospital. During periods with bad weather [such as the rainy or typhoon seasons], transportation to the outside can even be interrupted. (Resident B).

The magnitude of the concern was such that a Mitarai Tourism Association representative stated, "We don't want tourists to come here because we have so many elderly people, so we cancelled the local tour-guide services." (Mitarai tourism association interviewee; see table 9.1).

Implementing safety measures in a small community where the majority of residents are very vulnerable to the impact of the epidemic posed a new challenge for tourism businesses. The problem of how to take up the opportunities brought by the increasing tourist flow while at the same time considering elderly residents' safety thus became an important driving force behind the innovations introduced by tourism micro-businesses and their networks, which will be introduced in the following sections.

Creative Entrepreneurs, Diversified Networks

Small Means Diversification, Low Costs, and Flexibility

When asking micro-entrepreneurs about the merits of being small businesses located in a small town, the responses could be selectively coded by way of three themes or attributes: "multi-functionality," "flexibility," and "frugality." Multi-functionality refers to the fact that many, if not most, respondents are engaged in two or more occupations, including both tourism- and non-tourism-oriented ones. Mitarai's micro-entrepreneurs therefore either do not entirely depend on tourism income for their livelihood, or they have expanded into more diversified types of tourism businesses that can meet the needs of different types of tourists and locals. This is connected to their display of flexibility in their business operations.

Comparing the situations before and during COVID, it was evident that most micro-businesses were experimenting with new approaches that would allow them to survive and possibly even thrive. Examples include using the time without tourists to carry out self-maintenance of their businesses and to increase their online promotion. This flexibility is in turn connected to entrepreneurs' "make do at low cost" attitude, which results from their frugal approach. One way of reducing costs is to take advantage of the fact that the local government provides historical buildings to in-migrant entrepreneurs at very low rents, much cheaper than in nearby urban areas. Often renovations are undertaken by in-migrants themselves, thus further reducing costs. The cheap rent and relatively low cost of living in small peripheral communities helps micro-entrepreneurs survive even when their businesses are not flourishing, in a way that would be nearly impossible in cities. As the following respondent noted,

> I think the power of small overhead is the new big! It's difficult to survive in this environment if you have a lot of overhead and expenses. . . . Compared with urban tourism businesses that were used to receiving lots of visitors and that employ a lot of staff, we are in a better situation. (In-migrant entrepreneur C)

The three individual attributes of multi-functionality, flexibility, and frugality tend to be present, in different degrees, among all micro-business proprietors interviewed, and thanks to these attributes these micro-businesses displayed a striking capacity for resilience. Several businesses attributed this to their resource-constrained environment. One entrepreneur, for example, noted that

> the problems that were affecting the island before COVID [low visitor rates, lack of manpower] probably made Mitarai more resilient to the effects of COVID. (In-migrant entrepreneur B)

Through a combination of multi-functionality, bricolage, resourcefulness, and frugality (Michaelis et al. 2020; Qu, McCormick, and Funck 2022; Yachin and Ioannides 2020), during the three partial lockdown periods in 2020 micro-entrepreneurs and their networks initiated a variety of activities, from renovation of their closed businesses, to socio-technical innovation, to online networking and promotion. Moreover, their response to the COVID situation in a few cases also benefited the community more broadly. In line with Mitchell's creative enhancement, businesses that do not rely only on tourism in small-scale rural settings often maintain multiple functions (2013, 385).

This also shows that creative enhancement is more likely to happen through micro-businesses in resource-constrained areas with limited tourist flows (Mitchell 2013; Qu and Cheer 2020).

Small Island, Extended Networks: Co-creation between Competition and Collaboration

Business survivability and resilience do not only depend on the individual attributes mentioned above; the involvement of Mitarai's tourism micro-entre-preneurs in a variety of social networks also determines the types of community- and extra-community-level resource exchanges and integrations that will be present. We identified four major forms of micro-entrepreneur networks and classified them according to their position on a continuum extending from local to extra-local linkages and their roles as both businesses and gathering places for socially engaged community members (see figure 9.3). The four types are (1) private local or extra-local business networks; (2) community-level local business networks; (3) regional and cross-region-al creative co-operation networks; and (4) community-level revitalization networks.

Entrepreneurs' personal local or extra-local business networks (top-left quadrant in the above image) are often connected with urban places where they used to work or live, displaying "mixed embeddedness" (Kloosterman and Rath 2001) characteristics. This type of network is characterized by urban/rural and local to extra-local knowledge and resource flows and exchanges, which helps each entrepreneur in Mitarai maintain a business that is creatively distinct. Entrepreneurs localize the extra-local capital and crea-tivity in the regional context: for example, each business targets a different customer group, which results in the creative transformation of extra-local resources in the locally embodied context, while also maintaining a sense of creative uniqueness. Most entrepreneurs treat this kind of network as their private business resource and tend not to share it with other local entrepreneurs in Mitarai.

Due to the limited internal social resources of the community, however, the interaction among local tourism businesses is based not only on competition, but also on instances of collaboration informed by the desire to promote tourism within the community and to overcome common challenges, such as the impacts of COVID-19. These networks and interactions are shown

Extra-local
(From regional-scale to global-scale)

Private business network
(local to extra-local)
e.g., urban-rural/global-regional
business, culture creation, and
creative event network

Creative in-migrant network
(cross-regional)
e.g., collaboration with regional governments,
island immigration promotion, regional
revitalization corps program, university
research and on-site education

Socially oriented
(Rural lifestyle in-migrant, non-
tourism related works)

Business oriented
(Semi-competition/collaboration
among creative tourism businesses)

Local entrepreneur network
(local tourism)
e.g., local chamber of commerce, local
tourism association, community general
incorporated association

Community revitalization network
(community level)
e.g., community-engaged initiatives and
events, social volunteer, collaboration with
local resident association

Community

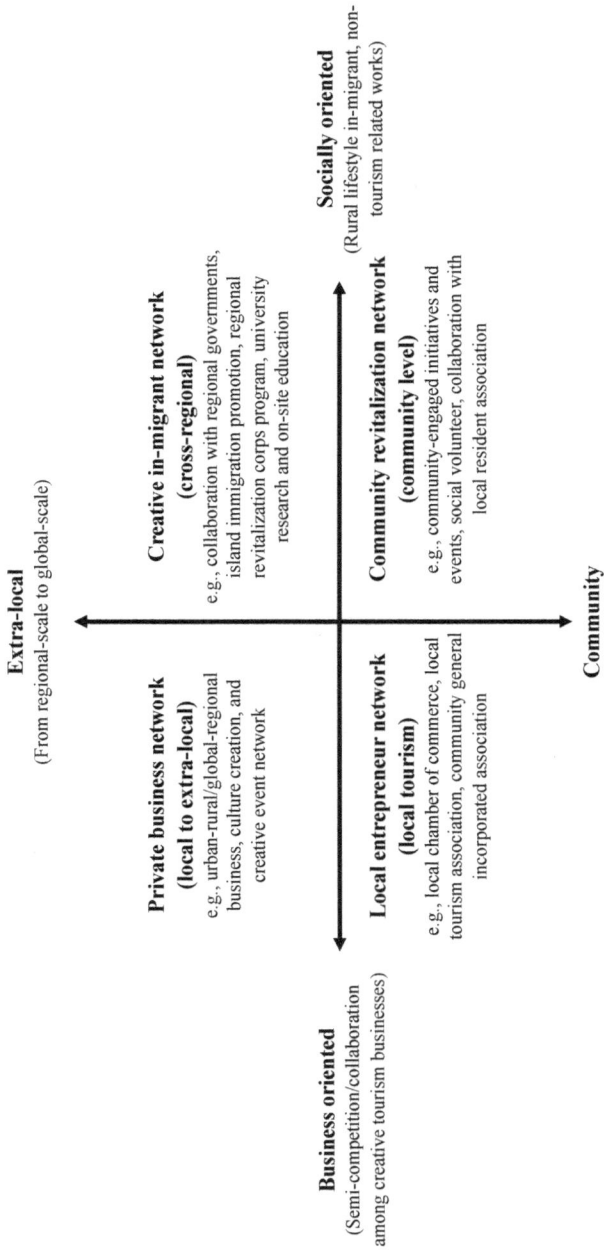

Figure 9.3: Type of creative in-migrant rural micro-entrepreneur networks.
Source: Authors.

in the bottom-left quadrant of figure 9.3. One example of such a network is Mitarailabo, a general incorporated association created in 2017 by a group of young entrepreneurs (both in-migrants and locals), not only to promote Mitarai's tourism development but also to engage with the community's social and cultural affairs. In 2020, Mitarailabo promoted the creation of a new audio tour guide device through crowdfunding (Mitarailabo 2020). The crowdfunding initiative opened in November 2020, and raised 315,500 yen (around USD$3,000) in one month with the support of thirty-seven people (Mitarailabo 2020). This initiative was launched because of the suspension of the community tour guide service that was managed by local elderly volunteers, yet again due to COVID-19. The content of the audio tour guide highlights the historical and cultural background of the town as well as its everyday life in the past, and the information was obtained with the participation of elderly residents who shared their collective memories. This small technical innovation therefore not only supports "socially distanced" tourism and indirectly benefits local tourism businesses, but also helps to preserve Mitarai's culture.

The introduction of this innovation is also connected to the resource constraints faced by the community even before the start of the pandemic. As one entrepreneur noted, "this idea came from a lack of guides rather than from COVID" (in-migrant entrepreneur B). At the same time, however, COVID-19 provided the stimulus for entrepreneurs to collaborate on the project, as it became more urgent to find a way to introduce the town to visitors while minimizing close contact with elderly residents. In terms of reciprocity (Olmedo, Twuijver, and O'Shaughnessy 2021), the role of the entrepreneur's "placially embedded' network is also reflected in their capacity to find mutually beneficial creative solutions through relational co-creation processes between entrepreneurs and residents.

Community-Engaged Social Innovation Networks

The socially oriented side (right quadrants of figure 9.3) shows how tourism businesses play a more than purely economic role by linking different stakeholders and supporting the community. Regarding extra-local networks (top-right quadrant), one example is a series of online promotional events co-designed by a Mitarai in-migrant entrepreneur and the prefectural government office that oversees the promotion of in-migration. The events were held in both English and Japanese between 26 November 2020 and 6 March

2021. The topics were designed to attract new creative in-migrants to the area, and the events had titles such as "My Setouchi Lifestyle" and "Your Next Challenge Can Be Done in Rural Japan" (HIROBIRO 2020). These events attracted a diverse range of participants, from aspiring in-migrants living in Japan's urban areas, to researchers, to members of the regional destination-promotion organization, to island residents. Creative entrepreneurs in small rural and island communities increasingly strive to connect with entrepreneurs and creative place makers from other rural areas—and even from outside Japan—to share their experiences. Through these promotional events, in-migrant entrepreneurs were able to put to good use their creative and communication skills to promote the community, connect it to the outside world, and sow the seeds of new collaborations.

At the community level, an important indicator of in-migrant entrepreneurs' social role is whether they participate in co-creating new activities that benefit the community, in collaboration with other entrepreneurs and community members (Qu, McCormick, and Funck 2022). In Mitarai, the best example is Shiosai, a regional-scale art festival created by one in-migrant artist and entrepreneur. In 2019 Shiosai attracted around 1,850 visitors in one week at the beginning of May (two and a half times more than the 2018 edition), a significant number in the context of Mitarai (Qu and Cheer 2021). Shiosai emphasizes the importance of using vacant historical buildings to host art events, and the need for the exhibited artworks to have a connection with the local community and history. It includes events in which community members (such as local children) engage in art creation together with artists.

Despite the growing success of Shiosai, however, organizers decided after the onset of the pandemic to put community safety first and cancel the 2020 edition, even though at that time the number of COVID-19 infections in Japan was still low. Subsequently, the Shiosai executive committee decided to hold two smaller-scale art and creative events in November 2020 and May 2021, while limiting participation only to artists living in or close to the community and involving community members even more in the festival creation process. For example, the November 2020 edition included events managed by local practitioners of traditional arts, such as tea ceremonies and traditional music. Although the festival was still open to tourists, the choice to reduce its scale and re-localize participation and content criteria increased the community's sense of ownership over the festival-creation process and encouraged the initiation of more locally embedded partnerships between in-migrants and residents.

To further protect the community from the threat of COVID-19, some tourism businesses managed by in-migrants also chose to implement stricter protective measures, despite the economic damage these would likely cause to their businesses. In the words of one entrepreneur,

> The problem [of being small-scale] is how to continue to cater for tourists while protecting the local population that is elderly. We've tried by separating locals and tourists. Tourists have the option to take away or sit outside; only locals can sit inside. (In-migrant entrepreneur C)

Small Businesses, Greater Capacity for Resilience

This research explored and categorized three types of migrant entrepreneurs encountered through our fieldwork. The findings discussed the role of in-migrant creative tourism micro-entrepreneurs and their networks under the double pressure of long-standing socio-economic and demographic rural decline and the COVID-19 pandemic. The research shows how small-scale, diversified businesses can be more sustainable to local contexts than large ones (Baixinho et al. 2020; Richards 2021), especially when faced with sudden and unpredictable shocks such as the COVID-19 pandemic. At the beginning of the epidemic, and later, during the recovery of the tourism sector, the flexibility of small businesses in keeping the balance between their tourism and non-tourism sides was particularly evident. The research also highlighted three attributes of individual entrepreneurs: multi-functionality, flexibility, and frugality. Furthermore, the findings show how COVID-19, despite its initial negative impact on tourism, also served as the catalyst for creative adaptation and innovation processes both at the individual and network levels. In line with research on the importance of diversified innovation networks for the building of resilience (Michaelis et al. 2020; Qu and Cheer 2020), the study found that four different types of networks contributed to greater community-level resilience and to sustainable tourism development. We observed how competitive and reciprocal behaviours (Olmedo, Twuijver, and O'Shaughnessy 2021) coexist, and how they largely depend on the type of network each individual entrepreneur is operating in and its business- versus community-oriented characteristics.

Finally, the findings add to the literature on the role of creative micro-businesses in small declining communities as a major driving force in supporting tourism development in ways that are respectful of the local community, enhance its social resilience, and promote sustainable tourism development and regional revitalization (Fleming 2010; Jóhannesson and Lund 2018; Qu, McCormick, and Funck 2022; Yachin and Ioannides 2020). The examples presented in this chapter show the social innovation encouraged by diversified micro-entrepreneurs and their networks, and their involvement in community-engaged initiatives. Small-scale businesses in small-scale destinations are more likely to develop through creative enhancement (Mitchell 2013); in our examples, the crucial role played by these enterprises' creative and relational attributes was demonstrated during the pandemic. The social role of micro-businesses can be described as the capacity to use innovative ideas to enhance community resilience.

Conclusion

Despite the challenges still posed by the COVID-19 pandemic, Mitarai's tourism micro-businesses have managed to survive, all while translating individual resilience into community-level resilience. From the perspective of long-term community resilience and revitalization in declining rural communities, small businesses established by in-migrants play a multi-faceted role. First, they create economic value for the in-migrants themselves, thus enabling them to keep living in the community. Second, they increase Mitarai's attractiveness as a tourism destination, thanks to the presence of new businesses and their creative activities. Third, they contribute to the improvement of local residents' quality of life, including by providing new services and community spaces. And lastly, the presence of in-migrants helps to attract other urban-rural in-migrants. This process, if sustained, has the potential to help stabilize the population and restore a sense of socio-economic vitality in the community.

Although this research was based on a single community case study, the findings broadly correspond to those reported in the recent literature on in-migrant-led revitalization in rural Japan (Ganseforth and Jentzsch 2021; Manzenreiter, Lützeler, and Polak-Rottmann 2020; Schrade 2019), which also confirm the importance of focusing on in-migrant entrepreneurs. This is further validated by research conducted in contexts beyond Japan (Bosworth and Atterton 2012), showing how similar processes are at play across the Global North. In addition, processes of social innovation connected to small- and micro-scale entrepreneurship are emerging as increasingly central to the social and economic resilience of small communities located in peripheral rural areas. In these contexts, being small is often an advantage, and combined with the common attributes of small-scale entrepreneurs, such as multi-functionality, flexibility, and frugality, as well as with the social innovation capacity and relational networks of these enterprises, smallness can contribute not only to the resilience of individual businesses, but to that of the whole community.

Acknowledgements and Funding

This research was assisted by many community members and micro-entrepreneurs in Mitarai. Special thanks are due to Tom Miyagawa Coulton for his invaluable assistance. Part of this study was financially supported by the JSPS KAKENHI (Grants-in-Aid for Scientific Research) No. 22K13251 and 21K20068.

Disclosure Statement

No potential conflict of interest was reported by the authors.

References

Arias, Ricardo Alonzo Cortez, and Allan Discua Cruz. 2019. "Rethinking Artisan Entrepreneurship in a Small Island: A Tale of Two Chocolatiers in Roatan, Honduras." *International Journal of Entrepreneurial Behavior & Research* 25, no. 4: 633–51. https://doi.org/10.1108/IJEBR-02-2018-0111.

Baixinho, Alexandra, Carlos Santos, Gualter Couto, Isabel Soares de Albergaria, Leonor Sampaio da Silva, Pilar Damião Medeiros, and Rosa Maria Neves Simas. 2020. "Creative Tourism on Islands: A Review of the Literature." *Sustainability* 12, no. 24: 1–25. https://doi.org/10.3390/su122410313.

Barraket, Jo, Robyn Eversole, Belinda Luke, and Sharine Barth. 2019. "Resourcefulness of Locally-Oriented Social Enterprises: Implications for Rural Community Development." *Journal of Rural Studies* 70:188–97. https://doi.org/10.1016/j.jrurstud.2017.12.031.

Borch, Odd Jarl, Anniken Førde, Lars Rønning, Ingebjørg Kluken Vestrum, and Gry Agnete Alsos. 2008. "Resource Configuration and Creative Practices of Community Entrepreneurs." *Journal of Enterprising Communities:*

People and Places in the Global Economy 2, no. 2: 100–23. https://doi.
org/10.1108/17506200810879943.

Bosworth, Gary, and Jane Atterton. 2012. "Entrepreneurial In-Migration and
Neoendogenous Rural Development." *Rural Sociology* 77, no. 2: 254–79. https://doi.
org/10.1111/j.1549-0831.2012.00079.x.

Burnett, Kathryn A., and Mike Danson. 2017. "Enterprise and Entrepreneurship on Islands
and Remote Rural Environments." *International Journal of Entrepreneurship and
Innovation* 18, no. 1: 25–35. https://doi.org/10.1177/1465750316686237.

Cederholm, Erika Andersson. 2018. "Relational Work in Lifestyle Enterprising: Sustaining
the Tension between the Personal and the Commercial." *Kultura i Społeczeństwo*
62, nos. 1–2: 191–201. https://doi.org/10.1300/J123v53n01_15.

Chugoku News Digital. 2021. "Hiroshima ken no kansenshasū to shisha-sū no suii
(tsukibetsu)" [Changes in the number of infected people and the number of deaths
in Hiroshima Prefecture (monthly)]. Chugoku News Digital, last modified 10
March 2021. https://www.chugoku-np.co.jp/local/news/article.php?comment_
id=707930&comment_sub_id=0&category_id=1167#hiro3.

Crawshaw, Julie, and Menelaos Gkartzios. 2016. "Getting to Know the Island: Artistic
Experiments in Rural Community Development." *Journal of Rural Studies* 43:134–
44. https://doi.org/10.1016/j.jrurstud.2015.12.007.

Creswell, John W., and J. David Creswell. 2017. *Research Design: Qualitative, Quantitative,
and Mixed Methods Approaches*. Thousand Oaks, CA: Sage Publications.

Cunha, Conceição, Elisabeth Kastenholz, and Maria João Carneiro. 2020. "Entrepreneurs
in Rural Tourism: Do Lifestyle Motivations Contribute to Management Practices
that Enhance Sustainable Entrepreneurial Ecosystems?" *Journal of Hospitality and
Tourism Management* 44:215–26. https://doi.org/10.1016/j.jhtm.2020.06.007.

Dinis, Anabela. 2021. "Tourism, Immigrants and Lifestyle Entrepreneurship: The (In)
Coming of People as a Key Factor for Sustainability of Low-Density Territories—A
Case Study in Portugal." In *The Impact of Tourist Activities on Low-Density
Territories*, edited by Rui Pedro Marques, Ana I. Melo, Maria Manuela Natário,
and Ricardo Biscaia, 149–82. Cham, CH: Springer. https://doi.org/10.1007/978-3-
030-65524-2_7.

Duxbury, Nancy, and Heather Campbell. 2011. "Developing and Revitalizing Rural
Communities through Arts and Culture." *Small Cities Imprint* 3, no. 1: 111–22.

Fleming, Rachel C. 2009. "Creative Economic Development, Sustainability, and
Exclusion in Rural Areas." *Geographical Review* 99, no. 1: 61–80. https://doi.
org/10.1111/j.1931-0846.2009.tb00418.x.

Ganseforth, Sonja, and Hanno Jentzsch. 2021. "Introduction: Rethinking Locality in
Japan." In *Rethinking Locality in Japan*, edited by Sonja Ganseforth and Hanno
Jentzsch, 1–17. London: Routledge. https://doi.org/10.4324/9781003032137.

HIROBIRO. 2020. "Online Event: My Setouchi Lifestyle." HIROBIRO, last modified 26
November 2020. https://www.hiroshima-hirobiro.jp/event/details/001819/

Jóhannesson, Gunnar Thór, and Katrín Anna Lund. 2018. "Creative Connections? Tourists, Entrepreneurs and Destination Dynamics." *Scandinavian Journal of Hospitality and Tourism* 18, no. S1: S60–S74. https://doi.org/10.1080/15022250.201 7.1340549.

Kalantaridis, Christos. 2010. "In-Migration, Entrepreneurship and Rural–Urban Interdependencies: The Case of East Cleveland, North East England." *Journal of Rural Studies* 26, no. 4: 418–27. https://doi.org/10.1016/j.jrurstud.2010.03.001.

Kankokeizai News. 2021. "[Data] Bankruptcy Trends in 2020 Travel Industry." Kankokeizai News, last modified 1 March 2021. https://www.kankokeizai.com/.

Karampela, Sofia, Charoula Papazoglou, Thanasis Kizos, and Ioannis Spilanis. 2017. "Sustainable Local Development on Aegean Islands: A Meta-Analysis of the Literature." *Island Studies Journal* 12, no. 1: 71–94. https://doi.org/10.24043/isj.6.

Kloosterman, Robert, and Jan Rath. 2001. "Immigrant Entrepreneurs in Advanced Economies: Mixed Embeddedness further Explored." *Journal of Ethnic and Migration Studies* 27, no. 2: 189–201. https://doi.org/10.1080/13691830020041561.

Korsgaard, Steffen, Richard Ferguson, and Johan Gaddefors. 2015. "The Best of Both Worlds: How Rural Entrepreneurs Use Placial Embeddedness and Strategic Networks to Create Opportunities." *Entrepreneurship & Regional Development* 27, nos. 9–10: 574–98. https://doi.org/10.1080/08985626.2015.1085100.

Lysgård, Hans Kjetil. 2016. "The 'Actually Existing' Cultural Policy and Culture-Led Strategies of Rural Places and Small Towns." *Journal of Rural Studies* 44:1–11. https://doi.org/10.1016/j.jrurstud.2015.12.014.

Manzenreiter, Wolfram, Ralph Lützeler, and Sebastian Polak-Rottmann, eds. 2020. *Japan's New Ruralities: Coping with Decline in the Periphery*. London: Routledge.

Michaelis, Timothy L., Jon C. Carr, David J. Scheaf, and Jeffrey M. Pollack. 2020. "The Frugal Entrepreneur: A Self-Regulatory Perspective of Resourceful Entrepreneurial Behavior." *Journal of Business Venturing* 35, no. 4: 105969. https://doi.org/10.1016/j.jbusvent.2019.105969.

Mitarailabo. 2020. "Furuki yoki mitarashi no kurashi o tsutaeru kankō onsei gaido jigyō o susumetai" [We want to promote the audio tour guide business to share the good life in Mitarai]. Mitarailbo, last modified 26 November 2020. https://camp-fire.jp/projects/view/334109.

Mitchell, Clare J. A. 2013. "Creative Destruction or Creative Enhancement? Understanding the Transformation of Rural Spaces." *Journal of Rural Studies* 32:375–87. https://doi.org/10.1016/j.jrurstud.2013.09.005.

Olmedo, Lucas, Mara van Twuijver, and Mary O'Shaughnessy. 2021. "Rurality as Context for Innovative Responses to Social Challenges—The Role of Rural Social Enterprises." *Journal of Rural Studies* 99:272–83. https://doi.org/10.1016/j.jrurstud.2021.04.020.

Prince, Solène. 2018. "Dwelling in the Tourist Landscape: Embodiment and Everyday Life among the Craft-Artists of Bornholm." *Tourist Studies* 18, no. 1: 63–82. https://doi.org/10.1177/1468797617710598.

Qu, Meng, and Joseph M. Cheer. 2021. "Community Art Festivals and Sustainable Rural Revitalisation." *Journal of Sustainable Tourism* 29, nos. 11–12: 1756–75. https://doi.org/10.1080/09669582.2020.1856858.

Qu, Meng, Tom Miyagawa Coulton, and Carolin Funck. 2020. "Gaps and Limitations- Contrasting Attitudes to Newcomers and Their Role in a Japanese Island Community." *Bulletin of the Hiroshima University Museum* 12:31–46. https://doi.org/http://doi.org/10.15027/50631.

Qu, Meng, A. D. McCormick, and Carolin Funck. 2022. "Community Resourcefulness and Partnerships in Rural Tourism." *Journal of Sustainable Tourism* 30, no. 10: 2371–90. https://doi.org/10.1080/09669582.2020.1849233.

Richards, Greg. 2020. "Designing Creative Places: The Role of Creative Tourism." *Annals of Tourism Research* 85:102922. https://doi.org/10.1016/j.annals.2020.102922.

———. 2021. "Conclusion: Creative Placemaking Strategies in Smaller Communities.' In *Creative Tourism in Smaller Communities*, edited by Kathleen Scherf, 283–97. Calgary: University of Calgary Press.

Schrade, Anna. 2019. "Depopulation, Abandoned Houses and Entrepreneurship: How Rural Communities in Hyogo Prefecture Try to Revitalise Their Locality." *Review of Economics and Business Management* 46:13–23.

Stockdale, Aileen. 2006. "Migration: Pre-requisite for Rural Economic Regeneration?" *Journal of Rural Studies* 22, no. 3: 354–66. https://doi.org/10.1016/j.jrurstud.2005.11.001.

Stone, Ian, and Cherrie Stubbs. 2007. "Enterprising Expatriates: Lifestyle Migration and Entrepreneurship in Rural Southern Europe." *Entrepreneurship and Regional Development* 19, no. 5: 433–50. https://doi.org/10.1080/08985620701552389.

Strauss, Anselm, and Julia Corbin. 2011. "Grounded Theory Methodology." In *The Sage Handbook of Qualitative Research*, edited by Norman K. Denzin and Yvonna S. Lincoln, 273–85. Thousand Oaks, CA: Sage Publications.

Woods, Michael. 2012. "Creative Ruralities." Paper presented at the Creativity on the Edge Symposium, Moore Institute, National University of Ireland Galway, June 2012. https://www.global-rural.org/wp-content/uploads/2018/11/Creative-Ruralities.pdf.

Yachin, Jonathan Moshe, and Dimitri Ioannides. 2020. "'Making Do' in Rural Tourism: The Resourcing Behaviour of Tourism Micro-Firms." *Journal of Sustainable Tourism* 28, no. 7: 1003–21. https://doi.org/10.1080/09669582.2020.1715993.

Zollet, Simona, and Meng Qu. 2019. "The Role of Domestic In-Migrants for the Revitalization of Marginal Island Communities in the Seto Inland Sea of Japan." *MIRRA (Migration in Remote and Rural Areas) Research and Policy Briefs Series*: 1–8. https://rplcarchive.ca/wp-content/uploads/2019/09/MIRRABrief.Zollet.Qu_.pdf.

———. 2023. "Rural Lifestyle Entrepreneurship: Opening Spaces of Possibilities for Resilient Community Economies and Local Agri-Food Systems." In *Rural Quality of Life*, edited by Pia Heike Johansen, Anne Tietjen, Evald Bundgård Iversen, Henrik Lauridsen Lolle, and Jens Kaae Fisker, 74–93. Manchester: Manchester University Press.

Small Tourism and Ecotourism: Emerging Micro-Trends

Ian Yeoman and Una McMahon-Beattie

Introduction

COVID-19 has changed the world, and from a tourism perspective, destinations have started to think about the values that are important to them. Therefore, tourists in general are thinking "local," "visiting friends and relatives," and "doing the right thing" (Carr 2020; Sharfuddin 2020; Sheldon 2021). Often, this means small trips to visit small groups. This return to basics encompasses a number of micro-trends that, when combined, are driving a focus onto everything that is small (Yeoman and McMahon-Beattie 2020; Yeoman, Fountain, and Meikle 2020). Penn (2007) and Penn and Fineman (2018) illustrate how micro-trend changes are occurring in society and ask what these mean for products and services, whereas Yeoman and McMahon-Beattie (2019) illustrate how these trends are shaping tourism experiences. The purpose of this chapter is to illustrate a series of micro-trends within the context of small destinations, whether that be a community festival or a small city. Additionally, the chapter explores these micro-trends from an ecotourist perspective.

Micro-Trends Driving the Ecotourist

Trend 1: Accumulation of Social Capital

As consumer-citizens we carry a vision of our better selves: that vision is how we like to be seen and appreciated by others. Increasingly we profile our skills, our accomplishments, and our experiences rather than merely our material possessions. This trend influences significantly the services we crave and the communication language that works best with us in the marketplace (Jones and Comfort 2020; Kallis 2011). In the tourism context, it may affect the holidays we want and what we do when we are on those holidays. Its essence is that, as we grow wealthier and better educated, we like to put our twenty-first-century sophistications on display. These are features of the ecotourist (Yeoman 2008). We want to achieve *savoir faire* and *savoir vivre* and thus endow our lives with quality experiences we can share with others (Bourdieu 2000; Robertson and Yeoman 2014). This sharing with others is an important feature, as Casado-Diaz and Benson's (2009) study of expat Brits who created a social network between English-speaking retirees located in Calpe, a municipality on the Spanish Costa Blanca, indicates. The study found the importance of smallness in creating community through social capital and networks. The research highlighted how a small community creates bonding and bridging through networks and activities, many of which are nature-based and related to tourism. As retirees, the expats became involved in the community, and in the process enriched their lives as well as those of the community. Similarly, a study by Situmorang (2017) of an ecotourism project within the Muara Baimbai community in Indonesia is an example of using a tourism project to bond a community together. Here a collective sense of purpose between community members and tourists was achieved by creating an experience based around the renovation of the mangrove area. As such, one of the outcomes from the study was a sense of community and achievement through the accumulation of social capital. Therefore, smallness in terms of tourism numbers and destinations can engender positive community outputs, and for the individual, can deliver quality experiences that build their social capital.

Trend 2: Authenti-seeking

As global consumers continue to embrace the convenience and reliability delivered by mass production, they also aspire to an alternative to the perceived "homogenization" of contemporary culture, food, and leisure experiences (Yeoman et al. 2014). There exists a craving among many consumers for products, services, and experiences imbued with a genuine sense of authenticity. We call this the authenti-seeking mindset (Factory 2018b). Authenti-seekers search for experiences that are real and original, not contaminated by being fake or impure (Yeoman, Brass, and McMahon-Beattie 2007). Cohen (2010) has argued that since the 1970s, escaping from the pressures of one's own home society in order to search for more authentic experiences is a primary driver in tourist motivation. He argues further that, on a broader level, escaping "from" in favour of "to" is reflective of Iso-Ahola's (1982) characterization of leisure and tourism experiences in two ways: it is dependent not only on an idea of escape or avoidance, but also on a process of seeking. As such, consumer experiences in tourism can be linked to a notion of searching, and thus seeking authenticity. The authenti-seeker is an individual who enjoys finding products or experiences that have clear links to a place, time, or culture—those that are produced in a traditional way, that are unique, and that have a genuine story behind them. Such authenticity is perceived as adding value. In tourism, authenti-seeking consumers pursue authentic experiences, distancing themselves from mainstream tourism providers and venturing into pastimes that they feel are more meaningful, that test them, and that help them discover themselves. There is a sense, too, of the consumer's desire to be individual, to be unique, to create a social profile that rivals that of any friend or colleague. In this respect, seeking and finding the authentic can increase one's social capital (Stringfellow et al. 2013). Laing and Frost (2015) note that modern holiday-makers wish to experience cultures and to sample foods and leisure activities endemic to a region or country. For example, authenticity in relation to food is about products that are simple, rooted in the region, natural, and ethically produced (Yeoman 2008). If we take this example further within the context of "smallness," Toast Martinborough[1] is one of New Zealand's most successful wine festivals. It is centred on the village of Martinborough in the Wairapara, about a one-hour drive north of Wellington, the capital city (Howland 2008). The festival started in 1992 and runs over a weekend every November. Martinborough is a small village with 1,920 residents whose entire focus is the production of wine. As the wines are boutique in style, many of them are sold at the cellar door or by local restaurants. The village has a strong tourism product that includes wine tasting rooms, delicatessens, women's clothes shops, cinema, boutique hotels, and fine restaurants that focus on pairing local food and wine. The purpose of Toast Martinborough is to create a brand, a story, and a permanent event to bind the community together as a successful tourism destination. This would be the event that defines Martinborough vis-à-vis the rest of New Zealand. Toast Martinborough sells out every year, mainly catering to the wider Wellington residential population. The participating vineyards open their doors for wine, music, and food. As such, wine is Martinborough's provenance (Murray and Overton 2011), and Toast Martinborough creates an experience for those seeking authenticity through place (Yeoman et al. 2005; Yeoman and McMahon-Beattie 2020). Small destinations with a clear sense of place, heritage, and culture are well positioned to deliver the unique experiences so keenly sought after by authentic-seekers.

Trend 3: Changing Meaning of Luxury

Previously, luxury was associated with materialistic goods, made only for the rich and unaffordable for many. But as society changes, the long-term trend is the growth of the middle classes because of education attainment, improved economic well-being, rising incomes, and capital growth. According to a report published by the Brookings Institution (Kharas 2020), by 2030 the middle classes will grow from 3.9 billion consumers to 5.5 billion consumers, mainly in Asia. Today, GDP per capita in advanced economies still dwarfs that in emerging economies, but growth is expected to accelerate in countries such as India and China over the next decade. By 2030, India's GDP per capita is forecast to rise to USD$11,727—growth of 88 per cent since 2020. However, this growth could be slower because of global inflation, the war in Ukraine, and global uncertainties (Yeoman, forthcoming).

Whatever the economic situation, the formulation of luxury is changing (Yeoman, Schänzel, and Zentveld 2022). Luxury has become accessible, democratized, and transformed. Luxury is often associated with conspicuous consumption (Kastanakis and Balabanis 2012)—that is, the buying of expensive items to display wealth, status, and income. However, luxury also has a double-edged face, showing both light and excess (Kastanakis and Balabanis 2012). Luxury can bring internal as well as external gratification. On one hand, it is about materialism and showing off designer brands; on the other, it is internal and inconspicuous, with a focus on experience, enlightenment, and achievement (Yeoman 2008). Hence luxury is a multi-discursive concept that is fragmented and unsolvable (Li, Li, and Kambele 2012). Within the travel sector, luxury is no longer about price or material goods but increasingly about experiences and other intangibles. These include the experience of time, space, authenticity, community, individuality, and well-being. All of these are dimensions of luxury that are beyond materialism. As such, luxury moves from being merely material to being about experience and enrichment, and tourism is a key beneficiary of this change. Experiential luxury is about consumers' prioritization of doing, seeing, and feeling over the need to possess material objects. Consumers want to do, learn, or experience something different and unique (Foresight Factory 2017; Yeoman and McMahon-Beattie 2018; Foresight Factory 2019; Athwal et al. 2019). Furthermore, luxury has an aspect of mindfulness that health products and service providers draw on. This is about extending spiritual well-being and looking beyond physical health. From an ecotourism perspective, Mtapuri and Giampiccoli's (2017) conceptual framework "Luxury Community-Based Tourism" (LCBT) focuses on the ecotourist who could be described with reference to the following characteristics:

- They are generally interested in culture, adventure, and interaction with locals. However, unlike the hard community-based tourism travellers, soft CBT travellers want some comfort. They are mainly interested in experiences they deem really unique and worthwhile.

- Are European, aged between fifty and seventy, and educated.

- Their children have left home so they take holidays all year round.

- They are mainly interested in soft adventure activities, combined with luxury and a range of authentic or eco-friendly experiences.

LCBT is the basis of holidays provided by companies such a Explore Worldwide,[2] Intrepid,[3] and Exodus Travel,[4] all of which cater to small groups (up to fourteen people), mainly singletons or couples travelling to offbeat destinations and staying in locally owned accommodations. These holidays will incorporate some community-based tourism activity and the meeting of locals. As such small tourism destinations have the potential to deliver luxury in terms of unique local experiences and opportunities for self-enrichment.

Trend 4: Supporting Local

As a consequence of COVID-19 there has been a renaissance of support for the local in all forms of products, services, and places. Consumers are invited to show their support for all that is local, to boost their neighbourhood or town or region by (a) buying products with proximate provenance; (b) choosing companies that engage actively with local communities; (c) participating in voluntary schemes or initiatives; (d) holidaying in one's own country; and (e) being an *all-around good local citizen*. And at a broader level, these desires propel customers toward supporting homegrown products at the expense of imported alternatives (Featherstone 2020; Towner and Lemarié 2020). This is not a new trend—the Foresight Factory[5] has been tracking it for over thirty years (Yeoman 2008). This trend leads to companies without obvious local credentials in a given market leveraging a sense of localism in their product ranges, focusing on regional tastes or customs. For example, global coffee chain Starbucks transformed an old bank vault in Amsterdam's Rembrandtplein into a new concept store (Interior Design Shop 2020). Described as the coffee chain's largest site in Europe, "its radical design departure and 'Slow' Coffee Theatre [offer] a new experience for coffee, design and food innovation." The interior, which was designed by over thirty-five local artists, features "a floor-to-ceiling 'tattooed' mural celebrating the history of Dutch coffee traders, repurposed Dutch oak throughout the space . . . a ceiling sculpture created from 1,876 hand-cut wooden blocks, and a wall clad in recycled bicycle inner tubes." Starbucks also says that "it was built under strict Leed® sustainable building guidelines" (Interior Design Shop 2020). According to the company, the store "will function as a test space for rare and exclusive coffees, diverse coffee brewing methods, and new food concepts (Interior Design Shop 2020)—including the Clover Brewing System, rare and exotic coffees, and an in-store bakery. Moreover, it said that "what works at The Bank will make its way to the rest of Europe" (Interior Design Shop 2020).

During the pandemic, many destinations have had to refocus on the domestic tourism market. New Zealand, with its closed borders, is a good example of this. According to Fountain (2021) there has been a renewed appreciation of local. In terms of food and wine, festivals based in small rural destinations offer something unique that is clearly associated with place (consider the Bluff Oyster Festival,[6] or the Hokitika Wild Food Festival[7]). Fountain (2021, 8) echoes the findings of Yeoman et al. (2022) saying that *supporting local* is a movement toward the slow, the small, and the local, with food being central to this trend.

Trend 5: The Experience Seeker

The experience economy dominates the philosophy of tourism (Yeoman and McMahon-Beattie 2019). It underpins how we engage with tourism and how we consume it. Research tells us that tourists want to engage a whole range of experiences, regardless of the particular activities they undertake: holidays abroad or at home, cultural events, fine dining, or cutting-edge leisure activities (Pine and Gilmore 2011). The experience economy is centred on the desire to enrich our daily lives by experiencing new things and undertaking activities that deliver a sense of improvement, enjoyment, and rejuvenation. Consumers prefer aspirational and experiential types of consumption that are based on the concept that sampling new and unique experiences provides them with the opportunity to develop new skills, acquire new knowledge, and thus boost their share of social and cultural capital (Bourdieu 2000). The desire to collect stories is fundamental to so many of our consumption choices: new experiences are sought in order to build memories, identities, stores of social capital. Hence consumers are experience seekers. Notably, social media has become a living journal and portfolio of consumers' daily lives, which naturally increases the demand for experiences to fuel these online story platforms. Snapchat and Instagram Stories allow travellers to display a constant stream of experiences, where the mundane or everyday sits comfortably with more glossy, performative content. Here, shareability and good story fodder is worth more than any material object or reward. Whether one is recording restaurant meals or music concerts, the sharing of every moment with one's followers appears to overtake living in the moment itself. Alongside this, increased access to those items once seen as luxuries has encouraged many people to place greater emphasis on the pursuit of experiences—whether in addition to, or in place of, more material-based forms of consumption. The ephemerality of the experience economy is also a common draw. Limited-edition events feel more exclusive, while transient pop-ups provide extra status for those who are in the know and reach the location first. And the most premium of experiences cleverly create even more hype by eschewing social media altogether—though shareability and status are still key considerations.

According to the Foresight Factory (2018a) the ephemeral experience has become an acceptable capitalist asset; it cannot be quantified or valued, yet it signifies authenticity, individuality, and solidifies personal positioning in the realm of the fascinating. One driving motivation for travel is the desire to collect unique experiences; the ultimate souvenir is a lasting memory. At its fringes this trend boosts interest in rarer experiences and unvisited places, because a story uncollected by others is more exceptional and thus more valuable. The increasing ability to personalize trips and create bespoke tours, even for travellers on a budget, gives rise to a wider range of unique experiences that everyone feels entitled to enjoy. Many experience-led holidays focus on disconnecting from the Internet so as to further absorb oneself in the present. A craving for meaningful human interactions and a sense of belonging in a world dominated by technology drives the desire for immersive, intense, off-the-beaten-track experiences. One of the best examples of this desire for experience and the search for localness, novelty, and authenticity has to be Airbnb Experiences,[8] in which every conceivable type of experience is available. Whether it is making pasta with a grandma in Palombara Sabina, Italy, or chainsaw carving in Salem, Oregon, Airbnb has allowed locals with a skill, interest, or hobby to take that experience and share it with tourists through their platform. The ability of small tourism destinations to deliver rare, bespoke, local experiences provides the tourist with opportunities to acquire, as noted above, the ultimate souvenir.

Trend 6: Fluid and Simple Identity

According to Yeoman (2016), there are two forms of identity, "simple" and "fluid," both of which are shaped by wealth, which in turn influences tourist behaviour. Rising incomes and wealth accumulation distributed in new ways alter the balance of power in tourism. Through the opaqueness of online booking systems for travel and holidays, the power base has shifted from the institution of the travel agent to the individual tourist. At the same time, modern life is rich with new forms of connection and association, allowing a liberated pursuit of personal identity that is fluid and much less restricted by the influence of one's background or geography. Today's society of networks in turn has facilitated and innovated a mass of options provided by communication channels leading to the paradox of choice; consumers can simply choose from an abundance of festivals and events (Yeoman 2016; Yeoman, Robertson, and Smith 2012). The concept of fluid identity is supported by Boztug's (2015) research on the hybrid tourist, which challenges the concept of market segmentation. The hybrid consumer buys cheaper generic and low-end brands but trades up on some occasions. They like to sample, try new experiences, and have no brand preference (Ehrnrooth and Gronroos 2013; Silverstein 2003). Boztog emphasized that the hybrid tourist's purchases vary dramatically. Yeoman and colleagues highlight the success of Visa Wellington on a Plate (WOAP) as a food festival in a small capital city that is in line with all the characteristics of fluid identity:

WOAP began in 2009 with 43 participating restaurants, 30 events, and sold approximately 400 tickets. In 2018, this had grown to 260 restaurants, 141 events and 11,024 tickets (Meikle 2019). WOAP is an annual festival held in the last two weeks of August that showcases the best of Wellington's culinary and hospitality industry through festival events, special menu offerings and industry activity.

The focus is on "from farm to plate" and the festival incorporates several products including specific lunch and dinner menus known as Dine Wellington. Other events include a best burger competition, free public lectures, events for pets, cookery classes, night markets, and a beer festival. Award winning events have included Rimutaka Prison Gate to Plate where celebrity chef, Martin Bosley, mentors prisoners to create a fine dining experience at the local prison and Dine with Monet which is a dining experience based on the food found in Monet's paintings. WOAP delivers experiences for foodies, innovations, and excitement. Although most events are focused in Wellington, they spread into the hinterland as far north as Kapiti and the Wairapa in the east. (2021, 168)

Yeoman (2020) and Fountain (2021) argue that in most developed countries, consumer behaviour is the product of uninterrupted prosperity (apart from the global financial crisis of 2007–09), driven by growth in real levels of disposal income, low inflation, stable employment, and booming property prices. Therefore, new consumer appetites emerged in which tourists could spend money on enriching and fun experiences in exotic locations. However, COVID-19 changed that, bringing global tourism to a grinding halt. As a consequence, tourists are travelling domestically, seeking simple experiences and getting back to basics. What we are starting to see are tourists reimagining travel within a local context. People still want adventure and novelty related to fluid identity, but at the same time they seek simplicity as they take refuge in nature, away from COVID-19 (Kock et al. 2020). In New Zealand, the trend has been in the direction of hinterland adjacent to populations centres such as Wellington and Auckland; indeed, the Department of Conservation (2021a) has seen a huge increase in the occupation of tramping (hiking) huts by domestic travelers. In other parts the world, many small places have been overwhelmed with success, bringing a new meaning to the concept of "over-tourism" (Oskam 2019). For example, Airbnb sold more overnight stays in rural Cornwall (England) than in London, as the BBC reported in 2021:

> "Rural nights booked in the UK used to be a quarter of our bookings, they're now half," Mr Chesky tells the BBC. Cornwall is the country's most-booked summer location in 2021, a title previously held by London. Globally, domestic bookings went up from 50% in January 2020 to 80% in 2021, according to Airbnb's newly released report, *Travel & Living*. (Shaw 2021)

In other parts of the United Kingdom, tourists' desire for space is overwhelmingly evidenced by visits to national parks and wilderness areas. For example, tourists are converging on Snowdonia National Park, and concerns have been raised about the potential devastation this could cause for rural health facilities. Park authorities reported their busiest visitor day in living memory, and that significant crowding on the mountain summits and trails made it impossible to maintain social distance (Mackenzie and Goodnow 2021). Overall, the desire for experiences and novelty has resulted in an increased demand for micro-adventures according to Mackenzie and Goodnow:

> Sierra Club encourages people to explore their backyard, not the backcountry. Local councils promote "isolation adventures" via webpages with adventure opportunities in nearby nature (e.g., DunedinNZ.com) and urban guidebooks revealing secret pathways connecting neighbourhoods to green spaces. . . .
>
> Neighbourhood "bear hunts" have sprung up internationally; social media overflows with images of backyard camping; and people are encouraged to "skip the climbing crag and rig a . . . station in [their] backyard. . . .

On a personal level, the first author has discovered trails around the corner and shifted focus to "pre-schooler paced" adventures exploring the local stream, identifying birdsongs, and practicing outdoor travel skills with her family "bubble." However, the pinnacle of micro-adventure creativity may be epitomized by the parents who built a homemade ski slope descending from their backyard treehouse, complete with pulley ski lift to hoist children atop. In the interest of disclosure, it must be said that neither author of this chapter has achieved this level of micro-adventure. (2021, 64)

Trend 7: Quietness—Our Inner Soul

Quiet and relaxation is a dominant motivation for going on holiday, and destinations are helping travellers find calm in their journeys (Quorin, Eeckhout, and Harrison n.d.). An increasing number of studies have begun to highlight the value of quietness in natural environments (Votsi et al. 2014). The emotional experience gained by tourists is often expressed as a sensory perception of silence and tranquility. Regardless of the terminology used, the absence of noise is often referred to as silence. Consequently, the visual and auditory perception of well-being related to an environment free from human disturbance (defined as tranquility) reflects the value of natural quiet. The importance of quietness has received broad acknowledgement within a series of projects and policies undertaken at both the national and international levels.

In the context of COVID-19, personal health is rapidly acquiring a high level of importance (Pfefferbaum and North 2020). Indeed, personal health focuses on the dual importance of both physical and mental well-being, with inner well-being becoming a new priority for the health-aware individual. According to the Foresight Factory (2018b), mindfulness techniques and other forms of exercise that emphasize mental and spiritual benefits are in the ascendant, beneficiaries of a newfound consumer desire to control and sharpen one's mental state. Against a backdrop of widely felt time pressure, stress, and competitive labour markets, mindfulness becomes an essential life skill to nurture and even parade in front of others for valuable social status. According to the Foresight Factory (2018b), a future beckons in which tools and offers that strengthen mental power and alleviate cognitive strain are delivered by technological, health-care, and commercial partners of all kinds. Inner perfection will be as keenly sought after as an optimized outer appearance is today. Meanwhile, exploration into our complex emotional states will inevitably strengthen, with next-generation, wearable devices promising to log our real-time moods alongside our activity in an effort to optimize both.

In fact, natural environments will be seen as therapeutic landscapes that encapsulate healing and recovery notions when associated with mental health, hence one of the reasons for the surge in ecotourism and outdoor activities in a COVID-19 world (Majeed and Ramkissoon 2020). Tourism is a participant in this trend, from well-being and detox retreats, to yoga, spas, and many more tourism products and experiences (Ma et al. 2021; Yeoman 2010). Examples highlighted by Jiang and Balaji include the following:

> Health house Las Dunas provides a two-night digital detox programme named "mobile fasting at the Costa de Sol," where the hotel guests have their phones kept at reception on arrival and stay in a sea-view room without TV or any mobile device. . . . Likewise, the Robinson Crusoe experience has been a novel appeal promoted by island destinations such as Maldives, St. Vincent, and the Grenadines (SVG), where travellers have to hand over their electronic valuables. Technology is discouraged on the beach and even alarm clocks are frowned upon. (2021, 2)

Small tourism destinations with fewer tourists offer ideal locations to provide this much sought-after quietness in natural environments, thereby promoting inner health and well-being.

Trend 8: Slowness

Mass tourism is dependent on a globalized system of large-scale industrial agriculture that, contrary to the claims made by the green revolution, has historically entrenched underdevelopment, dependence, poverty, and loss of food security. It is a significant contributor to climate change, the destruction of the local and global commons, and has adverse impacts on environmental and human health (Fusté-Forné and Jamal 2020). Calls for slow tourism and slow food experiences reflect the need for a conscious, active way of being and living, oriented not to speeded-up lifestyles driven by mass consumption, business competition, and jockeying for market position, but rather to slow, responsible, mindful relationships and practices that foster resilience, sustainability, and social and ecological well-being. As Fullagar, Markwell, and Wilson (2012, 18) explain "slow is embodied in the qualities of rhythm, pace, tempo and velocity that are produced in the sensory and affective relationship between the traveller and the world." Slowness is reflected in a number of social movements, including those of slow food, slow city, slow tourism, and slow travel (Williams et al. 2015). The slow food movement was initiated by Carlo Petrini in 1986 in response to the arrival of a McDonald's fast food restaurant in a culturally significant area of Rome. Its principles of good, clean, and fair guide aesthetic taste, promoting locally sourced ingredients, traditional recipes, and the need to take time to source, prepare, and enjoy food. Small tourism destinations that demonstrate a slow tourism or slow food approach emphasize the importance of local people, cultures, food, and music. Focusing on the moment, the here and now, they have the potential to have a marked emotional impact on the tourist, while remaining sustainable for local communities and the environment.

Caribbean tourism has faced various challenges in recent years (Walker, Lee, and Li 2021), with a focus on large-scale, mass tourism developments that create employment. However, this approach to tourism has been challenged over such issues as ownership, economic leakage, and climate change. Thus, an alternative model is advocated based on the principles of regenerative tourism and community. Whereas mass tourism is mainstream in Jamaica and the Bahamas, tourism in Cuba, a communist country, is focused on small-scale projects, community tourism, and entrepreneurship due to its political system and restrictions on inward investment and the size of businesses (Hollinshead 2006; Navarro-Martínez et al. 2020).

Trend 9: Ethical Choices

Tourists clearly distinguish between their holiday travels as something extraordinary and their everyday lives, where environmental factors are much more likely to be considered. Prillwitz and Barr's (2011) study of tourists' attitude to sustainable travel ten years ago saw insignificant acknowledgement of the willingness to change travel patterns because of climate change. Today, aviation is increasingly in conflict with societal goals to limit climate change and challenges related to air pollution, noise, and infrastructure expansion, and thus we see a movement away from aviation to rail travel, particularly in Europe (Gössling et al. 2019). COVID-19 has further accelerated our understanding of consumption, our environment, and how we live. These considerations then come to inform our understanding of tourism (Kock et al. 2020b), with small communities and rural destinations being the beneficiary, such as the Orkney Islands in the far north of Scotland (McGee and Arpi 2021), or the Chatham Islands in the Pacific Ocean (Cardow and Wiltshier 2010;

Sok 2022). These small islands are running at maximum occupancy due to the rise of ecotourism. One specific form of tourism that is booming because of COVID-19 is volunteer tourism (Dashper et al. 2021; Lockstone-Binney and Ong 2021). In New Zealand, the Department of Conservation's scheme for volunteers has seen a renaissance as people volunteer for a number of conservation projects such as laying new pathways, planting trees, monitoring bird numbers, and pest control measures (Department of Conservation 2021b). The period of COVID-19 has seen the rise of the first-time volunteer, according to Volunteering New Zealand:

> Some people learned about the importance of volunteering during the early stages of the COVID-19 pandemic. They realized they needed to do more and help their communities more. This resulted in a wave of new volunteers to enter the volunteering landscape in order to assist their communities. Traditionally, many first-time volunteers have been newly retired individuals or older people. This seems to be changing with more people across different age groups becoming first-time volunteers. (2021, 2)

Trend 10: Sense of Community

McMillan describes sense of community as follows:

> a spirit of belonging together, a feeling that there is an authority structure that can be trusted, an awareness that trade, and mutual benefit come from being together, and a spirit that comes from shared experiences that are preserved as art. (1996, 315)

This sense of community, belonging, and participation are the main factors that can affect processes of tourism development. The sense of community plays an important role in fostering community support for tourism development, and may enhance its long-term sustainability as a broad basis for tourism development planning (Aref 2011). Developing a sense of community contributes to participation by enabling people to feel connected and motivated to live in harmony and work together toward common goals. Sense of community can be seen as the capacity of the local people to participate in development activities (Joppe 1996). Alberti has commentated on the impact of COVID-19 on "community":

Something quite profound is . . . happening in terms of our relationships with people we don't know. Despite negativity about
the societal impacts of COVID-19—from increased levels of
loneliness to the limitations of social media—we are seeing some
positive and unexpected results, including widespread outpour-
ings of charity, togetherness and empathy for complete strangers. We might even be seeing a grassroots redefinition of what
"community" means in the 21st century. (2020)

This rallying cry can be seen at the centre of community tourism: here
tourism is owned by the people through a bottom-up approach (Butler and
Pearce 1999; Jamal and Stronza 2009; Aref 2011). Fundamentally, small com-
munities are taking ownership and developing their own tourism experience
that is fit for purpose (Sheldon 2021). This can be seen especially among
Indigenous groups (Ryan 1997; Yeoman et al. 2015; Howison, Higgins-
Desbiolles, and Sun 2017). For example, in Mexico, communities in the
Yucatan Peninsula have had to rethink their model of tourism because of
COVID-19. There has been a transformation to more nature- and farm-based
experiences, given that tourists want less commercial engagement, something more human-centred and imbued with the stories of the local people
(Noorashid and Chin 2021). Another notable example is Quebrada Verde,
Peru, a small rural community in the Andes Mountains (Gabriel-Campos et
al. 2021) with a nature-based tourism offering that, in response to COVID-19
and climate change, has developed a rural ecotourism tool in order to protect
the ecosystem in the hills.

Conclusion: A New Landscape

COVID-19 has hugely impacted tourism, without doubt. Many small communities that were dependent on tourism have been brought to a halt. For
example, the Small Island Development States such as Fiji in the Pacific or
Mauritius in the Indian Ocean have seen little or no tourism while at the same
time having to deal with the health impacts of COVID-19. As Carr points out,

Balancing the future industry so that tourism activities directly enhance the health and education of Indigenous peoples and
communities is essential. Slow Tourism or degrowth that is locally focussed and grass roots driven are compatible ways forward

for Indigenous Small and Medium Tourism Enterprises (ISM-TEs), Indigenous and non-Indigenous communities. (2020, 491)

Beyond COVID-19 there is the big issue of climate change and the debates about the future of tourism as a consequence big tourism (i.e., over-tourism). In order to find an alternative, maybe the future is about smallness, regeneration, and communities (Cave and Dredge 2020; Dredge and Jenkins 2007; Sheldon 2021) so that tourism can be part of the solution rather than part of the problem, and changing the debate in which the negative impacts of tourism are highlighted. Small tourism allows communities to address issues of social inequality, to create a sense of place, to gain ownership of the tourism-development process, and, most importantly of all, to allow the development of entrepreneurship and innovation. This chapter has identified ten micro-trends, the foundation trends of small tourism that, taken together, can provide a useful framework for those involved in small tourism and who are creating tourism experiences for a better world. Understanding the values, behaviours, and motivations of the tourist will result in the creation of suitable tourism products and experiences for that tourist to consume. We predict that, in the future, small tourism will become the venue in which the interests of ecotourists and destination communities will merge.

NOTES

1   https://www.toastmartinborough.co.nz/.

2   https://www.exploreworldwide.co.nz/.

3   https://www.intrepidtravel.com/.

4   https://www.exodustravels.com/.

5   https://www.foresightfactory.co/.

6   http://www.bluffoysterfest.co.nz/.

7   https://wildfoods.co.nz.

8   https://www.airbnb.com/experiences.

References

Alberti, Fay Bound. 2021. "Coronavirus Is Revitalising the Concept of Community for the 21st Century." *The Conversation*, 29 April 2020. https://theconversation. com/coronavirus-is-revitalising-the-concept-of-community-for-the-21st-century-135750.

Aref, Fariborz. 2011. "Sense of Community and Participation for Tourism Development." *Life Science Journal* 8, no. 1: 20–5.

Athwal, Navdeep, Victoria K. Wells, Marylyn Carrigan, and Claudia E. Henninger. 2019. "Sustainable Luxury Marketing: A Synthesis and Research Agenda." *International Journal of Management Reviews* 21, no. 4: 405–26. https://doi.org/10.1111/ijmr.12195.

Bourdieu, Pierre. 2000. *Distinction: A Social Critique of the Judgement of Taste*. Translated by Richard Nice. Cambridge, MA: Harvard University Press.

Boztug, Yasemin, Nazila Babakhani, Chrsitian Laesser, and Sara Dolnicar. 2015. "The Hybrid Tourist." *Annals of Tourism Research* 54:190–203. https://www.sciencedirect.com/science/article/pii/S0160738315001000.

Butler, Richard W., and Douglas G. Pearce. 1999. *Tourism Development*. London: Routledge.

Cardow, Andrew, and Peter Wiltshier. 2010. "Indigenous Tourism Operators: The Vanguard of Economic Recovery in the Chatham Islands." *International Journal of Entrepreneurship and Small Business* 10, no. 4: 484–98. doi:10.1504/ijesb.2010.034027.

Carr, Anna. 2020. "COVID-19, Indigenous Peoples and Tourism: A View from New Zealand." *Tourism Geographies* 22, no. 3: 491–502. doi:10.1080/14616688.2020.176 8433.

Casado-Diaz, Maria Angeles, and Michaela Benson. 2009. "Social Capital in the Sun: Bonding and Bridging Social Capital among British Retirees." In *Lifestyle Migration: Expectations, Aspirations and Experiences*, edited by Michaela Benson, Karen O'Reilly, and Anne J. Kershen, 88–108. Abingdon, UK: Taylor and Francis.

Cave, Jenny, and Dianee Dredge. 2020. "Regenerative Tourism Needs Diverse Economic Practices." *Tourism Geographies* 22, no. 3: 503–13. doi:10.1080/14616688.2020.176 8434

Dashper, Katherine, ShiNa Li, Mang He, Puyue Zhang, and Ting Lyu. 2021. "Ageing, Volunteering and Tourism: An Asian Perspective." *Annals of Tourism Research* 89:103248. https://doi.org/10.1016/j.annals.2021.103248.

Department of Conservation. 2021a. *2020/21 Visitor Insights Report*. Wellington: Department of Conversation. https://www.doc.govt.nz/globalassets/documents/about-doc/role/visitor-research/visitor-insights-report-2020-2021.pdf.

———. 2021b. "Volunteer Statistics." https://www.doc.govt.nz/get-involved/volunteer/search-volunteer-activities/.

Dredge, Dianne, and John M. Jenkins. 2007. *Tourism Planning and Policy*. Milton, AU: John Wiley and Sons.

Ehrnrooth, Hanna, and Christian Gronroos. 2013. "The Hybrid Consumer: Exploring Hybrid Consumption Behaviour." *Management Decision* 51, no. 9: 1793–820. doi:10.1108/MD-12-2012-0867.

Featherstone, Mike. 2020. "Whither Globalization? An Interview with Roland Robertson." *Theory, Culture & Society* 37, nos. 7–8: 169–85. doi:10.1177/0263276420959429.

Foresight Factory. 2017. "Luxury Sector Trends." https://www.foresightfactory.co/ffonline/.

———. 2018a. "The Experience Seeker." www.foresightfactory.co (subscription only).

———. 2018b. "Global World—Contextual Driver." www.foresightfactory.co.

———. 2019. "Once Is Not Enough." www.foresightsightfactory.co (subscription only).

Fountain, Joanna. 2021. "The Future of Food Tourism in a Post-COVID-19 World: Insights from New Zealand." *Journal of Tourism Futures* 8, no. 2. doi:10.1108/JTF-04-2021-0100.

Fullagar, Simone, Kevin Markwell, and Erica Wilson, eds. 2012. *Slow Tourism: Experiences and Mobilities*. Bristol, UK: Channel View Publications.

Fusté-Forné, Francesc, and Tazim Jamal. 2020. "Slow Food Tourism: An Ethical Microtrend for the Anthropocene." *Journal of Tourism Futures* 6, no. 3: 227–32.

Gabriel-Campos, Edwin, Katarzyna Werner-Masters, Franklin Cordova-Buiza, and Alberto Paucar-Caceres. 2021. "Community Eco-tourism in Rural Peru: Resilience and Adaptive Capacities to the Covid-19 Pandemic and Climate Change." *Journal of Hospitality and Tourism Management* 48, no. 27: 416–27. https://doi.org/10.1016/j.jhtm.2021.07.016.

Gössling, Stefan, Paul Hanna, James Higham, Scott Cohen, and Debbie Hopkins. 2019. "Can We Fly Less? Evaluating the 'Necessity' of Air Travel." *Journal of Air Transport Management* 81:101722. https://doi.org/10.1016/j.jairtraman.2019.101722.

Hollinshead, Keith. 2006. "The Shift to Constructivism in Social Inquiry: Some Pointers for Tourism Studies." *Tourism Recreation Research* 31, no. 2: 43–58. doi:10.1080/02508281.2006.11081261.

Howison, Sharleen, Freya Higgins-Desbiolles, and Zexuan Sun. 2017. "Storytelling in Tourism: Chinese Visitors and Māori Hosts in New Zealand." *Anatolia* 28, no. 3: 327–37. doi:10.1080/13032917.2017.1318296.

Howland, Peter. 2008. "Martinborough's Wine Tourists and the Metro-Rural Idyll." *Journal of New Zealand Studies* 6–7:77–100.

Interior Design Shop. 2020. "The Most Beautiful Starbucks Store: The Bank in Amsterdam." Interior Design Shop, 27 May 2020. https://www.interiordesignshop.net/the-most-beautiful-starbucks-store-the-bank-in-amsterdam/.

Iso-Ahola, Seppo E. 1982. "Toward a Social Psychological Theory of Tourism Motivation: A Rejoinder." *Annals of Tourism Research* 9, no. 2: 256–62. https://doi.org/10.1016/0160-7383(82)90049-4.

Jamal, Tazim, and Amanda Stronza. 2009. "Collaboration Theory and Tourism Practice in Protected Areas: Stakeholders, Structuring and Sustainability." *Journal of Sustainable Tourism* 17, no. 2: 169–89. doi:10.1080/09669580802495741.

Jiang, Yangyang, and M. S. Balaji. 2021. "Getting Unwired: What Drives Travellers to Take a Digital Detox Holiday?" *Tourism Recreation Research*: 1-17. https://doi.org/10.108 0/02508281.2021.1889801.

Jones, Peter, and Daphne Comfort. 2020. "A Commentary on the COVID-19 Crisis, Sustainability and the Service Industries." *Journal of Public Affairs* 20, no. 4: e2164. https://doi.org/10.1002/pa.2164.

Joppe, Marion. 1996. "Sustainable Community Tourism Development Revisited." *Tourism Management* 17, no. 7: 475–9. https://doi.org/10.1016/S0261-5177(96)00065-9.

Kallis, Giorgos. 2011. "In Defence of Degrowth." *Ecological Economics* 70, no. 5: 873–80. doi:10.1016/j.ecolecon.2010.12.007.

Kastanakis, Minas N., and George Balabanis. 2012. "Between the Mass and the Class: Antecedents of the 'Bandwagon' Luxury Consumption Behavior." *Journal of Business Research* 65, no. 10: 1399–1407. doi:10.1016/j.jbusres.2011.10.005.

Kharas, Homi. 2020. "Who Gained from Global Growth Last Decade—and Who Will Benefit by 2030?" Brookings Institution, 15 Hanuary 2020. https://www.brookings. edu/blog/future-development/2020/01/16/who-gained-from-global-growth-last-decade-and-who-will-benefit-by-2030/.

Kock, Florian, Astrid Nørfelt, Alexander Josiassen, A. George Assaf, and Mike G. Tsionas. 2020. "Understanding the COVID-19 Tourist Psyche: The Evolutionary Tourism Paradigm." *Annals of Tourism Research* 85:103053. https://doi.org/10.1016/j. annals.2020.103053.

Laing, Jennifer, and Warwick Frost. 2015. "The New Food Explorer: Beyond the Experience Economy." In *The Future of Food Tourism: Foodies, Experiences, Exclusivity, Visions and Political Capital*, edited by Ian Yeoman, Una McMahon-Beattie, Kevin Fields, Julia Albrecht, and Kevin Meetham, 177–93. Bristol, UK: Channel View Publications.

Li, Guoxin, Guofeng Li, and Zephaniah Kambele. 2012. "Luxury Fashion Brand Consumers in China: Perceived Value, Fashion Lifestyle, and Willingness to Pay." *Journal of Business Research* 65, no. 10: 1516–22.

Lockstone-Binney, Leonie, and Faith Ong. 2021. "The Sustainable Development Goals: The Contribution of Tourism Volunteering." *Journal of Sustainable Tourism* 30, no. 12: 1–17. doi:10.1080/09669582.2021.1919686.

Ma, Siying, Xueyi Zhao, Yuyan Gong, and Yana Wengel. 2021. "Proposing 'Healing Tourism' as a Post-COVID-19 Tourism Product." *Anatolia* 32, no. 1: 136–9. doi:10.1 080/13032917.2020.1808490.

Mackenzie, Susan Houge, and Jasmine Goodnow. 2021. "Adventure in the Age of COVID-19: Embracing Microadventures and Locavism in a Post-Pandemic World." *Leisure Sciences* 43, nos. 1–2: 62-69. doi:10.1080/01490400.2020.1773984.

Majeed, Salman, and Haywantee Ramkissoon. 2020. "Health, Wellness, and Place Attachment during and Post Health Pandemics." *Frontiers in Psychology* 11. doi:10.3389/fpsyg.2020.573220.

McGee, Jeffrey, and Bruno Arpi. 2021. "Wilderness Protection in Polar Regions: Arctic Lessons Learnt for the Regulation and Management of Tourism in the Antarctic." *Polar Journal* 11, no. 1: 239–41. doi:10.1080/2154896X.2021.1911764.

McMillan, David W. 1996. "Sense of Community." *Journal of Community Psychology* 24, no. 4: 315–25. doi:10.1002/(sici)1520-6629(199610)24:4<315::Aid-jcop2>3.0.Co;2-t.

Meikle, S. 2019. Private correspondence via email, 21 October 2019.

Mtapuri, Oliver, and Andrea Giampiccoli. 2017. "A Conceptual Coalescence: Towards Luxury Community Based Tourism." *African Journal of Hospitality, Tourism and Leisure* 6, no. 3: 1–14.

Murray, Warwick E., and John Overton. 2011. "Defining Regions: The Making of Places in the New Zealand Wine Industry." *Australian Geographer* 42, no. 4: 419–33. doi:10.1080/00049182.2012.619956.

Navarro-Martínez, Zenaida Maria, Christine Marie Crespo, Leslie Hernández-Fernández, Hakna Ferro-Azcona, Silvia Patricia González-Díaz, and Richard J. McLaughlin. 2020. "Using SWOT Analysis to Support Biodiversity and Sustainable Tourism in Caguanes National Park, Cuba." *Ocean & Coastal Management* 193:105188. https://doi.org/10.1016/j.ocecoaman.2020.105188.

Volunteering New Zealand. 2021. "Status of the Volunteering Sector: Post-COVID Recovery and Resilience." Volunteering New Zealand, May 2021. https://www.volunteeringnz.org.nz/wp-content/uploads/Status-of-the-volunteering-sector-post-covid-recovery-and-resilience-May-2021-v3.pdf.

Noorashid, Najib, and Wei Lee Chin. 2021. "Coping with COVID-19: The Resilience and Transformation of Community-Based Tourism in Brunei Darussalam." *Sustainability* 13, no. 15: 8618.

Oskam, Jeroen. 2019. *The Future of Airbnb and the "Sharing Economy."* Bristol, UK: Channel View Publications.

Penn, Mark. 2007. *Microtrends: The Small Forces behind Tomorrow's Big Changes.* New York: Twelve.

Penn, Mark, and Meredith Fineman. 2018. *Microtrends Squared: The New Small Forces Driving Today's Big Disruptions.* New York: Simon and Schuster.

Pfefferbaum, Betty, and Carol S. North. 2020. "Mental Health and the Covid-19 Pandemic." *New England Journal of Medicine* 383, no. 6: 510–12. doi:10.1056/NEJMp2008017.

Pine, B. Joseph, and James H. Gilmore. 2011. *The Experience Economy.* Updated ed. Boston: Harvard Business Review Press.

Prillwitz, Jan, and Stewart Barr. 2011. "Moving towards Sustainability? Mobility Styles, Attitudes and Individual Travel Behaviour." *Journal of Transport Geography* 19, no. 6: 1590–1600. https://doi.org/10.1016/j.jtrangeo.2011.06.011.

Quorin, Meabh, Laura Van Eeckhout, and Dominic Harrison. n.d. "The New Next: Which Consumer Trends Have Been Boosted by the Pandemic." Foresight Factory, accessed 5 April 2023. https://www.foresightfactory.co/webinar-on-demand/#boosted.

Robertson, Martin, and Ian Yeoman. 2014. "Signals and Signposts of the Future: Literary Festival Consumption in 2050." *Tourism Recreation Research* 39, no. 3: 321–42. doi: 10.1080/02508281.2014.11087004.

Robertson, Martin, Ian Yeoman, Karen Smith, and Una McMahon-Beattie. "Technology, Society, and Visioning the Future of Music Festivals." *Event Management* 19, no. 4: 567–87.

Ryan, Chris. 1997. "Maori and Tourism: A Relationship of History, Constitutions and Rites." *Journal of Sustainable Tourism* 5, no. 4: 257–78.

Sharfuddin, Syed. 2020. "The World after Covid-19." *Round Table: The Commonwealth Journal of International Affairs* 109, no. 3: 247–57. doi:10.1080/00358533.2020.1760 498.

Shaw, Dougal. 2021. "Airbnb Boss: 'Cornwall's More Popular than London.'" BBC News, 25 May 2021. https://www.bbc.com/news/technology-57240212.

Sheldon, Pauline J. 2021. "The Coming-of-Age of Tourism: Embracing New Economic Models." *Journal of Tourism Futures* 8, no. 2. doi:10.1108/JTF-03-2021-0057.

Silverstein, Michael J., Niel Fiske, and Butman. 2003. *Trading Up: The New American Luxury.* New York: Portfolio.

Situmorang, Rospita Odorlina. 2017. "Social Capital in Managing Mangrove as Ecotourism Area by Muara Baimbai Community." *Indonesian Journal of Forestry Research* 5, no. 1: 21–34.

Sok, Jenny. 2022. "Adversity Quotient." In *Encyclopedia of Tourism Management and Marketing*, edited by Dimitrios Buhalis. Northampton, UK: Edward Elgar Publishing.

Stringfellow, Lindsay, Andrew MacLaren, Mairi Maclean, and Kevin O'Gorman. 2013. "Conceptualizing Taste: Food, Culture and Celebrities." *Tourism Management* 37, SC: 77–85. https://doi.org/10.1016/j.tourman.2012.12.016.

Towner, Nick, and Jérémy Lemarié. 2020. "Localism at New Zealand Surfing Destinations: Durkheim and the Social Structure of Communities." *Journal of Sport & Tourism* 24, no. 2: 93–110. doi:10.1080/14775085.2020.1777186.

Votsi, Nefta-Eleftheria P., Antonios D. Mazaris, Athanasios S. Kallimanis, and John D. Pantis. 2014. "Natural Quiet: An Additional Feature Reflecting Green Tourism Development in Conservation Areas of Greece." *Tourism Management Perspectives* 11:10–17. https://doi.org/10.1016/j.tmp.2014.02.001.

Walker, Therez B., Timothy J. Lee, and Xiubai Li. 2021. "Sustainable Development for Small Island Tourism: Developing Slow Tourism in the Caribbean." *Journal of Travel & Tourism Marketing* 38, no. 1: 1–15. doi:10.1080/10548408.2020.1842289.

Williams, Lauren T., John Germov, Sascha Fuller, and Maria Freij. 2015. "A Taste of Ethical Consumption at a Slow Food Festival." *Appetite* 91, SC: 321–8. https://doi.org/10.1016/j.appet.2015.04.066.

Yeoman, Ian. 2008. *Tomorrow's Tourist: Scenarios and Trends*. London: Elsevier Science.

——. "Tomorrow's Tourist: Fluid and Simple Identities." *Journal of Globalization Studies* 1, no. 2: 118–27.

——. 2016. "The Future Tourist: Fluid and Simple Identities." Victoria University of Wellington. https://vimeo.com/181103735/ad143522da.

——. 2020. "Don't Leave Home—but Then Go See Your Country." *The Newsroom*, 19 April 2020. https://www.newsroom.co.nz/ideasroom/dont-leave-home-but-then-go-and-see-your-country.

——. Forthcoming. *Scenarios for Global Tourism*. Bristol, UK: Channel View Publications.

Yeoman, Ian, Amalina Andrade, Elisante Leguma, Natalie Wolf, Peter Ezra, Rebecca Tan, and Una McMahon-Beattie. 2015. "2050: New Zealand's Sustainable Future." *Journal of Tourism Futures* 1, no. 2: 117–30. doi:10.1108/JTF-12-2014-0003.

Yeoman, Ian, Danna Brass, and Una McMahon-Beattie. 2007. "Current Issue in Tourism: The Authentic Tourist." *Tourism Management* 28, no. 4: 1128–38. doi:10.1016/j.tourman.2006.09.012.

Yeoman, Ian, Alastair Durie, Una McMahon-Beattie, and Adrian Palmer. 2005. "Capturing the Essence of a Brand from Its History: The Case of Scottish Tourism Marketing." *Journal of Brand Management* 13, no. 2: 134–47. doi:10.1057/palgrave.bm.2540253.

Yeoman, Ian, Joanna Fountain, and Sarah Meikle. 2020. "Could Food and Drink Save the Tourism Industry?" *The Newsroom*, 8 June 2020. https://www.newsroom.co.nz/ideasroom/could-food-and-drink-save-the-tourism-industry.

Yeoman, Ian, and Una McMahon-Beattie. 2018. "The Future of Luxury: Mega Drivers, New Faces and Scenarios." *Journal of Revenue and Pricing Management* 17, no. 4: 204–17. doi:10.1057/s41272-018-0140-6.

——. 2019. "The Experience Economy: Micro Trends." *Journal of Tourism Futures* 5, no. 2: 1–8. https://doi.org/10.1108/JTF-05-2019-0042.

——. 2020. "Does the Past Shape the Future of Tourism? A Cognitive Mapping Perspective." In *Future of Tourism*, edited by Ian Yeoman and Una McMahon-Beattie, 243–307. Bristol, UK: Channel View Publications.

Yeoman, Ian, Una McMahon-Beattie, Elisa Backer, Martin Robertson, and Karen A. Smith, eds. 2014. *The Future of Events & Festivals*. Abingdon, UK: Routledge.

Yeoman, Ian, Una McMahon-Beattie, Katherine Findlay, Sandra Goh, Sophea Tieng, and Sochea Nhem. 2021. "Future-Proofing the Success of Food Festivals through Determining the Drivers of Change: A Case Study of Wellington on a Plate." *Tourism Analysis* 26, nos. 2–3: 167–93.

Yeoman, Ian, Martin Robertson, and Karen A. Smith. 2012. "A Futurist's View on the Future of Events." In *The Routledge Handbook of Events*, edited by Stephen J. Page and Joanne Connell, 507–25. Abingdon, UK: Routledge.

Yeoman, Ian, Heike A. Schänzel, and Eliza Zentveld. 2022. "Tourist Behaviour in a COVID-19 World: A New Zealand Perspective." *Journal of Tourism Futures* 8, no. 2. doi:10.1108/JTF-03-2021-0082.

Situating Small: Orienting Trajectories, Generative Journeys

Nancy Duxbury

Small tourism focuses on local experiences intentionally designed for a limited number of participants at a time, or for niche groups, and is offered by a micro-enterprise—ideally based in and supported by the community. This approach provides inspiration for touristic products in small places as well as those generated by neighbourhoods in larger cities. Organizers of small tourism experiences serve as a meeting point for artists and artisans, highlight diverse professions and living cultures, provide spaces for sharing cultural expressions and practices, and create collaborative social networks among individuals and community-based organizations. Through a small tourism lens, can we reimagine what the future could be? Is it possible that small tourism can be a part of a sustainable future, where the interests of travellers and destination communities can merge?

In the introduction to this book, Kathleen Scherf discusses various dimensions of thinking about small tourism today, from highlighting outside-the-mainstream approaches fuelled by motivations connected to altruism, education, experimentation, and immersion; to reconsidering and engaging with the significance of specific places (from neighbourhoods within urban centres to communities located in remote peripheries) and tapping into the life forces and dynamics that drive "everyday" cultures and communities. Rooted in very different contexts, the threads she traces relate to common ideas, concerns, and inspirational ideas across the case studies and stories presented in this book. She emphasizes the ways in which small tourism can enable deeper connections between the people engaged and facilitate connections between resident, visitor, and place. Ultimately, as she notes, when small tourism experiences are embedded in a community's desire to engage in tourism, and are rooted in local nature and culture, the participation of locals in crafting these intimate local tourism experiences creates social dynamics that, over time, serve to "strengthen, not deplete, the community's sense of place" (page 10). All in all, small tourism seems to be a win-win-win situation.

I share this interest in highlighting and (ultimately) strengthening alternative tourism approaches that can inspire and propel more sustainable and regenerative approaches to interlinking local cultures and tourism for local benefit and development (Duxbury et al. 2020, 2021). These imperatives are reinforced in the wake of well-known examples of damaging mass- and over-tourism situations; a return to emphasizing local well-being and community resiliency that was heightened during the COVID-19 pandemic; and the changing motivations and aspirations of travellers. As Yeoman and McMahon-Beattie elaborate, the COVID-19 pandemic has contributed to "a new landscape" that is reconfiguring our socio-economic contexts and redirecting our personal aspirations—influencing both the pathways for tourism going forward and the ways in which travel experiences will develop within more-than-tourism-sector mindsets.

In this context, I see resonating synergies between the inspiring initiatives presented in this book and my recent work (Duxbury 2021) examining a variety of tourism-influenced situations with a particular eye to enabling and strengthening cultural vitality and cultural sustainability through a strategic attention to tourism flows. In that work, four overarching, interconnected dimensions emerged as centrally important in what I now recognize as culture-centred small tourism:

1. *Caring for culture*—fostering cultural stewardship and sustainability while enabling cultural adaptations and new approaches to traditional and emergent resources.

2. *Enabling culturally sensitive modes of tourism*—encouraging locally beneficial modes of tourism which reshape relations between visitors and local residents and highlight the specificities of a place.

3. *Empowering community*—strengthening local community agency and designing inclusive and participative governance

frameworks and mechanisms to better understand and act upon dynamics and issues concerning tourism, local cultural vitality, and social well-being.

4. *Improving place*—leveraging the interactions between tourism and culture to engender positive placemaking dynamics that improve the cultural vitality, quality of life, and experience of place for both residents and visitors and thus contribute to sustainable development trajectories. (198)

Now, as I approach the design and writing of this concluding chapter, many possible directions and approaches swirl around me as I wonder how best to interweave the rich insights, perspectives, and distinct voices of the contributions in this book in ways that can inform and pull forward these streams of thinking and action. Three sets of questions have emerged top of mind:

- First, how are these small tourism initiatives rooted and fuelled by local specificities, both tangible and intangible? How do they engage with local culture, nature, and sense of place? How are these localized cultural assets and specificities of place taken up and "vitalized" in these initiatives?

- Second, how does the community benefit? What is fostered and nurtured by these initiatives? How can small tourism and similar localized initiatives provide generative dynamics toward the sustainable development of smaller communities?

- And, third, how can we address the fragility and vulnerabilities of small and micro-enterprises that comprise the core force designing and offering these small tourism experiences? What strategies and structures for resilience and ongoing sustainability might be found within the entrepreneurial ingenuity and practices of these initiatives?

With these wide-ranging questions in mind, I reviewed the chapters in this collection, aiming to identify insights and other "keys" that could help me understand these dimensions more deeply. As I did so, it became increasingly clear that these concerns were tightly interconnected, and it is the integrated-ness of these dimensions that can support and propel small tourism initiatives. In this concluding chapter, I aim to uncover some themes and trajectories that may illuminate strategic approaches to developing small tourism initiatives. While attempting to organize these points within the three areas identified above, I acknowledge that they are tightly interwoven—small tourism initiatives such as those presented in this book emerge from, embody, and enliven their locales in close and dynamic ways.

Rooted in Place, Engaging with Local Culture and Other Specificities

The diversity of initiatives presented in this volume present an array of approaches to how small tourism initiatives are rooted in and fuelled by tangible and intangible local specificities. The initiatives demonstrate an attentiveness and sensitivity to micro-cultures and the dynamics of communities and specific public sites. They offer strategic approaches to *integration*—of sites, activities, themes, stories, rituals/practices, and the knowledges and perspectives of local guides—in ways that, cumulatively, enable rich and meaningful experiences and exchanges, and enable visitors to temporarily tap into the socio-cultural and other dynamics of a specific place. It is in the intertwining of personal contacts, visitor perspectives, and mutual curiosities through such varied platforms that authentic cultural heritages, lifestyles, and meanings of place are revealed, shared, and—possibly—dynamized for local well-being and development.

Intangible Cultural Heritage, Realized through Personal Contact

It is in these integrative dynamics that the intangible cultural heritage of a place is revealed. As Diana Guerra Amaya and Diana Marcela Zuluaga Guerra observe in chapter 6, the intangible heritage of a place is "synonymous with the ordinary" and is found in "everyday life, in local people, in their routine and cultural practices, in the flavours, the colours, the crafts, the architecture, and the passersby" (page 156). In the case of Casa Bô in Porto (chapter 5), community-driven interactions and local cultural activity *is* the foundation and organizer of the small tourism experiences. In the southwestern Australia cases, the site and substance of the small tourism experience is caring and personally (re)connecting with the *Boodja* itself, "the biodiverse land biome with its entwined Noongar spirituality in all its realms" (page 113). The small, relational tourism experiences entail "a journey of landscape and cultural reconnection that focuses on tourists' brief immersion with land restorers at the site of recreation" (page 112) through which the entwined nature of ecological, cultural, and social values is encountered.

Throughout the small tourism examples, the focus is on people—individuals in "their" place, sharing their perspectives and knowledges of it with visitors. In southwestern Australia, the local residents and restorers are the "tourism providers": "they present their first-hand perspectives, offering authenticity in their ecotourism product" (page 114). In Maribor, the "walkers" are local residents who know the city's stories, who enable visitors to "feel, smell, taste, hear, and touch the cultural heritage in real time and space" (page 71). If the walkers are heritage bearers themselves, they become "active heritage interpreters" as well (page 74). At an individual level, small tourism organizers must be sensitive to and respect the desired involvement of locals, a point emphasized by Guerra Amaya and Zuluaga Guerra in chapter 6.

At the same time, the agency of the travellers themselves, and their own desire to obtain "a more nuanced understanding of the local area," is also important to keep in mind, possibly initiating local contacts through online communication conduits, as we see in Spencer Toth, Josie Vayrc, and Courtney Mason's chapter (page 43). Local residents (however contacted) are the mediators between visitor uncertainties and local realities, which is a significant role. For example, as Moira A. L. Maley and her co-authors point out in chapter 4, "The comfort and familiarity shown by restorers when in their landscape is a stabilizing factor for the visitors, most of whom will be out of their comfort zone to some extent, at least initially" (page 123).

Towards a Paradigm of Sharing and Connection

Altogether, the overriding perspective of carefully designed small tourism experiences is of *sharing*, rather than of *representing*. This focus on the sharing of *our* experiences means that small tourism is a carefully designed extension of ongoing activities, not a separate realm of enterprise. For example, the essence of 5Bogota's market visit and book-making activity is the sharing of "usual" practices—the workshop is an *extension*, not something new for tourists to do that locals do not do. The dynamics of crafting and implementing visitor experiences based on the traditional and everyday occurrences of local hosts and their cultural heritage can revitalize and stimulate "the recognition of their own cultural wealth, playing a central role in preserving intangible urban heritage assets" in Bogota (page 172).

Maintaining active social connections and creating long-term commitment and trust within the broader communities where small tourism activities are sited is imperative. Knowledge and social connections are maintained through ongoing active relationships: in the southwestern Australia cases (chapter 4), this means the "informal relationship building between restorers and traditional owners, as well as direct Noongar interpretation for visitors" (page 124), is both a context for and an integral core of the ecotourism experiences. It is also notable how these relationships have fostered cultural mapping and artworks capturing knowledges to become (again) part of the public knowledge base.

In an urban context, as chapter 6 points out, visits should occur regularly, without visitors, so that "the locals recognize you and allow you to become part of the community; only then will you be part of its daily life, able to share it with future guests" (page 158). In a festival context, Panyik and Komlós (chapter 7) note that while "events are held in central places in the villages to promote interaction with the local communities" (page 188), in addition, local cultural/community groups directly participate through cultural performances as well as in the organization of public forums within the festival to "draw attention to social problems such as segregation and discrimination" facing the local Roma community (page 187). Trust between hosts, residents, and guests is a necessary condition for small tourism.

Contextualizing and Grounding Local Experiences

Visitors are part of a broader context, beyond "tourism." For Casa Bô, visitor-welcoming activities are part of a constellation of already-occurring activities. For potential gay travellers to rural British Columbia, as chapter 1 points out, recognition that a place is "outwardly supportive" of the LGBTQ2+ community, indicating openness to inclusion, provides a welcoming message; in this context, symbolic gestures and concrete actions are both significant.

Donald Lawrence's experiences participating in arts festivals in small places has led him to stress the importance of ensuring the cultural activity is "true to the place," recognizing the close-knit identity and local traditions of smaller communities, being careful to enable "a meaningful encounter," and not misrepresenting a region and its cultural traditions. For visiting artist-participants, immersion into the local arts scene is part of the attraction: "the opportunity to be welcomed into the small cultural communities that congregate around places like Eastern Edge" (page 205). But he also notes that the organizers must also be careful not to stay "too insular" so as to appeal to and engage a broader audience (page 202).

Immersion and the direct experience of these broader scenes and dynamics is key for small tourism. For student-tourists living in a small village in Montespertoli, Tuscany, on-site insertion (temporarily) in a small community enables direct interaction with local producers and residents of the community, "not only to observe the circular socio-economy, but also to interact and participate in it" (page 97). With an emphasis on tradition, craftsmanship, and direct experiences, these "cultural creatives" seek meaningful experiences involving connections that demonstrate, for instance, the traditional art of producing food and directly participating in the process themselves.

The importance of direct "felt experience" is also mentioned in relation to the southwestern Australia ecotourism experiences: "The biodiversity needs to be felt through contact and actions before meaning can be made" (page 123). These examples pointed to the importance of centralizing learning and meaning making in the design of encounters and experiences. They also, for me, highlighted the value of rituals of visitation and learning, involving in this case "first, a journey into country; second, an orientation and intimate interaction inside country; and third, a journey back out from country" (page 122). In other cases, these journeys might be more symbolic and narrative-based than geographical, but this important aspect of transition is a valuable structure, providing time and space to build a relationship with a place, and returning, potentially transformed, into one's ongoing life trajectories. Integration of past, present, and future; of visitor, resident, and place; of cultures, perspectives, and voices; and of networks, nature, and community—all these syntheses are part of small tourism.

Fostering Community Benefits and Generative Dynamics

As repeatedly shown in the chapters in this book, in small tourism, localized initiatives can become the start-up engines for wider generative dynamics toward the sustainable development of smaller communities. These dynamics can realize a diversity of activities, such as youth training and talent development, incubation of emerging initiatives, and new cultural production. More widely, small tourism initiatives that are intentionally fostered with close attention to the particularities, needs, and resources of the community in which they are developed can contribute to greater community-level resilience, distribute benefits from tourism flows more widely and inclusively, provide pathways to preserve and sustain local cultures, encourage public dialogue, expand collective knowledge and know-how, enhance and diversify networks, and provide platforms for local change makers.

Training, Incubation, and New Cultural Production

From a cultural and economic development perspective, small tourism initiatives can become a training and incubation hub and an outlet for new cultural production. Beyond selling locally crafted products, Rajzefiber, for example, helps young people to create an idea, develop a product, and place the final product in their sales program, as we learn in chapter 2. And as Donald Lawrence observes, small-scale arts festivals, based in collaboration among locally engaged individuals and often with an eye to involving youth in planning and workshops, include a range of different types of activities in which people may engage. These events tend to attract "highly engaged visitors" to the host communities, who directly contribute to the local economy during the time of the festival but who are also "intent on building important linkages between small places, networks comprising members of an extended cultural community" (page 192).

Community-Level Resilience

Meng Qu and Simona Zollet (chapter 9) observe that the individual resilience of Mitarai's in-migrant-run tourism micro-businesses translates into community-level resilience. They explain how these small businesses play a multi-faceted role in their community: creating economic value that enables the in-migrant to continue to live in the community; increasing Mitarai's attractiveness as a tourism destination with businesses and creative activities; contributing to improving local residents' quality of life through, in part, providing new services and community spaces; and attracting, through their presence, other urban-rural in-migrants. As the authors note, "this process, if sustained, has the potential to help stabilize the population and restore a sense of socio-economic vitality in the community" (page 237).

More Inclusive Tourism Benefits

An important potential of small tourism initiatives is to strategically create new pathways of action that can diversify to whom and where benefits from tourism flow. The urban tourism initiatives of 5Bogota (chapter 6) create "thematic links between the outskirts and the inner city" and include "under-recognized locations as tourism territories" (page 166, 172). Through doing this, the company's initiatives foster both economic and social inclusion by "bringing wealth created by tourism to communities usually overlooked by the industry" (page 166). At a local level, the small tourism initiatives also create social capital through "integrating local communities as hosts" (page 172) and distributing earnings from these services into communities that would not otherwise receive them. Thinking beyond economics, small tourism initiatives like this are designed as "a bonding space for people" (page 172), which serves to reclaim "the dignity of the daily life of locals while at the same time impacting the lives of visitors in profound and moving ways" (page 172). Andre Luis Quintino Principe (chapter 5) also writes about how engagement between visitors and residents produced "mutual benefits, thereby promoting social cohesion and inclusion" (page 133).

As Panyik and Komlós discuss (chapter 7), within the organization of the Devil's Nest Festival, tasks are allocated to non-governmental organizations "to redistribute the profit generated during the festival for local development" (page 186). In addition, direct income for residents is generated through local accommodations and "tenting space" in backyards, sales of local products (e.g., food and souvenirs), expansion of basic foodstuffs in grocery stores, and second-hand clothes merchandized to cool festival visitors. More generally, the festival has created new tourism products, diversifying the tourism offer of the region, and elevated the profile of the small festival villages.

Cultural Sustainability and Public Dialogue

From a cultural perspective, the Devil's Nest Festival plays multiple roles, contributing to *cultural preservation*, through promoting "living ethnography" and almost-extinct cultural practices and incorporating local legends, myths, and oral traditions through new theatre pieces (sometimes supported by a cultural funding program); *new cultural production*, including new activities that are developed such as artistic workshops and new ideas and projects created in-process, from on-site sculptures to an "analogue Facebook" wall;

and enabling *attendance*, providing low-cost or free access for local residents to attend events and fundraising to support the participation of children from the poorest villages in the region.

Small tourism initiatives generate spaces and opportunities to voice and share personal stories of the place, allowing both visitors and locals to get to know their locale better, developing a collaborative sense of place. These initiatives can also generate a space for local public discussion. For example, the Festival of Walks in Maribor (chapter 2) "offers space and time to bring together stakeholders to discuss current issues and trends" on topics related to tourism, especially cultural and creative tourism, and culture in general (page 73). As mentioned previously, the Devil's Nest Festival in Hungary also incorporates a public forum dimension for this role.

Collective Knowledge and Know-How

Many of the entrepreneurs in small tourism serve to expand collective knowledge and know-how through regional networking and co-learning. In Tuscany (chapter 3), the emphasis on "local foodways" that provide regional distinctiveness, which encourages slower, smaller, and more interconnected food systems, simultaneously reinforces support for the local economy and the socio-cultural dimensions of these local ways of life. In Maribor, Rajzefiber established Potujočo Akademijo Kreativnega Turizma (PAKT) to enhance the development of regional creative tourism products; the initiative offers training through the sharing of experiences, peer learning, and discussions of theories and trends in small tourism. PAKT is "steadily growing to be the first regional, bottom-up educational platform for small tourist providers who live and work in the rural outskirts" (page 76).

Platforms for Change Makers

Small tourism can develop as an extension of local agents' personal mission as change makers. In the southwestern Australia cases (chapter 4), sharing the outcomes of restoration processes comprises an important dimension of the work during which "the restorers spread the word and mature their own wisdom" (page 125). The restorers' local actions aim to intentionally generate dynamics that flow from the community, directed outward, inviting visitors "to create their own [experiences] and to take with them into the future a new relationship with nature and biodiversity" (page 125). Their commitment to interweaving ancient knowledge with modern landscape assessment also influences residents in the region, with a generational change in mindset becoming evident: "The wider community now embraces First Nation People's cultural knowledge, ecological science, and lore related to land management. Emerging generations increasingly recognize and demand cultural connection and its integration into future restoration projects" (page 126). All chapters in this book attest to the cultural benefits offered by small tourism.

Strategies and Structures for Resiliency and Ongoing Sustainability

But how are such valuable encounters, activities, and experiences reliably sustained? While some of the cases presented in this book present successful year-on-year growing initiatives, the COVID-19 pandemic paused tourism-related activities internationally and introduced new dimensions of vulnerability that were not contemplated previously. This heightened sense of fragility continues to permeate a context of uncertainty, experimentation, and rethinking social foundations, and reconstructing networks of support. The situation has also provided insights into the structures and configurations that may be more resilient as careful steps forward are taken.

Organizational Resilience

The organizational contexts for small tourism initiatives in this book are varied, with Andre Luis Quintino Principe (chapter 5) elaborating how a not-for-profit cultural association can be a location of "emergent creativity" that can develop open and accessible approaches to welcoming local residents and visitors. Such an organization can operate in a flexible and autonomous manner, and in the case of Casa Bô in Porto, with low fixed expenses and a high number of volunteers. Nonetheless, economic sustainability was strained by the pandemic restrictions, and new approaches to sustaining the organization were adopted, such as using its space for artistic residencies.

An important aspect of the operations and sustainability of small tourism providers, Casa Bô or the creative tourism entrepreneurs in the CREATOUR project in Portugal, is the constellation of associated or complementary activities that align with their small, creative tourism initiatives (see Duxbury et al. 2020). Small tourism and creative tourism providers, such as Rajzefiber in Maribor (chapter 2), find themselves working across both culture and tourism, with different regulations in each field and limited experiences in cross-sector collaborative working practices. It is important to recognize how such systemic challenges can be substantial hurdles to innovating sustainable initiatives. The "boundary spanners" in this volume are reworking approaches in practice, and demonstrating new collaborative arrangements that may, over time, contribute to changing these broader regulatory contexts.

Qu and Zollet (chapter 9) highlight three keys to the resiliency of the micro-entrepreneurs they interviewed: "multifunctionality, flexibility, and frugality." They note the pragmatic importance of adopting multi-faceted functions and creating flexible and frugal organizational approaches with small overheads. At the same time, they point to the importance of "advancing strategies for balancing both community and tourism needs" (page 220), and it is this embeddedness in and responsibility to the community that characterizes these small tourism entrepreneurs. It is also this orientation that enables competition among micro-entrepreneurs to exist alongside collaborative networks with broader issues in mind. These insights resonate through many of the chapters in this collection.

The nature of the activities that locals and visitors share may enhance the resilience of their relationships. Chapters 3 and 6 highlight how gastronomic experiences, potentially embracing circular economy principles and "de-marketed or de-commodified tourist practices" (page 89), address an area of growing interest among contemporary travellers. Such experiences are crafted with local collaborators, enabling visitors to engage with the everyday life of a destination on a personal, experiential basis. Moreover, as John S. Hull, Donna Senese, and Darcen Esau point out, the close nature of host-guest relationships and the sense of place that is engendered can motivate and spread altruistic behaviours that may support the sustainability of small-scale tourism programs, creating ripples in the broader host community. This theme also resonates through the examples from southwestern Australia.

For small arts festivals such as those presented by Donald Lawrence (chapter 8), maintaining a balance among local and visiting participating artists serves to keep such events "rooted in the community, while at the same time enjoying a national profile and significance" (page 202). He notes that such festivals attract dedicated members of the arts community as well as "visitors who come upon such projects unexpectedly" (page 204). The character of such events "welcome and encourage visitors to engage in the experience at hand in different ways, to not stand back as passive observers" (page 201)—a memorable and desired-to-be-repeated role. Regularly scheduled arts festivals enable their visibility, programming, and a "dedicated" audience to be built and augmented over time. These are ways to encourage organizational resilience.

Networks of Collaborators and Supporters

The authors in this book, like those in its companion volume, *Creative Tourism in Smaller Communities*, note the significance of local clusters in sustaining small tourism. Repeatedly, the chapters attest to the vital importance of collaborative networks in organizing small tourism initiatives, sometimes coupled with external support. For example, Donald Lawrence (chapter 8) notes how small-scale arts festivals are typically "organized by a small collaborative network in a local community, including artists, and perhaps some artists from other places" (page 192), and externally supported (e.g., by an arts council) through a well-networked organizational partner. Rajzefiber (chapter 2) relies on a small core team and a strong system of volunteers who help it implement its events, with organizational support obtained from public funding agencies. It is interesting to note here Toth, Vayro, and Mason's observation in chapter 1 that a better-organized approach would aid in the promotion of rural British Columbia to gay travellers.

Castello Sonnino/SIEC (chapter 3) began with the cultivation of a network of university educators, researchers, and students with interests in preserving the natural environment and the cultural heritage of place for future generations. Over time, in addition to this network of scholars, local practitioners, entrepreneurs, and leaders from the local community have come to use the site—"a preserved but functioning family-run agricultural and viticultural operation" (page 93)—for educational initiatives and to support the local community. Here we see a successful example of networking. The importance of "early-in" local municipal support of these small initiatives appears in a number of stories. For instance, in Rajzefiber's initial five years, the municipality provided a rent-free space in the city centre, and the initiative received funding from the national employment agency to hire unemployed people. Panyik and Komlós note how the Devil's Nest Festival in Hungary has had ongoing municipal support in pragmatic infrastructure logistics and space needs, with close collaboration among various entities: "local wine cellars and municipalities are part of the organization as they do not only provide venues but accommodation as well" (page 188).

Wide and varied collaborative networks are also part of these initiatives, marked by the proactive role of small tourism organizers. Rajzefiber intentionally connects across culture, cultural heritage, creative industries, and tourism, although intersectoral work continues to be a core challenge. The organization has worked closely with a wide range of public and private organizations, agencies, and public bodies, and has built networks between stakeholders in the town with those in their region. Rajzefiber's success is attributed to this "strategic and systematic methodology of collaboration and co-creation" (page 70). For the Devil's Nest Festival, both organizational and geographic connectedness appear as priorities: "each of the villages [nearby the central festival site] became a festival location linked by a free festival bus" (page 174). The sense of collaboration around the festival also extends to its programming, which draws on local values and resources and "grows spontaneously in accordance with the interests, ideas, and feedback of the visitors, residents, and organizers alike" (page 174).

These networks connect outward, as mentioned by Donald Lawrence (chapter 8) and emphasized by Meng Qu and Simona Zollet (chapter 9), who discuss how "the involvement of Mitarai's tourism micro-entrepreneurs in a variety of social networks also determines the types of community- and extra-community-level resource exchanges and integrations that will be present" (page 232). However, it is also important to note how downscaling of activities can deepen local re-engagement: as Qu and Zollet explain, in 2020, "Although the festival was still open to tourists, the choice to reduce its scale and re-localize participation and content criteria increased the community's sense of ownership over the festival-creation process, and encouraged the initiation of more locally embedded partnerships between in-migrants and residents" (pages 235–36). Clusters and networks are an important factor in sustaining community-based small tourism.

Marketing and Profile

The challenges of marketing small tourism initiatives are well recounted by Katja Beck Kos, Mateja Meh, and Vid Kmetič (chapter 2), including a more widespread lack of marketing infrastructure that establishes channels to foreign markets for the diverse array of small tourism providers, including appropriate digital channels of sale and promotion. Although the support of local destination marketing organizations is a piece of this picture, their resources are limited and their scope is geographically and thematically focused, as Toth, Vayro, and Mason vividly demonstrate in chapter 1. This marketing issue is becoming more pronounced as a growing number of small producers are emerging and as travellers increasingly search for "authentic," embedded, and even transformative experiences through travel. It would seem that there is an opportunity for creating a co-operative international network that is open to and supportive of diverse small tourism initiatives without it becoming a branch of a multinational corporation already in the travel-booking market. Put another way: Can small tourism become a bigger presence in tourism while maintaining an approach that is also small and collaborative in nature?

In Closing: A Butterfly Effect?

The butterfly effect refers to the fact that small, barely perceptible changes can have a big, non-linear impact on a complex system. In other words, small matters can generate significant impact.

At the beginning of this chapter, I introduced four aspects of small, culture-based community tourism: caring for culture, enabling culturally sensitive modes of tourism, empowering community, and improving place. It is clear that the small tourism initiatives presented in this volume all mirror these themes. They demonstrate an ethics of care for people and a stewardship of places, embracing both traditional and emergent resources. The initiatives are intentionally engaging in locally sensitive and locally beneficial modes of tourism that are reshaping relations between visitors and local residents, as well as highlighting the specificities of a place. We see how they are empowering community, strengthening local economies and agency, and leveraging the interactions within tourism to engender positive dynamics in the broader community/place in ways that improve the cultural vitality, quality of life, and experience of place for both residents and visitors and thus contribute to sustainable development trajectories.

However, the volume also speaks to some of the issues that small tourism stakeholders must address. Specifically, the chapters reveal three concerns that are underdeveloped at this point. First, as I mentioned earlier, we might look to a (co-operative?) marketing "infrastructure" that establishes channels for marketing the diverse array of small tourism providers internationally. These channels should leverage the emerging roles of "disruptive" technologies and social media to engage new generations of young, "connected" travellers, who can enhance the takeoff and propel this type of "alternate" infrastructure. Even doing this regionally, and then perhaps nationally, would be a start. Second, there is a need for closer attention to how to manage the growth of successful small tourism, which may become much larger over time, and to envision various prospects and strategies for small-scale tourism in the context of the continued growth of travel and tourism internationally. Third, there seems to be room for discussing the development of inclusive and participative governance frameworks and mechanisms that can appropriately nurture and support these small tourism initiatives, facilitate cross-sectoral connections and innovations, and enable communities to better understand and act upon the dynamics of tourism to foster and improve local vitality, socio-economic well-being, and generate other local and regional benefits.

Collections like this book serve a valuable role in highlighting how small, seemingly isolated actions may be collectively contributing to wider changes—for tourism and for local communities and places. Those of us interested in small tourism require a greater awareness of how other small tourism sites are experiencing their situation, what issues they are facing, and what actions they are taking. We require more sustainable platforms to learn from each other, and we must participate in intentional, international connections; these seeds will generate the garden in which small tourism and its potential local community benefits could flourish.

References

Duxbury, Nancy, ed. 2021. *Cultural Sustainability, Tourism, and Development: (Re)articulations in Tourism Contexts.* London: Routledge.

Duxbury, Nancy, Sara Albino, and Cláudia Pato de Carvalho, eds. 2021. *Creative Tourism: Activating Cultural Resources and Engaging Creative Travellers.* London: CABI.

Duxbury, Nancy, Fiona Eva Bakas, Tiago Vinagre de Castro, and Sílvia Silva. 2020. "Creative Tourism Development Models towards Sustainable and Regenerative Tourism." *Sustainability* 13, no. 1: 1–17. https://doi.org/10.3390/su13010002.

Scherf, Kathleen, ed. 2021. *Creative Tourism in Smaller Communities: Place, Culture, and Local Representation.* Calgary: University of Calgary Press.

Contributors

DIANA GUERRA AMAYA is a Colombian business administrator trained at the Pontifical Xavierian University in Bogotá, Colombia, with twenty-five years of experience as an entrepreneurship consultant with the Inter-American Development Bank and the Foundation for Sustainable Development in Latin America. She taught for five years at the Colombian Tourism and Hotel Management School. She is a co-founder of 5Bogota, a creative tourism alternative in Colombia, where she focuses on budget management and financial analysis, thus creating value and protecting corporate assets. She has led the group of hosts at 5Bogota for seven years, overseeing tours for over three thousand travellers. She is also a winning participant in social entrepreneurship contests through 5Bogota. Moreover, she is a co-author of the book *Bogotá through the 5 Senses.*

KEITH BRADBY, OAM, is a landscape restorationist and CEO of Gondwana Link, a large-scale connectivity conservation program in southwestern Australia. He is a former chair of the Western Australian Landcare Network.

NANCY DUXBURY, PhD, is a senior researcher and coordinator of the transdisciplinary thematic line "Urban Cultures, Sociabilities and Participation" at the Centre for Social Studies, University of Coimbra, Portugal. She is also a member of the European Expert Network on Culture. Her research has examined creative tourism development in smaller places, cultural mapping, and culture in local sustainable development, among other topics. She was the principal investigator of "CREATOUR: Creative Tourism Destination Development in Small Cities and Rural Areas," a national research-and-application project (2016–20) that catalyzed creative tourism pilot projects in small cities and rural areas across four regions of Portugal (Algarve, Alentejo, Centro, and Norte). She currently leads the European Commission–funded project "IN SITU: Place-Based Innovation of Cultural and Creative Industries in Non-urban Areas" (2022–26). Her most recent edited books are *CREATOUR: Desenvolver Destinos de Turismo Criativo em Cidades de Pequena Dimensão e em Áreas Rurais* (Imprensa da Universidade de Coimbra,

(2020); *Cultural Sustainability, Tourism and Development: (Re)articulations in Tourism Contexts* (Routledge, 2021); and *Creative Tourism: Cultural Resources and Engaging Creative Travellers* (CABI, 2021).

DARCEN ESAU is a market researcher specializing in both consumer behavior and sensory evaluation, with over a decade of experience designing and implementing research studies. He completed his master's at the University of British Columbia Okanagan, where he studied the sensory experience of wine and how this impacts consumer decision making. At the 13th Pangborn Sensory Science Symposium, Darcen was selected as one of the top eleven early career researchers in sensory science. Darcen is part owner and head of research at TasteAdvisor, which developed a white-labelled wine tourism platform that helps wine regions recommend wine, wineries, events, and experiences, all based on an individual's personal preferences. He also conducts consumer and market research studies on wine through his company, Terroir Consulting.

MOHAMMADREZA GOHARI is an Iranian tourism management/ecotourism graduate. His research concerns the impact of tourism, with a focus on socio-cultural and economic impacts.

DIANA MARCELA ZULUAGA GUERRA is a Colombian advertising professional trained at the Palermo University in Buenos Aires, Argentina, with a specialization in in creative entrepreneurship management from the Cordoba University, in Argentina. With seven years of experience in the tourism industry, she is a co-founder of 5Bogota, a creative tourism alternative in Colombia. She is experienced in public relations and in the creation of entrepreneurial networks through the conception and development of innovative tourism products. She is also a winning participant in social entrepreneurship contests through 5Bogota. Additionally, she is a co-author of the book *Bogotá through the 5 Senses*. She holds a master's in planning and management in tourism systems from the University of Bergamo in Italy.

JOHN S. HULL completed his PhD at McGill University in Montreal and currently works in the Faculty of Adventure, Culinary Arts and Tourism at Thompson Rivers University. He is also affiliated with Harz University of Applied Sciences in Wernigerode, Germany, the Sonnino Working Group in Tuscany, Italy, and the New Zealand Tourism Research Institute. John does research in economic geography and community-based tourism. His current research is focused on mountain/peripheral tourism, food/wine tourism, festivals/events, and health/wellness tourism. He presently serves on the Province of British Columbia's Minister of Tourism Engagement Council.

VID KMETIČ is a walking city stories book, a software technician, and, since 2018, a member of the society Hiša! In Rajzefiber, he is mainly responsible for the development and preparation of new tourist products and is the program manager for the Festival of Walks. He also provides assistance in the preparation and implementation of the Living Courtyards, Lumina, and Elf Town. He has accumulated work experience in various fields, including the cultural. From 1997 to 2010, he participated in most of the excavations and archaeological inspections of the Institute for the Protection of Cultural Heritage of Slovenia—Maribor Regional Unit. Since 2015 he has authored more than forty articles about the past of Maribor, which he published as an ongoing column, "Once Upon a Time," for the newspaper *Večer*. Vid is also author of two books, *Fünfek vas ima rad, pa pohano tudi* (Fünfek loves you—but breaded as well) and *Mi, otroci socializma z našega dvorišča* (Us, kids of socialism from our courtyard).

ATTILA KOMLÓS holds an MSc in geography with a specialization in tourism management (University of Pécs, Hungary.). He has been working toward a PhD on issues of socio-economic activity at the University of Pécs. His current position is at the Duna-Drava National Park Directorate (Pécs, Hungary).

KATJA BECK KOS studied cultural studies in Ljubljana, working for NGOs in Ljubljana and Maribor (among other roles, serving as the backbone for the internationally renowned choir Carmina Slovenica), trained in cultural management in Germany (three years of assistance of program director at Tanzhaus NRW in Düsseldorf and serving as Robert Bosch cultural manager). These experiences made her strong enough to return to Maribor on the verge of an economic crisis in 2010. She stayed. Working as a cultural producer and urban changer, she initiated a community-based art program for neglected spaces called Living Courtyards (part of ECOC Maribor 2012), co-founded the Living City initiative aimed at urban change, helped to establish a new program resident platform, GuestRoomMaribor, helped develop the nano-touristic program Rajzefiber, and initiated a regional travel academy of creative tourism, the PAKT. At the same time, she successfully maintained and steadily expanding the academy's international network, including through collaborations with the Robert Bosch Alumni Network, TANDEM Cultural Managers Exchange, and as an active member of the Network Actors of Urban Change. She was nominated as personality of the year for Styria (region of Maribor), and her group Nanoturizem won the BIO50 Award. She remains curious and in love with her region.

DONALD LAWRENCE, professor (BFA, University of Victoria, 1986; MFA, York University, 1988), teaches in the Visual Arts program at Thompson Rivers University, Kamloops, BC. In both the creation and dissemination of his artistic works, Lawrence merges traditional and experimental/performative practices to investigate two broad areas of interest: (1) the meeting place of urban and wilderness cultures, with particular interests in the ocean environment and the culture of recreational sea kayaking, and (2) pre-photographic optical apparatuses, particularly the early projection device of the camera obscura. Lawrence was the lead researcher of the SSHRC-funded Camera Obscura Project (2013–19), in which a group of artists, scholars, and students realized the 2015 Midnight Sun Camera Obscura Festival in Dawson City, Yukon, followed by a travelling exhibition in partnership with the University of Lethbridge Art Gallery. Donald Lawrence has received the Distinguished Researcher and Undergraduate Research Mentor Awards from Thompson Rivers University and has received the inaugural Undergraduate Research Mentor Award in Humanities from the Council on Undergraduate Research.

SYLVIA M. LEIGHTON is a farmer and ecological researcher from the south coast of Western Australia. She has a deep commitment to incorporating wildlife conservation and healthy soil systems back into commercial regenerative agricultural farming systems in Australia. Wilyun Pools Farm won the WA State Landcare Farmers Award in 2021 and the Australian National Landcare Farmers Award in 2022.

ALISON LULLFITZ is a biologist living on and managing a conservation property in the Fitz-Stirling area. Dr. Lullfitz undertakes collaborative post-doctoral research in Noongar plant conservation and land management in southwestern Australia.

MOIRA A. L. MALEY is an Australian education / ecotourism academic with a life-long interest in transformative learning in multiple settings, from medical education to understanding landscapes.

COURTNEY W. MASON is a professor and Canada Research Chair in Rural Livelihoods and Sustainable Communities at Thompson Rivers University in British Columbia. His work examines locally driven initiatives in rural and Indigenous communities that enhance regional food security and tourism development. His research on parks and protected areas informs public policy on land use management frameworks and conservation practices. He is the author of *Spirits of the Rockies: Reasserting an Indigenous Presence in Banff National Park* (University of Toronto Press, 2014) and the co-editor of *A Land Not Forgotten: Indigenous Food Security and Land-Based Practices of Northern Ontario* (University of Manitoba Press, 2017).

UNA MCMAHON-BEATTIE is professor and head of the Department of Hospitality and Tourism Management at Ulster University (UK). Her research interests include tourism futures, tourism and event marketing, and revenue management. Una is co-editor of Channel View's Tourism Futures series and sits on the editorial board of the *Journal of Tourism Futures*. She is the author/editor of a number of books, including *The Future Past of Tourism: Historical Perspectives and Future Evolutions* (Channel View Publications, 2019).

MATEJA MEH received her bachelor's degree in science from the Faculty of Electrical Engineering and Computer Science (University of Maribor), where she studied media communications. As an undergraduate, she was part of the organizing team for the international student film festival Student Cuts. Between 2014 and 2016 she was head of public relations at the Faculty of Electrical Engineering and Computer Science. During that time, she became part of the organization team for Tedx Maribor, where she served as head of public relations and executive producer. After leaving her job in the faculty she worked briefly as a journalist at one of the country's biggest newspapers, *Večer*. In the last four years she has worked on such projects as the Festival of Walks, Living Courtyards (Festival Lent), and Elf Town, serving as executive producer for the latter event's inaugural 2019 edition. From 2017 to 2019 she helped with the Creative Europe–funded project LUCity. She is also a mentor to young people joining Hiša! through different Erasmus+ programs.

EMESE PANYIK is assistant professor in tourism at the Catholic University of Portugal, Braga Regional Centre, and a member of the Governance, Competitiveness and Public Policy Research Unit (GOVCOPP) of the University of Aveiro, Portugal. She holds a PhD in tourism management from the University of Aveiro. She has a decade of teaching experience in tourism management. Her research interests include local governance and stakeholder relations in tourism, EU tourism policy, and thematic tourism routes.

CAROL PETTERSEN, OAM, is a Menang Ngadju Noongar Elder from Albany, Western Australia. She grew up on her family's home country in a traditional Noongar family, and culture is central to all aspects of her life. She works to empower her people and to build sustainable pathways for Aboriginal people, including as an adviser to the Western Australia Department of Premier and Cabinet. In her retirement, Carol continues to work in a voluntary capacity on land-care issues utilizing her traditional knowledge.

ANDRÉ LUIS QUINTINO PRINCIPE is an independent researcher with a focus on themes connected to cultural associations, creative industries from the cultural sector, and their role in creative tourism. He is currently an IT coordinator at the Brazilian company Vector Two Technology. He holds a bachelor of laws from São Judas Tadeu University (São Paulo). He earned a postgraduate certificate in project management from New York University, and has more than twenty years of experience in the business field as a senior consultant. He has recently completed an MSc in innovation economics and management from the University of Porto. He is the proud father of his newest project, named Miguel.

MENG QU holds a PhD from Hiroshima University and is an associate professor in the Center for Advanced Tourism Studies, Hokkaido University, Japan, and co-convener at the Small Island Cultures Research Initiative. He is a board member of CREATOUR International. His research draws from interdisciplinary perspectives, especially creative tourism, geography, and rural and island studies, particularly in East Asia. His work emphasizes socially engaged rural art festivals, interactive aesthetics, sustainability, and community revitalization.

DONNA SENESE earned a PhD in geography at the University of Waterloo before moving to the Okanagan Valley of British Columbia, where she is now an associate professor of geography at the University of British Columbia—Okanagan Campus, and associate dean of students in the Faculty of Arts and Social Sciences. Dr. Senese has research and curricular interests in the geographies of rural tourism and development at the intersection of sustainability, vulnerability, and resilience thinking. Dr. Senese is a member of UBC's Centre for Environmental Impact Assessment, the UBC Graduate Studies Sustainability Theme, the UBC Wine Research Centre, Kwantlan Polytechnic University's Institute for Sustainable Food Systems, and is founding director of the Sonnino Working Group, an international trans-disciplinary research and writing collective with curricular and research interests in food and wine tourism and rural sustainability.

KATHLEEN SCHERF holds a PhD from the University of British Columbia. She is professor of communication at Thompson Rivers University in Canada. Most recently, her edited volume *Creative Tourism in Smaller Communities: Place, Culture, and Local Representation* was published by the University of Calgary Press in 2021. Also in that year, she published chapters in Nancy Duxbury, Sara Albino, and Cláudia Carvalho's *Creative Tourism: Cultural Resources and Engaging Creative Travellers* (CABI, 2021).

M. JANE THOMPSON is a botanic artist, nurse, and citizen-scientist in spider and floral projects for the Queensland Museum and Herbarium. She and husband Bill owned Yarraweyah Falls and completed a 100-hectare biodiversity carbon sequestration restoration as part of Gondwana Link. They now run boutique ecotourism visits.

SPENCER J. TOTH is a 2SLGBTQI+ tourism and diversity, equity & inclusion professional based in Kamloops, British Columbia, Canada. He is passionate about the tourism sector and its role in rural community economic development. Spencer holds a BBA honours in marketing and entrepreneurship from Simon Fraser University and an MSc from the Erasmus Mundus European Master in Tourism Management program (jointly offered by the University of Southern Denmark, University of Ljubljana, and University of Girona).

JOSIE V. VAYRO is a behavioural ecologist, primatologist, wildlife researcher, and social scientist with twenty years of international and national experience working in Asia, West Africa, and Canada. Her education and career are highly multidisciplinary, having earned a bachelor's of environmental studies, a master's of science in environmental biology, a PhD in biological anthropology, and a postdoctoral research fellowship in human-wildlife interactions, Indigenous food security, and wildlife conservation. Josie is currently the wildlife research lead at Bailey Environmental Consulting, where she oversees and supports a variety of wildlife-related projects.

JOHANNES E. WAJON is an environmental and water-treatment scientist who has spent more than thirty years trying to protect and restore the environment. He and his wife, Donna, were the first buyers of land in the Gondwana Link project. Dr. Wajon is currently the national conservation officer for the Australian Native Plants Society Australia. He is a photographer and the self-publisher of books on Western Australian wildflowers.

IAN YEOMAN is a professor of innovation, disruption, and new phenomena at NHL Stenden Hotel School in the Netherlands. Ian holds visiting professorships at Victoria University of Wellington and Ulster University. Dr. Yeoman is co-editor of the *Journal of Tourism Futures* and co-editor of Channel View's Tourism Futures series. Author and editor of over twenty books, including *Scenario Planning and Tourism Futures* and *Global Scenarios for World Tourism*. Outside the future, Ian is a keen photographer and Sunderland AFC football fan.

SIMONA ZOLLET holds a PhD from Hiroshima University, where she is an assistant professor in the Department of Academia-Government-Industry Collaboration and a USASBE research fellow. Her doctoral research examined sustainability transitions in agri-food systems through organic and agro-ecological farming and alternative rural lifestyles in Italy and Japan. She believes in the importance of social entrepreneurship and small business creation, particularly in the areas of sustainable farming and food systems, and of leveraging local culture in the creation of resilient and sustainable rural futures.

Index

www.ingramcontent.com/pod-product-compliance
Lightning Source LLC
Chambersburg PA
CBHW040146270326
41929CB00025B/3401